]

LONG SLOW TARGET

"A thrilling yet hilarious memoir of a young naval officer's life aboard an amphibious ship in Vietnam. But the real protagonist is the USS *Hampshire County* (LST-819). A love story with all its ups and downs, and feeling of loss when it ends—except it's about a ship. Few understand the attachment men and women have to a Navy ship on which they served. Lindsey pulls back the curtain and shows us why in this engaging account of life on the sometimes overly bounding main. He brings humor to shipboard life in Vietnam, while revealing the dangerous circumstances in which he served."

—Ron McManus
Vietnam veteran and award-winning author of the Jake Palmer series.

"Lieutenant Lindsey continually walked a fine line between success and disaster."

—G. C. Heffner
Rear Admiral, SC, USN

"Terrific! Larry Lindsey superbly conveys his personal experiences in the Vietnam era, US Navy, and does so with insight, self-awareness, and humor. He adeptly captures the flavor and complexity of serving his nation during an extremely tumultuous period in American history. A wonderful and thought provoking-read, not so removed from current-day events."

—James Curry
Lieutenant Colonel, USMC retired, DoD instructor

"So far beyond the realm of imagination, it has to be true. And I should know since my own existence is often imagined."

—Joseph D. Oznot
Princeton Class of '68, professor of para-psychology, non-emeritus

"A great read; this book is a hoot! Brings back fond, and not so fond, memories. Sights and smells are superbly done. Had tears running down my cheeks from laughing."

—Skip Meinke
Vietnam veteran, US Navy

"Lindsey's manic, anti-heroic account of a rust-bucket LST during the Vietnam War is immensely engaging. If Hunter S. Thompson had served in his place, this is the memoir he might have written."

—J. I. Merritt
Navy Vietnam veteran, and author of *Goodbye, Liberty Belle: A Son's Search for His Father's War*

"Completely enthralled! Any guy deployed to Vietnam would love this book. Some without these experiences would probably think it far-fetched. But I know better."

—Terry Seymour
Vietnam veteran, Lieutenant, US Navy

"Brings back the smells and sounds, and the camaraderie of men in war. Well written, the humor balances the unpleasant and scary parts perfectly."

—Mikk Hinnov
Vietnam veteran, US Army

"Many thanks. It brought back many memories. Some of the stories are pretty raw. But hey! That was the Navy and life on a ship."

—Benjamin McCleary
Vietnam veteran, US Navy

"Superb! Gripping! The combination of humor, suspense, and danger rolled together to make for a great reading."

—David Baraff
GM of Ultra Voice, former *Shades* guitarist

"Really fun read! Rings true."

—Stephen Cook
Captain, US Navy (Retired)

"You're one damn fine writer!"

—Robert N. Chester
Former CEO Lions Gate Films

Long Slow Target

By Larry Allen Lindsey

© Copyright 2022 Larry Allen Lindsey

ISBN 978-1-64663-721-8

All rights reserved. No part of this publication may be reproduced, stored in a retrieval system, or transmitted in any form or by any means—electronic, mechanical, photocopy, recording, or any other—except for brief quotations in printed reviews, without the prior written permission of the author.

Published by

köehlerbooks™

3705 Shore Drive
Virginia Beach, VA 23455
800–435–4811
www.koehlerbooks.com

LONG SLOW TARGET

PORK CHOP CANDY

THE TRUE STORY OF LIFE ONBOARD THE SLOWEST,
UGLIEST, WORST RIDING SHIP IN THE US NAVY . . .
OR ANY NAVY FOR THAT MATTER

LARRY ALLEN LINDSEY

VIRGINIA BEACH
CAPE CHARLES

"We sailors are jealous of our vessels. Abuse us if you will, but have a care for what you say of our ships. We alone are entitled to call them bitches, wet brutes, stubborn craft, but we will stand no such liberties from the beach."

—Sir David William Bone.

"A ship is always referred to as a 'she' because it costs so much to keep her in paint and powder."

—Admiral Chester William Nimitz

"They sailed away, for a year and a day. . .
they went to sea in a Sieve, they did . . .
in spite of all their friends could say."

—Edward Lear, "The Owl and the Pussy-Cat"

TABLE OF CONTENTS

MILITARY RANK (NON-FLAG)

NAVY	COLLAR DEVICE	MARINE
Ensign	One gold bar	Second Lieutenant
Lieutenant junior grade	One silver bar	First Lieutenant
Lieutenant	Two silver bars	Captain
Lieutenant commander	Gold oak leaf	Major
Commander	Silver oak leaf	Lt. Colonel
Captain	Silver eagle	Colonel

Note: A Navy captain is three ranks higher than a Marine captain. Even more confusing, in the Navy the commanding officer of a ship is addressed as "Captain," no matter his/her rank. Even if he/she is a lowly ensign. To avoid confusion, I have maximized the use of "Skipper" throughout the book.

PROLOGUE

In the military, *chest candy* means medals. It comes from the bright, candy-like colors radiating from a service member's chest when he or she is decked out in their dress uniforms. The chests of those who brave the perils of combat dazzle the eye. The chests of pork chops (the Navy's nickname for their supply officers) are often drab in comparison, as they perhaps should be. Supply types serve a vital function, but as a famous admiral once said, "You don't earn medals counting beans."

During my tours in Vietnam, I qualified for three medals. *Whaddya want Lindsey? A medal, or a chest to pin it on?* Given to me for enlisting in a time of national crisis, one was awarded to everyone who joined up during the Vietnam era. My other two were for longevity—the first for merely setting foot in 'Nam and the second for accumulating six months in and about that war-torn country. Although I wore all three proudly during my military career, in effect, they were little more than a matter of timing. No daring deeds were done on my part, no heroic efforts made. Other than a paper cut or two, I wasn't wounded. And for that, I'm grateful.

This book is an accurate, albeit sometimes tongue-in-cheek, account of how I earned my limited array of *chest candy* serving on a rust bucket of a ship called the USS *Hampshire County* (LST-819), the same type and vintage vessel that deposited my father on the beaches of Normandy some seventy years ago. Officially designated by the Navy as a *Landing Ship Tank* to the Viet Cong up and down the Mekong River, she was not so affectionately known as the *Long Slow Target*. The hundreds of green-gilled Marines who staggered across her decks on any of her transits from Cua Viet to Okinawa called her the world's best seasick machine, also without affection.

This book is an example of creative nonfiction. As popularized in Michael Shaara's *Killer Angels* (later transformed into the award-winning film *Gettysburg*), I use cinematic techniques to introduce and expand the many colorful characters. Lee Gutkind, author of *You Can't Make This Stuff Up*, explains it as a way to "introduce the characters behind the facts with action and excitement in a more compelling story-oriented way than with straight exposition or traditional journalism."

In *Long Slow Target*, I have utilized dialogue as a literary element, expanding or creating it when needed to complete a narrated scene. One final disclaimer, as the narrator intoned at the opening of the *Dragnet* series, "The names have been changed to protect the innocent." To those famous words, I respectfully add the phrase "and/or the guilty."

My birth certificate lists me as Lawrence Allen Lindsey. To my friends, I'm Larry, Lar for short. And this is the story of my ship.

ONE

Goodbye, Cleveland. Hello, Saigon!

In 1969, a loaf of bread cost a whopping two dimes, a gallon of gas all of thirty-three cents, and a first-class postage stamp set you back a nickel and a penny. *Midnight Cowboy* won best picture that year and on the small screen *Rowan & Martin's Laugh-In* and *The Carol Burnett Show* were knocking them dead. On the gridiron, the New York Jets upset the heavily favored Baltimore Colts and the "Amazing Mets" won the World Series. On July 20, the whole world held its breath as Neil Armstrong set foot on the moon. All things considered, 1969 was a pretty good year.

On the flip side, 1969 was also the year of the Manson murders and the Chicago Seven. Ike died, Tricky Dick became president, and a handsome senator from Massachusetts accidentally drove his car off a bridge, drowning his female passenger. There was also that cloud on the horizon called the Vietnam *conflict,* soon to be designated a war. I had a low number in the upcoming draft so that cloud loomed especially dark for me.

The best laid *schemes o' men,* and especially *mice,* I joined the Navy in the late sixties to avoid the Army. And hopefully, Vietnam. Since I didn't speak Canadian all that well, an intelligent choice of military service seemed to be a viable option. Any day I was expecting a terse letter from the government, the kind that starts out *"Greetings. . . "*

Since my father had been attached to the 5th Armored Division under Patton during World War II, he was none too thrilled about the prospects of me becoming a foot soldier. As always, his opinion was short and to the point:

"I didn't spend three years freezing my butt off in a Sherman tank chasing goddam Nazis all over Eastern Europe only to have the Army yank my number one son off to fight another friggin' war!"

Or something to that effect.

Having landed at Normandy, my father knew what he was talking about. Like so many of his generation, he thought he'd fought the war to end all wars, that the next generation wouldn't be at risk. Since they didn't have rice paddies on ships, I marched down to the nearest Navy recruiting office and signed on the dotted line. With a college degree in psychology, I was pretty sure they'd make me an officer of some kind. So what if I didn't know port from starboard?

On June 1, I trundled my GI butt off to Newport, Rhode Island, home of the Navy's Officer Candidate School, OCS for short. The most important thing I learned at OCS was the difference between a boat and a ship. Hint: you can put a boat on a ship, but not a ship on a boat. I also learned how to tie a double sheepshank. To this day, whenever I'm asked to tie a knot at parties, I can whip out the old double sheepshank to impress the ladies.

After months at Newport, I found myself standing tall at graduation with one shiny gold band on my dress blue jacket sleeve that officially classified me as an ensign, the Navy's lowest ranking officer. Everyone else in my graduating company had this impressive gold star embroidered above their shiny gold band, indicating they were line officers, people capable of driving ships. Above my shiny gold band, however, was a strange blob that looked like three half-inflated balloons tied together by a string of three small balls.

"It looks like a lop-sided pork chop," I said to my drill instructor. "What the hell gives?"

"Funny you should say that," he said. "That's what the Navy calls its supply officers—*pork chops*. Looks like you're gonna be one, lad. Whether you like it or not."

Because of my poor vision, I'd been classified as a candidate for the Navy's Supply Corps School and branded with their special insignia. When I held up my sleeve for closer inspection, the blob didn't look any more stylish.

"What's this . . . this *thing* supposed to be?" I asked.

"It's a patch of oak leaves," said the instructor. "And those three balls represent nuts. Acorns, I think."

"Why three?"

"Simple, he said. "A doctor's insignia has two nuts. A nurse's has none, of course. And pork chops have three. Supply types always carry a spare."

"That's just great," I moaned. "I'm a bean counter."

———

At the Navy's Supply Corps School in Athens, Georgia, I studied enough multipart forms to choke a horse. In my dreams, I can still fill out a *1348-6* in ten seconds flat. If it hadn't been for the fact that NSCS was located near the University of Georgia, the six months I spent there would have been a total wash excitement-wise. When it comes to warm hospitality, there's nothing finer than a Southern belle undergrad.

Upon graduating from Bean Counter U, the ensign receiving the worst set of orders is awarded a joke plaque. It depicts a fuzz-faced junior officer bending over, his pants down around his ankles, getting ready for a proctologist's fickle finger of fate. Usually a close race, the year I graduated, I won going away. The fact that I was going to independent duty, which was supposed to reward you for good grades, was no consolation. The commander reading from my orders list even balked twice.

"Mr. Lindsey, you have been ordered to the USS *Hampshire County*, hull number 819. It's a twice recommissioned World War II LST. . . " First balk, ". . . home ported in Guam and arduously deployed to. . . " Second (and even longer) balk, ". . . Vietnam."

I'd been given the orders from hell. *World War II LST? Guam? Vietnam?* I felt weak in the knees. The room began to spin. My classmates shuffled away from me, as if I'd been stricken with a communicable disease. Several gasped. Two crossed themselves. Opting for bravado, I took a deep breath and forced a plastic smile. Stiffened my upper lip.

"Ah, well," I managed, "it could have been worse."

Knowing full well it couldn't. My best laid plans had gone up in smoke.

"At least I won't be going up and down the rivers," I added, trying to make lemonade out of lemons.

That night, I looked up LST in *JANE'S FIGHTING SHIPS*, the Navy almanac for vessels of the line. There on page 522 was a black-and-white photo of my ship under full steam. Sort of. According to *JANE*, LST meant *landing ship tank*. I would discover later that those three letters actually stood for *long slow target*.

Less than sleek and blunted at both ends, LST 819 looked like an overcooked sausage. If destroyers are the greyhounds of the sea, then LST's are Neptune's warthogs. An important part of our amphibious fleet, they are nicknamed the "Gator" navy. Three hundred and twenty-eight feet long, with a top speed of twelve knots (the pace of a brisk trot), faster only than a rowboat on one oar, a *T* isn't capable of leaving anything in its wake.

Hollow down her middle with a keel as flat as your dining room table, an LST is the worst riding ship in anyone's navy, bar none. With a fifty-foot beam and manned by a crew of 110, she displaced 1,640 tons. Propelled by two 900-horsepower diesel engines and built to beach herself on purpose, she was twin shafted with two recessed rudders and had two gigantic doors imbedded in a pug-nosed bow that opened to admit all sorts of cargo up a tongue-like ramp. Like tanks and two-and-a half-ton trucks. Efficient when it comes to moving men and material, instead of cutting through the water she pounded into it, vibrating every nut and bolt onboard. Along with all living things nearby.

I didn't know whether to laugh or cry. I'd seen trimmer looking garbage scows. Miles from any body water larger than a bathtub, I felt myself getting seasick.

I'll never forget the drive to Cleveland Hopkins Airport the day I left for Vietnam. Due to an overturned eighteen-wheeler on the freeway, definitely a bad omen, it ended up being the longest two hours of my life. My father, bless his heart, tried to put on a brave front, joking about this and that and how my deployment would be over sooner than we both thought. How I was finally getting a chance to see the world, supposedly one of the Navy's biggest selling points.

But I could tell my impending departure was tearing him up inside. Not once in my young life had he ever brought up World War II, but I knew his experience at Normandy was eating away at him. However, being macho males, we both tried to make light of the situation. "No big deal . . . silver lining . . . this too shall pass. . . "

"Bottom line, you'll be on a ship," he said. "You might not even have to set foot in Vietnam. You'll get three square meals a day, not something out of a tin can like we got in the Army."

"The Navy *does* eat well," I said. "At least I won't starve."

My poor mother, on the other hand, sat speechless in the back seat, looking out the window, dabbing at her swollen eyes. I have to give her credit, though; she didn't let loose with the real waterworks until I was walking up the ramp to my plane.

———

I spent the first ten minutes of the flight staring out the window, watching numbly as Ohio faded into the contrails of our 727.

"On your way to 'Nam?" said a stew, offering me a pillow. Back then they called them stewardesses, not flight attendants.

"How can you tell?" I asked.

"The uniform's a dead giveaway."

Dead? I thought to myself. Not a word I wanted to hear.

"And no offense," she continued, "but you've got the look. I've seen it too many times this year. Um . . . care for a cocktail?" Adroitly changing the subject.

"No, thanks. I don't drink," I said, mustering up a weak smile.

I've never been against the idea of drinking. I just don't like the bitter flavor of alcohol. Booze is an acquired taste, much like asparagus, blue cheese, or coffee. At heart, I'm a simple man with simple philosophies. When it comes to things I put in my mouth, if it doesn't taste good, why bother?

"You may not drink now," said the stew, "but you probably will soon enough." Blushing a bright red, she put a hand to her mouth. "Sorry. I don't mean to imply . . . um, is there anything else I can get for you?"

"A few peanuts would be nice."

"Coming right up."

In the sixties, people treated you *nice* when they found out where you were headed. Some people anyway.

The rest of the flight shot by in a blur. Before I could finish my third bag of peanuts, we were landing in San Francisco.

San Francisco! The Golden Gate Bridge, Fisherman's Wharf, Coit Tower, and Lombard Street! Rolling hills and trolley cars. And of course, Haight-Asbury, a place we buzz cuts were told to avoid.

After a long bus ride, I checked into the transient officer barracks at Travis Air Force Base. They weren't the greatest accommodations, but at least I had a nice warm bunk for the night. The following morning, I boarded a Texas Air Charter flight, a military aircraft packed with nothing but uniforms. When they slammed that 747's door shut, I knew I was finally on my way to Vietnam.

No turning back now, said the lump in my throat.

———————

The sailor sitting next to me on that jumbo jet looked eighteen going on twelve. His eyes brimming with moisture, his right hand held a snapshot of his girlfriend. His left hand fingered a set of rosaries. Both not good signs.

"H-her name is Carol," he said. I hadn't asked. "We're gonna get hitched when I get back. Been sweethearts since the fifth grade."

I'd seen enough war flicks to recognize the set up: *Young lad just out of high school, first time off the farm, with a girl waiting back home. Ten minutes into the movie, he walks into a bullet and is sent back in a coffin. You name the war.*

"*Run, kid, run!*" I wanted to scream. "*They're going to write you out in the first reel!*"

He held up the snapshot and I nodded.

"She's very pretty," I said. "You'll make a nice couple."

"She's working at the Colonel's, frying up chicken," he continued. "Mom takes care of the baby during the day. We've got another one on the way."

Babies, too? Oh, Jeez!

"We're saving our money so we can get married when all this is over. Buy a place of our own. Maybe a little farm."

I envisioned the picket fence, a German shepherd in the backyard, lots of chickens, and maybe a few cows.

"That's nice," I said, trying for optimism.

With relief, I noticed the dental tech insignia on his shoulder. DT's always stayed in the rear, far away from the action. At least he wasn't a corpsman. In World War II, the life expectancy of a corpsman at Normandy was a few minutes. Odds were this kid would return to his Carol. Raise more kids, plant corn, maybe some wheat.

Subconsciously I hoped the survival rate for dental techs also applied to supply officers. I'd been told pork chops never, *ever* saw action, that Charlie didn't waste ammunition on bean counters. That the worst malady a supply officer endured was an acid stomach when they tried to balance the books.

At Honolulu, our plane came down with mechanical difficulties, something to do with leaking hydraulic lifters. Faced with a two-day layover, I decided to make the best of it and see the sights. *Gather ye rosebuds while ye may.*

I rented a car to drive around the island for most of that first day. I marveled at Diamond Head, gawked at the big surf around the North Shore, and enjoyed the cool breezes at Waikiki. Breathtaking flowers, gorgeous beaches, exotic food—I enjoyed them all. Right up until I boarded the launch out to the USS *Arizona* Memorial. I'd always wanted to see the final resting place of the grand old lady and figured it was as good a time as any.

Big mistake. When I stared down into that blue-green water and saw those dots of oil trickling up to the surface, a constricting feeling washed over me. Perhaps being bound for Vietnam had something to do with it, but I blubbered like a baby.

That was it for playing tourist. I returned my rental, went back to the barracks, and stayed in my room until my flight was called. No snorkeling, no surfing, no Don Ho and his "Tiny Bubbles," just me in my safe bunk, staring up at the ceiling.

It was the seventh of April, a Wednesday I think, and my first glimpse of Vietnam came at the crack of dawn out a window on the port side of the plane. With the sun inching over the horizon to shadow our tail, it was a sight I'll never forget.

We were coming in low over the ocean, heading straight for the Mekong River Delta. Ahead lay the still blazing lights of Saigon. Twinkling in a lazy morning mist that seemed to hover over a blue-green jungle, Saigon almost looked inviting. Like something out of a tropical paradise. At least it did from twenty thousand feet. In reality, the morning mist was actually steam, and we were about to set down in the world's biggest sauna.

The blue green soon faded to gray green, then finally to a muddy brown to match the widening delta. I could see what was left of the jungle had been pock-marked with craters. Goodbye tropical paradise, hello war-torn country. At two thousand feet, the kid next to me was back to manhandling his rosaries. As an officer, you're often forced to accentuate the positive. Even if it's nowhere to be found.

"It doesn't look so bad," I said. But my heart wasn't in it. When we flew over a bombed-out village, I realized we weren't in Kansas anymore.

Get a grip, Lindsey, I told myself. *What did you expect? Manicured lawns and swimming pools? This is Vietnam, for chrissake! Toto's been dead for years and the Tin Man was sold for scrap eons ago.*

After a steep, high-speed approach and bumpy landing (to avoid snipers, I was told), the plane came to a roaring stop at Tan Son Nhut Airport's main terminal, the hub of traffic in and out of Saigon. Drinking in the last remnants of our air-conditioned cabin, I ventured a glance out my window.

Other than the strange flag flying from atop its control tower, Tan Son Nhut looked much like any big city airport. A host of familiar support vehicles scurried around beneath several planes nuzzled up to a modern facility, much like baby chicks scrabbling to their mother hens. A reassuring motorized ramp, like the one I'd climbed up way back in Cleveland, headed our way.

There were a few differences, of course. At least two dozen heavily sandbagged machine-gun bunkers dotted the runways. More disturbing was the burned-out skeleton of an F-4 Phantom jet fighter pushed over the embankment to my left. The two gutted Huey helicopter gunships hunkered next to it added to the stark ambience.

I make it a rule never to be first off the plane. Any plane. That day, I was the last to leave. Dead last.

"Sir?" said a stew. "I'm afraid you'll have to get off now. Everyone has de-planed already."

De-planed? I wonder about the derivation of that word. You don't *de-train* Amtrak. And nobody has ever *de-automobiled* or *de-boated* anything.

With a black cloud coagulating overhead, I took a deep breath, unfastened my seat belt, and headed for the door.

Like my dad, I'm not much of a churchgoer. Sitting on a rock-hard pew for an hour on every Sunday seems like a waste of time. But I had a religious experience when I first stuck my head out of that plane.

For a terrifying few seconds, I couldn't breathe. It was as if I'd walked face-first into a burning pillow. The air was so humid—you swallowed it. Every last one of my sweat glands went into overdrive, and by the time I wobbled down to the tarmac, I was sopping wet. Staggering in the vague direction of the terminal, I left a trail of puddles.

I'm melting! I'm melting! I thought. *How can anyone live in this ungodly heat? Much less fight in it.*

With sweat dripping off my nose and without the foggiest notion of where I was going, I must have looked pathetic.

"Your ride's over there," said a sympathetic Marine corporal. "Don't worry, sir. The hotel where you officers stay is top notch. Most of the rooms are air-conditioned."

Thank God!

My *ride* turned out to be an open-air cargo truck. An Air Force major, two Army second lieutenants, a Marine captain, and I piled into the back with our gear. All five of us soaked to the skin. Too hot for conversation, we panted instead.

After being checked out by mirror-toting guards at two separate bunkers on the outskirts of the airport (the Marine captain informed me they were searching for satchel charges attached to the undercarriage), the driver speed-shifted into second and we lurched onto a modern thoroughfare packed bumper-to-bumper with vehicles. Classy looking Citroens, elongated jitney-Jeeps, overloaded pickup trucks, banged up Toyotas, a few vintage Cadillacs, dozens of ox carts, and at least a million scooters, all within ten yards of us, fender first being the right of way.

After a quick right turn, the truck slowed to a crawl. Then stopped altogether. A collision between a Jeep and an ox cart ahead had mired traffic to a standstill. Two groups of people were full-volume babbling at each other. Three large barrels were in the middle of the road, cargo from the overturned cart. One of the barrels oozed a dark brown fluid that stunk so bad it made my eyes water.

"What is that godawful stench?" I asked.

"That's nuoc mam," said the Marine. "It's everywhere in 'Nam. This is my second tour, and I still haven't gotten used to it."

"Holy crap! It smells like fish guts ten days in the sun."

"That's actually what it is," he said. "Nuoc mam is a staple over here. The Vietnamese eat it five times a day. Carry it around in a container to pour over their rice."

"It stinks like hell."

"The worse it smells, the better it's supposed to be. They pack fish heads into those big barrels you see in the street. After a month, they drill holes at different levels and work from the top on down. The good stuff comes from the bottom hole. Costs more because it ages longer. Like fine wine, I guess."

"Fine wine? You gotta be kidding."

On a dare, I'd once eaten a *balyut* at a Philippine restaurant back home. It's a fermented duck egg one day away from hatching. Considered a delicacy in Manila, it smelled like a bag of sulfur farts. It was a breath of fresh air compared to nuoc mam.

While we all breathed through our mouths, a steady stream of mopeds zipped by. One overloaded Honda caught my eye. Carrying a man, his wife, a baby, a cat, a piglet, and what appeared to be two rooms of battered furniture lashed across the back, it also pulled a full-grown goat tethered to a bumper. I watched with amazement as the tottering menagerie weaved around the crashed vehicles with the grace of an Olympic figure skater. How the driver managed that tight left turn was beyond me.

Welcome to Vietnam!

The *Hampshire's* main deck, crane, bridge, and LCVPs.

An LST's bread and butter.

Hampshire (aka the Seasick Machine) in action.

TWO
Waiting for the Fat Lady

My quarters that first night in country turned out to be at a Parisienne hotel. Preceding the United Sates in Vietnam by at least twenty years, the French had cut their losses and run. Since Saigon was a war zone, I'd expected C-rats for dinner. What I got instead was a full-blown French cuisine buffet. Complete with baguettes, *coq au vin*, quiche, escargot (ugh!), and crepes for dessert. For those of us with less sophisticated palates, they also provided a side table heaped with burgers, fries, and all the trimmings.

After gorging myself à la Big Mac, I retired early for a much-needed shower in my private air-conditioned room with clean sheets and a view of the river.

Not bad, I thought. *Maybe in time I'll get used to the heat and humidity.*

Exhausted from my travels, I was sure I'd have no trouble falling asleep. Like clockwork, however, every few minutes, weird sounds trickled up from the street. Starting with a high-pitched faraway whine, they rose to a crescendo to terminate in a muffled explosion. After an hour of tossing and turning, I decided to investigate. Not a smart thing to do in a war zone. Reminding myself the hotel was located in the most secure section of the city, I headed out the door.

The sounds seemed to be coming from somewhere down the promenade. The streetlights around the hotel and the ubiquitous illumination flares lit up the area as bright as day. My ears soon brought me to the edge of a river where I discovered the source of my insomnia. Several villagers were cremating the day's dead on the far bank.

Curiosity satisfied, and now weak in the knees, I hustled back to my room where I spent the rest of the night staring at yet another ceiling. With visions of funeral pyres and rotting fish heads swimming in my brain, a few blinks before dawn, I managed to fall into a fitful sleep. I'd worked up my first respectable snore when the messenger of the watch nudged me awake.

"Sir? You're set to go."

"Go?" I mumbled. "Go where?"

"To Vung Tau. Your ship is due to dock there sometime this week. A Jeep is waiting at the front entrance to take you back out to the airport."

Not sure where (or even who) I was, it took me a few seconds.

"Vung Tau?"

"You'll love it," said the messenger. "It's the R & R capital of Vietnam." But before I could fumble out my next question, he was gone.

My crumpled uniform of dried sweat felt like twenty pounds of crusty salt when I put it back on. Smelling like a walking mound of moldy sweat socks, I gathered my gear and headed for the front desk.

"I'm Ensign Lindsey," I told the duty clerk. "The messenger said there's a ride waiting for me outside somewhere?"

Covering his nose with his left hand, he pointed at the hotel's revolving front door with his right. My uniform was *that* ripe.

"Thanks," I said. "Sorry about the stink."

Outside, I was greeted with another blast of liquid heat. The sun had only nudged the horizon and already the temperature was in in the upper nineties. Humidity—110 percent.

"Lieutenant Lindsey?" said a young Army corporal with long hair and a fu manchu moustache, clearly unfamiliar with Navy ranks. "We've been assigned to take you to the airport."

Leaning nonchalantly on a 50-caliber machine gun in the back of his Jeep stood a private with a red do-rag wrapped around his afro. His weapon of choice was an ominous reminder of where we were. The do-rag, a reminder of where we weren't. By the time I manhandled my bags into the back, I'd sweated through my jacket again and developed a wedgie of epic proportions.

"Thanks for the promotion," I said, returning the driver's salute. "But it's *Ensign* Lindsey. And I appreciate the ride."

Before sliding into the shotgun seat, I surreptitiously pulled my skivvies out of my butt cheeks.

"Tell me, Corporal. Does anything ever dry out in this country?"

"Not uniforms, that's for sure, sir."

On the way to Tan Son Nhut, the driver had his hands full navigating through the morning commute, so I turned my attention to our gunner. The minute we passed through the hotel gates, he cocked his weapon and assumed *the stance*. Sweeping his weapon back and forth in front of the Jeep, he began to sing the chorus of a familiar Animal's song.

"*We gotta get out of this place. . .* " I would soon learn it was the most popular tune in 'Nam.

"Um . . . what's Vung Tau like?" I asked, ducking low when the barrel of his gun passed over my head.

The gunner spat a brown glob of tobacco juice. It barely missed the chicken running alongside us.

"Tau is better than some and safer than most. At least you can walk the streets at night without fear of getting knifed. Most times, that is. They say you don't have to carry your weapon around during the day, but I always do. Just to be on the safe side."

He spat again, this time hitting the unfortunate fowl on head. Then he looked me square in the eye.

"Just like I do in Mississippi."

At the airport again, I was directed to a staging area on the far side of the field. After seeking out the only shade available, I asked an Air Force captain where the flight to Vung Tau was boarding. Before he could answer, a battered Huey helicopter gunship barreled overhead, its deep-throated rotors one of Nam's unforgettable sounds. After kicking up a dust storm, it slammed into the tarmac with a resounding thud, scattering debris everywhere. The landing was so hard, two bolts and a nut dribbled off the chopper's fuselage.

"Damn!" Yelling to be heard over the din. "Do they always come in so steep?"

"They have to!" yelled back the captain. "To keep snipers from drawing a bead!"

This was the second time in two days I was having a conversation about snipers.

"Doesn't that damage the choppers?" I asked.

The captain nodded, pursed his lips.

"Better to damage a chopper than the men inside!"

Equipment could be replaced. Men couldn't. When the dust cleared, he pointed to a squat aircraft parked in front of a corrugated tin hangar.

"That's your ride over there. She may not be the sleekest filly in the barn, but she'll get you where you want to go. Even if you aren't anxious to get there."

Letting out a stream of expletives, he was off to chew out a private who had tipped over a cart of repair parts on the ramp.

As I plodded across the sunbaked tarmac, the heat from it boiled up through the soles of my shoes. The closer I got to the C-130, the more I doubted the *getting me to where I wanted to go* part. The transport plane looked like a loaf of bread with wings. A fat, dumpy loaf of bread infested with weevils.

When the pilot cranked over a port engine, it coughed four times before catching. The oil dripping off a starboard engine hinted my chances of making it to Vung Tau in one piece were at best fifty-fifty. After quietly genuflecting in my mind, I followed three other uniforms up the lowered boarding ramp into the back of the plane.

What the hell, I figured. *When in Rome. . .*

While handing my orders to the plane's load master, another stench, not quite as bad as nuoc mam, hit me.

"Jesus! What *is* that disgusting smell?"

The sergeant barely glanced at my papers.

"Last week, we had a pallet of hamburgers defrost on us and the juice dripped into the support struts. We cleaned what we could reach but couldn't get it all. You get used to the stink after a while."

"It smells like somebody died in there. And what are those?" I said, pointing to several holes in the plane's outer skin.

"That's our special ventilation system."

"They look like bullet holes to me."

Turning to the next idiot in line, the sergeant grinned. Tapped a finger to his head.

"Can't get anything by you, can I, sir?"

My seat on the C-130 turned out to be a canvas strap suspended by two wires from the overhead. Bullet holes and canvas straps? Something told me I wasn't about to fly the friendly skies.

Thankfully the trip lasted no more than an hour. A quick power up, a skidding turn onto the runway, and we were off the ground in less than a thousand feet. After what couldn't have been two seconds, we leveled off and headed east into the rising sun.

A minute later, I chanced a peek out a butter-plate-sized portal to my right. When flying at altitude, people on the ground should look like ants. Not so this time. I could almost read their wrist watches.

"Um . . . Sergeant? Just how *high* are we?"

The sergeant put down his Louie L'Amour paperback. Looked out his own window.

"About two hundred feet. Give or take a few inches."

"Two hundred feet! Do you always fly that low? Wait, don't tell me. Snipers, right?"

He pointed a forefinger at me. Winked.

"Bullseye! We've got ourselves another winner."

Fifty minutes of terrified silence later, something scraped along the plane's bottom. Instinctively, I ducked. As if that would have done any good.

"What the hell was *that*?" I asked.

"Not to worry," said the sergeant. "We always brush against that tree. Brace yourself, we're about to land."

Something clanged beneath my feet.

"*That* didn't sound like a tree!" I said.

"Just some local taking potshots. No sweat. It was only a pistol. Nothing that could penetrate our skin."

"Do they always shoot at us?"

"It wouldn't be a war if they didn't," said the sarge returning to his paperback.

We hit the runway at full speed, hard enough to rattle my back fillings. A sudden roar shook the entire plane as the pilot reversed engines and stood on his toe brakes. A screech of tires and the smell of burning rubber almost overpowered the stink of last week's burger juice. A hairpin turn bounced me and my canvas seat off the bulkhead. Two protracted shudders from the starboard engine and the plane came to a quivering stop.

"Welcome to Vung Tau," said the sergeant, unfazed by the jostling.

It took me several seconds to catch my breath. And make sure my heart was still in my chest.

"Are all your flights like that?" I asked.

"Nah. Sometimes they're pretty rough. You're lucky. Today was a piece of cake."

Piece of cake?

With rubbery legs, I headed toward the makeshift terminal at the end of the runway. There, a grizzled gunny sergeant took pity on me. It probably wasn't the first time he'd seen a lost expression on a boot officer. Less than a day in country and I'd already mastered the look.

"Over there, Ensign," he grunted, pointing to two orange crates connected by a plank. "That's the check-in counter. They'll tell you where to go."

"Thank you, sir," I said, saluting him first. When you're discombobulated, you tend to forget military protocol.

"I ain't no *sir*," he said. "I work for a living."

I'd heard that line before. Probably in a John Wayne movie.

"Bit of advice, sir," added the sergeant. "We don't salute in country. Officers are prime targets for snipers."

Snipers again?

"Sorry about that," I said. "My bad."

An hour after presenting my orders to the orange crate clerk, I boarded yet another Jeep, this one bigger than the one in Saigon, with *two* machine guns.

"Hold tight," said the driver. "It's gonna be a bumpy ride. We're in the rainy season and the road to Cat Lo is full of ruts."

When I looked back at the Jeep's gunner, I swore I'd seen him somewhere before. Maybe it was the gigantic Afro under his red do-rag. I was about to ask him if he had a brother in Saigon but decided against it. The last thing I needed was to piss off someone with a 50 caliber in his hands.

And so, it was off to Cat Lo. Wherever or whatever that was.

———————

Our Jeep ride through Vung Tau lasted no more than twenty minutes. Nestled into a prime sliver of delta bottom land, the sleepy Vietnamese village was a step down from the hustle and bustle of Saigon. Local traffic plodded along. Fewer Citroens, more bikes and oxcarts, punctuated by a sea of pedestrians with animals in tow. Pigs, goats, cows, water buffalo, even a few monkeys. I did a double take when I spied a bowlegged woman with blackened teeth on the side of the road, a large snake in a basket balanced on her head.

"Is that a python?" I asked the driver.

"Yep," he said. "She probably caught it upriver. Snake that size makes for good eating. Add some hot sauce and it tastes a lot like chicken."

Going through town, I noticed every other shop had long strips of meat hanging out front. Spiked to rough-hewn boards, they looked a bit like beef jerky, my favorite snack back home.

"What's that they're selling?" I asked.

The driver shook his head. Let out a slow whistle.

"Stay away from that stuff. It's monkey meat. I tried it once and got sicker than a dog. Which is also something else the Vietnamese like to eat. Both are loaded with parasite eggs."

My appetite for jerky fading, I turned my attention to the crowd around us. Like bees in a hive, they seemed to be getting to where they wanted to go without trampling each other. Once again, I inhaled the stench of nuoc mam. Before my eyes stopped watering, we were out of town.

"No offense," I said, "but there's not much to Vung Tau."

"Don't let appearances fool you," said the driver. "Come nightfall, Tau really rocks. When the sun goes down, you can get anything you want dirt cheap. And a few things you *don't* want. The creepie-crawly kind that burn when you piss . . . if you catch my drift."

"Creepie-crawly?"

"According to my sergeant, Vung Tau has the highest VD rate

in the Western Hemisphere. Bareback it in town and there's a good chance your Johnson shrivels up by morning."

Contemplating celibacy, I changed the subject.

"I heard Vung Tau is fairly safe. Never gets attacked."

"We haven't been hit once since I got here. And that was over eight months ago. Charlie doesn't like to fight where he parties."

I was shocked.

"The Viet Cong come into town?"

"Hell, I've probably clinked beers with one or two. And I *know* I've shared some of their women."

"You can't be serious," I said. "How does that work?"

"Fifty miles upstream, we fight tooth and nail during the week. Come the weekend, we all party hearty down here. There's an unspoken truce when we come to town. The local police make you check your guns at the city outskirts. Ala the Earps in Dodge City."

"Aren't there any . . . altercations?"

"A fight breaks out now and then," said the driver, "but they're mostly push-and-shove affairs. A few broken noses, maybe a black eye or two, but nobody gets greased."

"Amazing," I mumbled. And left it at that.

———————

Cat Lo turned out to be a small Army base three miles south of Vung Tau. It was also home to two squadrons of PBRs—the small river boat Martin Sheen lionized in *Apocalypse Now.* The site of a refueling pier for LST, Cat Lo's accommodations were sparse compared to Saigon. Officer quarters consisted of a corrugated tin hut that looked and acted like an old-time radiator.

"The fan switch is over there," said the duty sergeant. "Although nobody ever turns it off. Showers and the head are one hut over. Chow hall, behind that. We don't stand on ceremony here, so everyone eats at the same mess."

I pointed to a rusted Mail Pouch thermometer nailed to a post. Its mercury was pegged out at 110 degrees.

"Is that thing accurate?" I asked.

"Don't rightly know," replied the sergeant. He tapped the glass with a finger. Grinned. "In the six months I've been here, it hasn't moved once. To my mind, she's reading a tad low."

Sweating profusely now, I plopped my gear onto a sagging cot.

"Got any other discouraging words for me?"

He handed me a sheet of paper.

"Just this. It's your battle station duty. I guess you Navy types call it *general quarters*."

"General quarters? But I'm only a transient. And I thought this place never got attacked."

"Regulations," he said. "There's always a first time, so base commander says everyone has to be included in the *battle* plan." Finger quotes around *battle*. "Even temporaries. I did you a favor and put you on tower four. It's close to the water and the coolest place in camp at night. If you're lucky, you might catch a breeze up there."

"Thanks . . . I think. And what am I supposed to do in this tower?"

"Don't worry, it's skate duty. All you have to do is direct a few illumination flares. But don't sweat it. As I said, we haven't been hit in a month of Sundays. Haven't had a drill in over four weeks."

Don't sweat it? Standing in a puddle of my own fluids, I couldn't fathom the logic.

"I appreciate the special assignment, sergeant. You're all heart."

He tossed me a thin booklet.

"You might want to browse through this in your spare time. Just in case. It's a manual on how to use a star scope."

Just in case? Those three words sounded familiar. I'd gone to high school with a guy named Justin Case. Little did I know his name would pop up a lot in the next few months. I flipped through the manual, then tossed it aside, a decision I would soon regret.

"You should take that with you to read on the beach," said the sergeant.

"Beach?"

"Cat Lo's got one of the finest beaches this side of Hanoi. White sands, blue water, the whole nine yards. Surf's not bad for boogie boarding. If you don't mind the jellyfish. We call it Malibu West."

Surfing in Vietnam?

After three days of lounging on the beach, I'd worked up a respectable tan and gone through two worn paperbacks. My nights consisted of camping out in front of that fan in my skivvies until I drifted off into a sticky sleep. By day five, I was bored silly. With my ship still a no-show, I struck up a friendship with a Navy chief at the mess hall. An avid Browns fan also from Ohio, he ran the local PBR repair facility at Cat Lo. The second night of our friendship, he came up with a novel solution to my boredom.

"We just finished refitting boat number six, and me and the boys are getting ready to head upriver for a test run tonight. Want to come along?"

"What do you mean *test run*?" I asked.

I'd heard stories about PBRs and was leery about riding on one—no matter how bored I was.

"If you're worried about getting into a firefight, we won't be going anywhere near the enemy," said the chief. "Just a quick trip up and back, no more than ten miles. We'll test the engine, fire off a few rounds to check out her guns, and be back in time for midrats."

Midrats were rations served at midnight to those on the late shift. Milk and cookies, peanut butter and jelly sandwiches . . . that sort of thing. Sometimes the Navy was all heart.

"Hell, why not?" I said from a place nowhere near my brain.

The typically masculine response of *Why not?* is the most ill-thought, hands down dumbest reason for doing anything a human being is capable of contemplating. I knew I'd stepped into it ankle deep that night when the chief tossed me a flak jacket as I boarded his boat.

"What's this for?" I asked.

"Just in case," said the chief, spider to the fly.

Too late to back out, I took a deep breath and strapped the thing on. The newfangled Kevlar jackets hadn't reached us yet, so the vest felt like a forty-pound armored corset. Which is exactly what it was. Curious about its efficiency, I rapped a knuckle on one of its plates.

"What will this contraption stop?" I asked.

"Anything short of an AK-47," replied the chief.

Since the Viet Cong's weapon of choice was an AK-47, his answer was anything but reassuring.

There were three boats in our little run up the river. After casting off from the dock, we headed down one of the river's many tributaries single file, spaced about two hundred yards apart. My PBR being the second in line, at least I wasn't cruising point. About three quarters of a mile later, we were the only boat to turn off its running lights. After another half mile, the chief cut the engine and we began to coast. Boat number one continued on its merry way and boat number three soon caught and passed us. Drifting backward with the current, nobody in my boat said a word. When the lights of the two other boats disappeared around a bend ahead, we were swallowed up by a suffocating darkness. A lump the size of a golf ball inched up my throat.

"Uh, Chief?" I whispered. "Is this standard procedure?"

"All part of the exercise. As long as we're on the river, we might as well do something productive. We call it the *ol' switcheroo*. If any VC are about, they'd see two sets of lights come up the river, then two sets of lights pass by. Our job as the middle boat is to lay low in the reeds for a while and see if anybody pops up. If they do, we blow them to smithereens."

That wasn't what I'd signed on for.

"We're laying an ambush? Um . . . just how successful do you expect this little ruse of yours to be?"

"Depends on how well coordinated we are. If we're sloppy, *we* might be the ones getting ambushed."

Great! Just friggin' great!

We drifted under an overhanging palm tree, and the forward lookout grabbed a low frond to pull us stern-first toward the bank. *Just in case* we had to make a quick exit. After securing the boat, the crew hunkered down to listen. Yours truly included. As nervous as I was, I mastered hunkering down real quick.

The jungle at night emits a variety of ominous sounds. Across a body of water, those sounds are amplified three-fold. A gentle gust of wind, a rustle here, a snap there, and within sixty seconds, I was sure an entire battalion of black pajamas lurked in the bushes.

"Did you hear that?" I whispered, my mouth suddenly dry.

"Nothing but a wild pig rooting around," said the chief.

"How can you be sure?"

"If it was Charlie, you wouldn't hear a thing."

With that, I got even better at hunkering down, behind the thickest patch of metal I could find. After thirty nerve-racking minutes, lights reappeared up the river, and boats one and three rejoined us.

"Another dry run," said the chief as he steered his boat away from the bank. "So much for an ambush. Ready for some fireworks, sir?" he asked with a grin.

Not waiting for a response, he turned to the forward gunner.

"Light up the Zippo! It's barbecue time!"

Zippo?

Before I could get my question out, a huge flame shot from the forward turret. Stretching at least two hundred feet, it reached all the way to shore to incinerate the palm tree we'd been hiding under. At the push of a button, we had been transformed into a fire breathing dragon. I didn't even know we'd been packing.

"Jesus Christ!" I blurted. "What is that stink?"

"Napalm," said the chief. "It smells like shit and burns everything in sight. Handy stuff when it comes to clearing things out."

Always the pessimist, I had to ask. What I'd been hiding behind was fifty pounds of ammo.

"Uh . . . what would happen if we took a hit?"

"We'd all turn into swiss cheese. Two seconds flat."

After that startling revelation, the chief decided it was time to crank up the fifties.

"Just a few rounds to clear out the barrels," he called it.

A few rounds?

I often exaggerate. But I swear on a stack of Bibles, we must have fired off more bullets than the French did in all of World War II. With tracers whizzing off into the night like a steady stream of angry red bees, I breathed, tasted, and smelled cordite through every orifice, every pore. After what seemed like a week, the chief finally ordered "Cease fire!"

When the firing subsided, I looked down to find myself standing ankle deep in warm, spent shell casings. Soon, an eerie silence settled over the water. Not a leaf on shore stirred; no insects chirped. Even the gentle breeze had lost its whistle. For a second or two, I thought the river had stopped flowing. Fearing I'd gone deaf from the din, I snapped a finger in front of my left ear. Thank God I could still hear.

With such awesome weaponry at our disposal, I couldn't fathom why America hadn't won the war by then. One thing for certain, I was glad I wasn't on the receiving end of what our PBR put out that night.

That boat ride taught me a valuable lesson. There would be no more nocturnal excursions for this lowly pork chop—aquatic or otherwise. For the duration of my stay in Cat Lo I limited my circle of activity to the chow hall, the latrine, and my trusty cot. Maybe a midday trip to the beach. Until my ship showed up, I could live with being bored silly. Emphasis on the word "live."

My ride to Vung Tau—Hamburger juice and bullet holes.

Officer's quarters in Cat Lo—definitely a no-star rating.

Navy swift boats—one ride was more than enough.

THREE
Battle Stations! Are You Kidding Me?

Two nights after my PBR adventure, I was settling into my cot with a new paperback when a siren shattered the night. Its high-pitched whine was followed in short order by several not distant enough explosions.

"What's going on?" I asked a half-dressed soldier trying to pull his pants on as he scrambled for the door. The second I got the words out, another explosion set off a ball of flame three huts over.

"We're under attack!" he yelled, his eyes wider than pie plates.

Just my luck. Eight months of peace down the drain, and it had to happen on my watch. Struggling with my own pants, I tried to remember my general quarter's station.

Was it tower four or tower three?

It didn't make much difference, since I didn't know the location of either one. As an afterthought, I grabbed the untouched stars scope manual from a shelf, then dashed for the door.

You REALLY should have read the thing, Lindsey!

Heaven help Cat Lo if I was actually called on to do something important.

Outside, I was met with a Chinese fire drill of epic proportions. Daunted by the hectic activity swirling all around me, I grabbed the slowest person I could latch on to. When I looked into the poor guy's eyes, I could tell he was more confused than me.

"Tower number . . . FOUR!" I managed. "Where is the damn thing?"

"Down by the beach," he said, pointing off to the right. "Head for the boat docks. You can't miss it." After mumbling something that might have been a prayer, he dashed off.

"Of course . . . the beach!" I said to his vapor trail. "Where else would it be?"

I hustled off toward the smell of water, hoping against hope my tower mates would know what to do when I got there. After all, I was only passing through, an uneducated transient. One who had never stood a battle station of any kind in his life. On ship or on shore. They had to be more competent than a lowly supply puke. Right?

If wishes were fishes. . .

At the base of tower four's ladder I was met with a disturbing sight. A Navy lieutenant even younger than I sat on the ground, legs splayed out in front of him, his back leaning against the first wrung. He was wearing a doctor's insignia on his left collar. The goofy expression on his face told me he'd tipped more than a few beers that evening.

"I'm not going up there," he said, wobbling a finger back and forth in front of his nose. "No how, no way. Heights scare the crap out of me. Anything taller than a bar stool makes me woozy. I'd only barf all over you."

"Have you been drinking?" I asked. Stupid question.

A slow, shit-eating grin spread across the doc's face.

"Ever since I got to Cat Lo." He looked up at the ladder. "Funny. I been here two whole months and I never noticed this tower before. Must be new."

"Do you know what's up there?" I asked.

"Haven't a clue," he said.

"But I'm supposed to assist you with . . . with whatever it is we're supposed to do up there."

The doc raised himself to one elbow. Offered a sloppy salute. Then slouched back down.

"Good luck with that. I'm sure you'll do a bang-up job. Whatever it is."

"Don't tell me you didn't read the manual, too?"

"Manual? What manual?"

"Out-fucking-standing!" I said. "The blind leading the blind."

Further conversation pointless, I climbed the ladder, the phrase *Why me, Lord?* rolling around in my brain. When I got to the top and opened the tower's trapdoor, I could see the real reason why Doctor Drunk hadn't wanted to come up.

At least ninety feet high, Tower Four had a commanding view of the entire area. I could see for miles. Given its height, however, it was also a *commanding* target. The enemy could see *me* from miles. After assuming the hunkered position I'd mastered on the PBR, I took a quick inventory of my surroundings. The only item of import seemed to be a small rectangular black box with an antenna on the far wall. It looked to be a portable radio of some kind. One I had no idea how to operate since I hadn't read a word in the manual.

"Is this black box thing a walkie-talkie?" I called back down to Doctor Drunk.

"Got me by the elbow," he shrugged.

That tears it!

"Goddamn it! I've had it up to here with your shit! Get your drunken ass up this ladder or I'll shoot you myself!" Wishing I actually had a gun.

My request brought another half-assed salute from the doc.

"I don't make house calls," he said. "Besides, what are you going to shoot me with? I may be shit-faced, but I can tell you aren't packing."

And he was right. The only weapon I saw fit to bring with me was my wits, leaving me unarmed. Out of options, I crouched against the thickest wall I could find. No sense in wasting more words on a useless pill pusher.

May the fleas of a thousand camels infest your armpits, Doc!

I tried to settle down for the night, but before I could get comfy, a mortar round hit a wooden beach chair fifty yards to the right of our tower. The one I'd been sunbathing in just that afternoon.

The explosion and subsequent shower of splinters sent the doc scrambling up the ladder as fast as his bandy little legs could propel him. After slamming the trap door shut behind him, he huddled against the wall next to me, out of breath, his eyes saucer-wide and alabaster white.

"I got lonely down there," he said.

I was about to cuss him out when the walkie-talkie thing went off with a loud buzz. Startled as we both were, we only stared. Three more buzzes quickly followed. Each more insistent than the last.

"Well," said the doc. "Aren't you going to answer it?'

"Me? Why not you?"

He tapped a finger to his collar insignia.

"I'm only a doctor. Talking into a walkie-talkie isn't in my job description."

"Big deal. I'm only a pork chop. And in the Navy's scheme of things, that's lower than a doctor."

"But I'm also drunk," added the doc.

"So what? I'm also a coward. And that trumps being drunk any day of the week. You've also been here ten times longer than me. Longevity should count for something. You also outrank me."

Despite our juvenile banter, the walkie-talkie thing kept buzzing its fool head off.

"What do you suppose it wants?" I asked.

"Why don't you answer it and find out?" said the doc.

"I wouldn't know what to say."

"How about ordering us a pizza? I'm starved. Pepperoni and sausage would be nice. Hold the anchovies. And no onions. I don't think my stomach could handle them."

Just what I needed, a soused-to-the-gills standup comic with a scalpel. The doc glanced over the railing. Rolled out a loud burp that smelled like a baked-bean fart.

"Then again," he said, "now that I think about it, maybe pizza isn't a good idea."

With that, he upchucked a quart's worth of whatever he'd eaten for dinner. At least he had the good manners to do it over the side. I almost felt sorry for the shirker.

"I'm curious," I said when he finished. "What's a doctor doing up in a tower anyway? Shouldn't you be assigned to a triage or something?"

"Maybe I'm a lousy doctor. Besides, I could ask you the same question. What's a supply officer doing in the cheap seats?"

He had a point. I guess counting beans wasn't high on anyone's pecking order. No matter where you were.

The doc sat back to pull a Coors can from his vest pocket. Popped the top with a loud fizz. Then gulped a large swig. I couldn't believe it.

"You brought *beer* to a fire fight?"

"Yeah," he nodded. "A martini would have been too much trouble. Besides, I ran out of olives last week."

From another pocket, he retrieved a flattened bologna sandwich. Took a huge bite.

"Late night snack," he grinned. "Care for some?"

"No, thanks. I think I'll pass."

Meanwhile, the walkie-talkie thing continued to buzz. Realizing it wasn't going to stop, I swallowed my pride, took a deep breath, and answered.

"Yes," I ventured into what I hoped was its mouthpiece.

I probably should have come up with some military sounding words. Like *Bravo, Tango, Echo,* or *Mike.* But I had no idea what any of those meant.

"Roger, over," I said as an afterthought. Probably from yet another John Wayne film.

Silence from the walkie-talkie.

Oh, great! Whoever's on the other end of this thing thinks I'm an idiot.

Finally, a distant sigh came over the line. Followed by, "Where do you want the first one, sir?"

"First what?" I asked.

"First flare, of course."

"I don't see any flares up here."

Another sigh from Mr. Walkie-Talkie.

"Have you looked through the starlight scope yet, sir?"

When another mortar round exploded on the beach, the doc peed himself. I almost followed suit.

"There's nothing up here but this damn radio I'm holding," I said.

"Look in the metal box hidden in the corner," said the voice.

"The one bolted to the wall?"

"That's the one."

"But it's got a huge padlock on it."

"The key's hanging on a peg hidden behind the second portside rafter."

After remembering *port* meant *left*, I found the key and opened the box. Then pulled out the largest, heaviest pair of binoculars I'd ever seen.

"Now what?" I asked.

"Turn the scope on then strap it to your head."

"Everything looks green," I said.

"That's the way it's supposed to look."

I felt like a kid with a new toy. When I looked off toward the field by the north gate, I could see three white objects slithering through a patch of tall grass. My instincts told me they shouldn't be there.

"Bandits at 1000 hours!" I shouted without thinking.

"Bandits?" said Mr. Walkie-Talkie.

"Bad guys, bogeys, intruders! Whatever you want to call the white things sneaking around in the weeds about a hundred yards due east of the north gate."

"As good a place to start as any," said Mr. Walkie-Talkie.

Three seconds later, the first illumination flare was on its way with a loud *thwoosh*. Our first attempt was way off target. Instead of illuminating the field where the bad guys were getting ever closer to gate two, it lit up the chow hall bright as day.

"Redirect?" asked Mr. Talkie.

I didn't know what the devil he was talking about. Undaunted by my poor sense of direction, he must have wanted me to try again. *If at first you don't succeed . . .* or something like that.

"Um . . . put your next one fifty degrees right of the last one. This time about two hundred yards out."

Thwoosh!

Now the boat dock to our left was bathed in bright light, sending several confused sailors scrambling for cover.

"No, no," I said, spinning around to take a hasty sight line. "Make that one hundred twenty degrees right of your last. About three hundred yards out."

Thwoosh!

Time for the latrine to shine. Struggling to pull their pants up, two bare-assed Marines dived into a nearby bunker, cursing loudly.

"No, damnit! Try eighty degrees left of your last! At one hundred yards!"

Thwoosh!

As it turned out, Mr. Wallkie-Talkie was as proficient with his flare launcher as I was with my scope. Our final effort detonated twenty feet in front of Tower Four. *My* Tower Four! With me staring through that scope, dead center at the explosion. It was like a gazillion-watt flashbulb going off in my face.

I wouldn't regain my sight until the following morning. So, for the rest of the night, I was pretty much useless as a flare spotter. Eventually, the mortar attack dwindled, and the white objects in the field tired of our fireworks show and crawled somewhere else. No thanks to me and my soused tower partner. Charlie probably got bored and headed off to Vung Tau for a couple of beers and a hooker or two.

Although my vision eventually returned, it took another full day before the big red dot in front of my eyes faded away. I hadn't even set foot on the *Hampshire County* yet, and in the short span of a few days, I'd already gone deaf, dumb, and blind. Heavy emphasis on the *dumb* part. My second ironclad vow in Vietnam was to never again touch anything that resembled a starlight scope. The experience wasn't a total loss, however. When my eventual captain learned of my less than heroic exploits at Cat Lo, he put me in for a tongue-in-cheek citation (a copy of which is included in the appendix). Since pork chops are notorious for their lack of chest candy, I would wear the medal proudly.

━━━━━━━

For the next five days, it was back to boredom. With the words *tower* and *boat ride* now dead to me, at least I didn't go blind or suffer a heart attack. I had just returned from another afternoon at the beach, lobster red in my shorts and flip-flops, when I felt a tap on my shoulder.

"You wouldn't happen to be Ensign Lindsey would you, sir?" asked a guy dressed in a sloppy green uniform. Thirty pounds overweight and missing a front tooth, I knew right away he wasn't a Marine. Then I recognized the logo stenciled on his shirt pocket.

"That's me," I replied, wondering why a Seabee would be interested in me.

Mr. Green snapped off a salute. Smiled.

"I've been looking all over for you, Mr. Lindsey. I see by your sunburn you found Cat Lo's beach. I'm SK3 Michael Mantle. But everyone calls me Mickey." No surprise there. "I'm one of your storekeepers. I'm here to drive you to the ship."

"Ship? What ship?"

Confused, I pulled a sand wedgie out of my butt. After being shuttled up and down the Vietnam coast, I'd almost forgotten I'd been ordered to an LST.

"The *Hampshire County*, of course," said Mantle. "You *are* our new supply officer, aren't you?"

"Yes . . . or I think so. I was beginning to have doubts the *Hampshire* even existed."

"Oh, we exist, all right. Unfortunately. I've got a truck waiting. As soon as you change, I'll help you with your gear."

"Do I have time for a quick shower?" I asked. "To wash all this sand off."

"Good idea. We've been on water rats for a month now. The vaps are offline again."

"Come again." I'd never heard the term *vaps* before.

"Evaporators," said Mantle, "the equipment that makes fresh water for the ship. When they go on the fritz, we have to shower in salt water. Ain't too good in the cleaning department. Leaves you itchy all over."

I scratched at my pubescent moustache. I'd discovered facial hair was a must in 'Nam.

"And just how often are these *vaps* down?" I asked.

"About fifty percent of the time," Mantle said, smiling. "You get used to it after a while."

After a not-so-quick shower, I found myself staring at the *Hampshire County*'s twenty-year old smelly Dodge pickup.

"I hope that stink isn't coming from the truck," I said.

"Depends on what you're smelling," said Mantle.

"I think it's diesel oil, with maybe a dash of grilled onions thrown in."

"Then that would be me," said Mantle. "The truck smells like gasoline and rotten eggs."

"Diesel oil and onions? Odd combination for a sailor."

"We all smell like that on the 'Fat Lady.' You will, too, sir. Since she runs on diesel fuel, her exhaust smoke gets into everything." Mantle made a sour face. "And we had liver and onions for lunch today. Again! Everybody onboard hates the stuff. Maybe your first order of business should be to tell the cooks to cut back on it."

"I'll see what I can do," I said. "I'm not a big fan of liver myself."

It was a little white lie, the first of many I was destined to tell. According to the Navy, liver was good for you, so it had to be on the menu at least once a week. Come inspection time, they checked on such things. Inventoried your stock to make sure you were ordering your fair share. Even went so far as to rummage through the garbage, which is where most of the liver ended up anyway.

"That explains the liver smell," I added. "What about the diesel stink? Don't the ship's stacks carry away the exhaust?"

Mantle blurted a laugh.

"Exhaust stacks? Ain't no such things on a *T*."

"We don't have stacks?"

"Nope. Just two big openings on either side of the ship. When we're not buttoned up tight, which is pretty hard to do in this heat, the fumes drift down the passageways and get into everything. Our clothes, our bedding, the food. We've learned to live with it."

Mystery solved, I turned my attention to the truck. At some time in the distant past, it might have been a fine vehicle, but those days were long gone. Decked out in battleship gray, the old Dodge was rust-streaked, tilting to the left, and squatting low in the stern on what was left of its back springs.

"Are you sure this thing is seaworthy?" I asked.

"Susie may not look like much, but she runs like a top. Her engine's just been overhauled, and her tires are almost new. She'll get us to where we're going."

Susie? Get us to where we're going?

I'd heard that last phrase before. And not that long ago.

"I guess I've ridden in worse looking vehicles," I said. But I couldn't remember when.

As I slid into Susie's sagging passenger seat, I noticed the window crank was missing and my armrest dangled by a single crooked bolt. A cushion spring goosed my left butt cheek with a painful prong.

"Comfy seat," I said.

When I looked down, I saw a four-inch rust hole to the left of my right foot. Directly in front of me, three large cracks stretched across the front windshield. At least it appeared to be functional, which was something I couldn't say about my armrest. Susie may have looked and smelled like a junkyard dog in heat, but when Mantle cranked the engine over, it purred like a kitten. The phrase *"Never judge a book by its cover"* came to mind.

"She's got a powerful sound to her," I said.

"We have several piston heads onboard," said Mantle. "I put the four barrel in myself."

Four barrel what? I thought. When it came to engines, I couldn't tell a carburetor from an alternator.

Mantle slammed Susie into first and we were off—in the opposite direction of the water, where I expected the ship to be.

"Where have you guys been?" I asked. "I got to 'Nam ten days ago."

"Our last stop was a dink-water settlement upriver to deliver supplies," said Mantle. "We've been to so many places; after a while, they all look the same. Places order stuff; we deliver it to them. Toilet paper, plywood, C-rats . . . you name it. Back and forth, week in, week out."

Mantle widened his grin to expose another missing tooth.

"'Course we got it better than some. At least we're not up to our asses in some rice paddy. With gooks in black pajamas trying to slit our throats every night."

My curiosity got the better of me.

"I notice you aren't wearing dungarees. Any reason for the greens?"

"You mean my Seabee costume?" Mantle laughed, doffed his cap. "It's uniform of the day when I go on one of my special runs."

"Since you work for me, this *special run* of yours wouldn't be anything illegal, would it? I'd hate to get thrown in the hoosegow before I even report."

"*Illegal*? Nah. There ain't no such word in 'Nam. Besides, it's only illegal if we get caught."

We?

"So, this run? It's the reason we're heading away from the ship?"

"I'm impressed, Mr. Lindsey. You've got a good sense of direction.

A huge shipment of gear arrived yesterday over at the Seabee camp and it's ripe for the picking."

"Hence the Seabee uniform you're wearing," I said. "I take it, then, you're planning to rob them."

"You got it."

I could tell I was in the presence of the most important man on the ship, *Hampshire County*'s resident scrounger.

"And just what kind stuff are you, uh, *we*, looking for?"

Mantle shot a thumb over his shoulder.

"Whatever we can fit into that big crate in the back."

"I hate to bring it up," I said, "but the Navy just spent big bucks and six months of my time training me to be on the lookout for questionable behavior like this. According to regulations, some would say it would be my duty to clap you in irons."

"You might want to rethink that, sir. By the grace of God, the book of Cumshaw, and my sneaky disposition, so goes the *Hampshire*."

Cumshaw was the light-fingered art of bartering. Loosely translated, it meant *stealing*.

"If we need this *stuff* so badly, why don't we just order it? That's why the Navy gives us a budget. You know, the ship's OPTAR (operating target), the amount they allocate to its ships to keep them afloat?"

"No disrespect, Mr. Lindsey, but you've got a lot to learn about how we do things out here in the real world. If we had to depend on what the Navy gives us, we'd be dead in the water within a week."

"We could always ask for more funds."

Mantle smiled. Raised a slow eyebrow.

"Ever hear the phrase *blood from a turnip*? Ask the Navy for more money and the first thing they'd do is jump all over you for not managing your resources properly. Then send out a tight-assed inspector to stick his boot up your ass."

I hadn't laid eyes on my ship and already a lengthy prison term teetered on the horizon.

"So," I sighed, "you're telling me we have to rob from the rich and give to the poor? Namely, us?"

"You might put it that way. You're not going to turn me in, are you?"

"Not yet, anyway. I suppose that uniform you're wearing is to get us through the Seabee's front gate?"

"You catch on quick, sir."

"What do you want me to do?"

"Just relax and follow my lead," said Mantle. "I've done this a few times, so I know the ropes. The Seabees are good people. They can build anything out of nothing. Anywhere, anytime. Under the worst conditions possible. But up here—" A tap to his forehead, "they ain't got a grasp of how it works paper-wise. It'll be like stealing candy from a baby."

Obviously, my man was an expert *thief.* One I would come to depend on in the months to come.

Typical Vietnam street scene.

Doctor Drunk's ill-fated tower #4.

FOUR

Robbing Peter to Pay Paul

A soldier with an M-16 strapped over his left shoulder stopped us at the Seabee gate. Standing tall in his pressed greens, he strode forward. Raised his right hand.

"Halt! Show me some identification."

Oh, shit! I thought. *Prison, here I come.*

"This is new," whispered Mantle as he braked to a stop. "The Bees must be on some kind of alert. They don't usually carry rifles."

The guard bent to read Mantle's name tag.

"Never seen you around before . . . *Smith*. And I know every Seabee face here at Cat Lo. What outfit you with?"

My sweat turning cold, I knew it wasn't long before I'd be donning prison garb. Alcatraz or Folsom, I didn't know which. But Mantle didn't bat an eye.

"I'm from NMCB 62, of course," he said. "Ain't but one battalion in-country this time of year." Then he whipped out an ID card. The one with a *Smith* on it.

A fake ID? Expert, hell? The guy's a friggin' mastermind!

The guard looked down at the ID, back at Mantle. Then at our low-riding truck.

"What's in the back?"

My man didn't miss a beat.

"The transmission from our number two D-8 cat. Needs to be sent back to the States for overhaul. Her connecting rods are shot. Guess we rode her too hard."

What the hell was he talking about?

"She slips a gear every time we put power to the blade," continued Mantle. "So, it's shit city when it comes to grading."

Huh?

"I know what you mean," said the guard. "But all of the supply types from '62 have been by here more than once. How come this is the first time I've seen you?"

"They just transferred me in from the Okinawa detachment to help with the MLO pack out. It's a real mess, and Commander Bagley is scared shitless about flunking inspection. Alpha Company's been cannibalizing so much of the rolling stock, there ain't nothing left but bare bones."

Double huh?

"You got that right," chuckled the guard. "Our grease monkeys are worse thieves than those gator Navy assholes."

"You been hit by *T* bandits, too?" asked Mantle.

"All the time. We're on the lookout for a skinny dude, name of Jones. Two weeks ago, the bastard carted off an entire oven. And half our supply of shit paper. How he got that big oven in his truck by hisself is beyond me. Damn thing must have weighed over a ton." After shaking his head, the guard waved us through the gate.

Mantle leaned out the window as we were going by. "If I ever run across the guy, I'll kick him in the slats."

"Much obliged," said the guard. "The oven's no great loss, but I'm getting sick and tired of wiping my ass with yesterday's *Stars and Stripes*. Newsprint itches like hell."

When we were out of earshot, I turned to Mantle.

"Don't tell me. *Jones* is also one of mine, right?"

"Best seaman storekeeper this side of Guam. I taught him all he knows. But his name is Markovich, not Jones. We call him the perverted Pollack."

"Because he steals toilet paper?"

"Because of his way with women. He'll screw anything that moves. And a few things that don't."

Great, I thought. *I've inherited a light-fingered Laurel and Hardy team.*

But having taken part in the heist, there was no turning back. In for a penny, in for a pound, I was now officially a felon. Although the guard hadn't asked me for identification, I'd never be able to show my face on that base again. Come tomorrow, the Seabees would be on the lookout for a chubby dude and a tall ensign with a bad moustache. Still, I was impressed with my new storekeeper's savvy. And his gigantic brass balls.

"That was quick thinking on your part back there, Mantle. You rattled off that garbage like you knew what you were talking about."

"Actually, I *did* know what I was talking about. And it wasn't garbage."

"So there really *is* an Okinawa detachment?"

"Yep. There's also one in Guam and one in Diego Garcia. I picked Okinawa because it's closer, more plausible."

"CDR Bagley is actually 62's commanding officer?'

"He relieved CDR Thompson last month."

"MLO?"

"Material Liaison Office."

"And what the hell is a D-8 cat?"

"A big bulldozer. Standard earth mover for the Seabees."

I shook my head. Let out a long, slow whistle.

"Now I'm *really* impressed."

"Pays to do your homework, sir."

Turning the corner, Mantle made sure no one was looking. Then backed down a narrow alley between two Quonset huts. Leaving the truck running, he went to the back and lowered the bed gate. When he popped open one side of the crate, I was surprised to find myself staring at two huge rocks, at least a hundred pounds each.

"I could use some help with these," he said. "They're heavy suckers."

It took our combined strength to roll those rocks out of the truck. They came to rest next to two other rocks that looked like a matching set. Gaping at the foursome, I scratched my head.

"I'm sure there's a reason for this madness," I said.

"It would have looked suspicious to waltz in here with an empty crate. I needed the weight to set Susie down on her springs. The gate guard would have noticed the discrepancy right off."

I pointed at the four rocks.

"I take it these shenanigans are nothing new for the *Hampshire County*."

"Standard operating procedure. Next time, though, I'll have to come up with something different. Eventually even Seabees catch on."

During my tour, the inventive mind of Michael "Mickey" Mantle, SK3 par excellence, never ceased to amaze me.

Many years later, I would serve a tour of duty with the Seabees. And wherever we went, I always kept an eye out for LST sailors wearing greens. Fat, skinny, or otherwise. To make sure we weren't *robbed blind. Just in case,* I always left a standing order with our gate guard to admit no one smelling of diesel oil and grilled onions.

———

Going out of the Seabee encampment, Susie rode low on her springs. Just like she did when we pulled up to the gate. Several cases of TP were among the booty stashed in our crate, and I felt a twinge of guilt. That poor gate guard's already chafed behind was destined for more newsprint. I had to admit, however, it had been a successful outing. Both satisfying and exhilarating.

"Not bad for your first trip out, Mr. Lindsey," said Mantle. "You've got the makings of a top-notch scrounger."

I chanced a quick glance over my shoulder. To my relief, no alarms had been sounded in Seabee-ville. So far, so good; at least nobody in greens was chasing us. Not yet, anyway.

"That or a first-class jailbird," I said. "Not to nitpick, Mantle, but do you have any idea what the stuff in the back is worth?"

"Nine, maybe ten thousand dollars on the black market."

"Omigod! We're up for grand larceny?"

"Not to worry, sir. It's not like we're going to sell it. Take my word, every last bit will be put to good use on the ship. I didn't go hog wild back there. We only took things we needed. Before suiting up, I went to every department on board and asked for a wish list. Even the captain added his two cents worth."

I couldn't believe my ears.

"Our commanding officer was in on this raid?"

"He always is. How'd you think I came up with the fake ID?"

Apparently, this was a community effort; if one went down, we *all* would. I imagined the entire crew standing tall at our court martial.

We were only doing it for the good of our ship, Judge.

Mantle slowed to point out a few of the sights. Swerving to avoid a peasant woman and her two goats, he nodded at a rusty tin shack to our right.

"That hole in the wall over there . . . that's the Wagon Wheel Club. Come Friday night, it's the most popular place in town. Packed to the rafters. Hot music and even hotter women."

A rickety claptrap a healthy sneeze would blow over, the Wheel's front door dangled by a single leather strap nailed to a rotten wooden frame. A mangy mutt dozed on its ramshackle porch, legs spread out.

"*That* tiny place?" I said. "You couldn't cram ten people nuts to butts in there if they all held their breath."

"Try a couple hundred," said Mantle. "The dance floor is underground where it's cooler. On weekends, you'll find half our crew bellied up to the bar. Markovich has been tossed out of the Wheel over twenty times. As skinny as he is, he never puts up much of a fight. The bouncers, good Joes all, know him well. As a courtesy, they just pick him up by the belt and throw him out. Make sure he lands on something soft. Kris is always so drunk he walks away without a scratch. No harm, no foul."

"And he keeps going back? You'd think he'd wise up."

"Hell, Kris expects to get thrown out. Be disappointed if he didn't."

Curiouser and curiouser, I thought.

Mantle followed a slow right turn with a quick left. Another right and there she was, tied up to the pier in all her glory—the USS *Hampshire County* (LST 819). Pride of America's amphibious Navy.

The picture in Jane's Fighting Ships didn't do her justice. Not much longer than a football field, she looked like a rectangular loaf of very old, very tired rusting metal. I'd seen sleeker looking dog turds. My new home was quite possibly the scurviest ship ever to displace water. In the hard-on-the-eyes Olympics, she took the gold, silver, and bronze all by herself. Mantle saw my jaw drop. Tried for a reassuring smile.

"Kinda takes your breath away, doesn't she, sir? She may look like she fell out of an ugly tree and hit every branch on the way down, but she's damn near unsinkable. Although—" Pausing to rub his chin. "Truth be told, she rides worse than she looks."

Just what I wanted to hear.

"You gotta be kidding me," I said.

"Nope. Wish I was. Hate to say it, but the Fat Lady is a real seasick machine."

A flurry of activity near the gangplank caught my attention. Two sailors in working dungarees and ball caps were engaged in a shouting match. Mantle noticed my stare right off.

"The tall skinny one on the right is SK2 Spratt," he said. "He's—"

I put up a quick hand.

"Don't tell me," I said. "His first name is Jack, and he doesn't eat any fat. Right?"

"Good one, sir. Actually, Ed there is your head storekeeper. He's the real brains of the outfit. I may be good at scrounging, but he's the one who keeps us out of jail. Ed knows the regulations like the back of his hand. And how we get around them."

I could only make out bits and pieces of the shouting. Spratt kept pointing at a huge crate on the back of an elongated flatbed truck. The crate had to be seventy feet long, ten feet high, and weigh at least fifty tons. As we got closer, I picked up the gist of the argument.

"You can't be serious!" spewed Spratt. "I didn't order that fucking monstrosity! It's a catapult piston, for God's sake! Do we look like a goddam aircraft carrier? Hell, you could put three LSTs on a carrier's hangar deck. With room left over!"

The driver crossed his arms. Stuck out his jaw.

"I was told to deliver this here crate to this here pier. And you're the only ship in sight."

"What's the identification code on the paperwork?" asked Spratt.

The driver pulled out a crumbled invoice.

"72766, it says here."

"That's for the USS *America*! Like I said, a goddam *AIRCRAFT* carrier! Our code is 50819. Close but no cigar, my friend. Even *you* should be able to tell the difference. Open your eyes, numbnuts, not even a single digit matches!"

The driver would have none of it. He'd been given his orders and that was that. Not about to take any more guff, especially from a supply puke, he stood his ground. If it came to blows, so be it.

"All I know is my boss told me to deliver this to that there ugly ship. Now, are you going to sign for it or not?"

"Over my dead body!" said Spratt, his jaw tight. "Wake up, stupid! Something that big would sink our ship!"

"Fucking asshole!"

"Stupid prick!"

At that point, I decided to intervene. I stepped between the two. Puffed out my chest to make my collar device more visible, then asked to see the invoice. A cursory glance told me my man was in the right. A sympathetic look on my face, I turned to the driver.

"Your shipping department obviously misrouted this," I said. "It's a shame they put you to all this trouble. But if you tell them you noticed the wrong code before you came down to the pier, it'll save them a lot of embarrassment. They'll owe you."

I'd like to think it was my coolheaded voice of reason and not the fact that I was an officer that convinced the driver to get back in his truck and drive away. But I'm probably kidding myself. At least I impressed SK2 Spratt.

"Nice job, sir," he said, then saluted. "You must be Ensign Lindsey. Welcome aboard."

"Glad I could be of assistance. Although, from what I saw, you had the situation well in hand."

Another commotion at the other end of the pier caught Spratt's eye.

"Sorry, sir," he said. "Gotta run. This onload is turning out to be a real pain in my ass. As they always do."

Watching my lead storekeeper hustle off to handle another snafu, I thought back on my day. The morning wasn't half over and already I'd committed a crime and broken up a fight. And I haven't even set foot on the *Hampshire County* yet.

Time to report for duty. At the top of the gangplank, I saluted the ensign (the flag, not me), then turned to address the quarterdeck watch.

"Ensign Lindsey, reporting as ordered. Permission to come aboard?"

Before the watch could respond, a paint chipper clattered to the deck. A foot to the right and it would have split my skull.

"Look out below!" rang out too late from above. "Sorry about that!"

"Johnson, you worthless piece of shit!" shouted the watch. "You could have killed somebody! That's the second time you dropped that damn thing. One more and your scrawny ass goes on report!"

More yellow than white, the watch's uniform looked as if it hadn't been washed in a year. He sported a thick Fu Manchu moustache a full three inches below his chin line. Well beyond regulation. The only things missing were an eye patch and a parrot on his shoulder.

"Permission to come aboard?" I repeated.

"Permission granted," he said. "If you got the guts."

Before I could respond, a screwdriver tumbled from above.

"Godammit, Johnson!" yelled the watch. Deciding the poor man had enough problems of his own, I turned back to Mantle.

"Lead on," I said.

"The captain's anxious to meet you," he said. "I'll show you to his cabin. I'm sure he wants to lay a few words on you."

Two steps later, I tripped over one of the many cables crisscrossing the deck.

"What's the captain like?" I asked.

"Captain Davidson is gruff, but fair as the day is long. Old school mustang, he came up through the enlisted ranks. Made lieutenant three years ago."

In the Navy, the commanding officer of a ship is always referred to as *Captain*, no matter the rank on his collar.

"He's one smart cookie," continued Mantle. "Used to be an aviation electronics chief, so he knows his stuff. Can't get anything by the man. The one time I went to captain's mast, he saw right through my cockamamie excuse and nailed my ass to the wall."

"He's strict?"

"Yeah, but I had it coming. When it comes to this ship, there ain't no one more savvy than the skipper. He can tell you where every bolt goes, where every pipe leads to. Unfortunately for us storekeepers, he also knows a lot about supply."

Just what I needed. A boss who knew my business better than me.

"Does he hover over your shoulder?"

"Not really. But don't try to baffle him with bullshit. He even knows how to fill out all our forms. He'll go to bat for you when needs be, but you'd better have your ducks in a row. The dude's from Missouri."

Dodging a low overhang, I stumbled over a coiled section of chain. Then banged my shin on an open crate.

"Damn! Is the ship always this cluttered?" I asked.

"This is nothing," said Mantle. "We're empty now. Wait until we're loaded and packed chockablock to the rafters."

A stubbed toe and knocked knee later, I'd learned to walk crouched over with my head on a swivel. By the time we crossed to the other side of the ship, I'd been permeated with a diesel oil smell that wouldn't leave me for the next two years. Mantle had been right. The stink was everywhere.

As we made our way down the only passageway in officer's country, I noticed the rubber deck tread extending three feet up the bulkheads.

"Um . . . Mantle? I'm sure there's a good reason for that, but I'm afraid to ask."

"It's for heavy seas. As I said, the Fat Lady can be a rough ride when the weather turns bad."

I bent for a closer look. The footprints on the bulkhead indicated someone had actually *walked the walls* not that long ago.

"Holy crap!" I said. "That's a twenty-degree angle! The ship rolls *that* much?"

"More like thirty," said Mantle. When we get caught in a trough, we can push forty. Chief Holms has been onboard longer than anyone and he swears we once pegged out at fifty during a real blow."

"A *fifty*-degree roll? You can't be serious. Wouldn't that capsize the ship?"

"A destroyer or a cruiser, maybe," said Mantle. "But not an LST.

With our flat bottom, we only wallow out and snap back. Something to do with our longer riding arm."

I remembered hearing the term in one of my navigation classes back at Officer's Candidate School. Using both hands, Mantle demonstrated.

"Since we ride so flat in the water, and because of our low center of gravity, whenever we take a hard roll, the ship tends to—"

"That's okay," I said. "I'll take your word for it."

FIVE
Shavetail Ensign Learns the Ropes

At the end of a dark passageway, Mantle knocked on the skipper's open door. Lieutenant Rick Davidson sat at his desk pondering the mound of papers in front of him.

"Cap'n?" said Mantle. "Sorry to disturb you, but I finally found our new supply officer."

"Ah, Ensign Lindsey," said the captain. "Welcome aboard. I'm glad you caught up to us. Have a seat."

He motioned to the only other chair in the cabin, then turned to Mantle.

"Did you get everything we needed?"

"And then some, sir."

"Any problems?"

"Piece of cake."

"Excellent," said the captain. "Should I expect an angry call from the Seabees?"

"They didn't know what hit them, sir."

Davidson shot a thumbs up at Mantle, who nodded an appreciative smile and then left. Something told me the two had had this conversation before.

"I'll be with you in a sec, Lar," continued the captain. "Got to finish this SITREP. It's due out to today."

As I watched him chicken scratch some figures, I liked him already. He had called me "Lar." Not Ensign or Lindsey. Even though he was only a lieutenant, he was still my CO, my commanding officer. That meant he could call me anything he wanted. Including dumbass. As in, "What took you so long to get here, *dumbass*?"

Even while he was sitting, I could tell Lieutenant Davidson was a big man. Not quite as tall as me but broader in the shoulders. And a lot more muscle. As he labored over the report, every few seconds, he'd take a puff from his cigarette. The dead soldiers in an ashtray by his elbow told me he was a chain-smoker.

Richard Peter Davidson was only thirty-four, but his leather worry lines made him look much older. Eighteen months in command of a relic LST had taken its toll. His eyes were still razor sharp, however, and he exuded the aura of a no-nonsense skipper, a man who knew where he wanted to go and how to get there. His mangled left ear and crooked nose indicated he'd been in a few fights. And probably won all of them. Sporting a massive set of hairy forearms that would have made Popeye jealous, he looked like he could tear a phone book in half without breaking sweat.

The most impressive thing about the man was his hands. Obviously working man's hands, they told me he wasn't afraid of getting down and dirty with his crew. Hands that you'd want on your side when things got rough.

As he labored over his papers, my eyes began to roam. As far as sea cabins went, the captain's wasn't half bad. Fold down writing table, built in bunk on one wall, long table on the other, modest closet, two portholes, and an adjoining private head (bathroom). Basic but livable. Hanging on the far bulkhead was the grungiest looking officer's hat I'd ever seen. A mass of crumples and wrinkles, its cover was blacker than khaki. Salt stained and frayed, it broadcast volumes about life aboard an LST. While waiting, I wondered what could drain the starch out of both a man's face and his hat in such a short period. Swallowing hard, I realized I'd probably find out soon enough.

"There!" said the captain, slamming his pen down. "The son of a bitch is done! And if headquarters doesn't like what I'm telling them, they can kiss my hairy ass. Sorry to keep you waiting, Lar, but the higher-ups get their panties in a bunch if they don't get this friggin' report on time. No matter what garbage I feed them."

"Paperwork!" I snorted. "The final act of a good crap."

Skip slapped his knee. Laughed from the belly.

"Good one! I'll have to remember it at our next squadron meeting." Sucking in deeply, he blew out a perfect smoke ring, then leaned back to cross his arms.

"Something tells me we're going to get along just fine, Lar. Great minds always roll along the same gutter."

Now it was my turn to laugh.

"It's a good thing you showed up with a sense of humor," said the skipper. "You'll need it in the weeks to come."

He leaned forward on his elbows to blow another smoke ring. Donned a more serious expression.

"This is the part of the conversation where I'm supposed to give you a welcome aboard speech, or some such crap. Well, I ain't much for mincing words, so here goes."

He scratched at his bad ear before taking a deep breath.

"Welcome to purgatory, lad. As you can see, we"—he always referred to the ship as *we*—"are old, tired, dirty, and stink to high heaven. And as you've probably been told, we are also the worst riding ship in the fleet. You may have also noticed we don't do spit and polish well. After the day is done, we don't got much spit left. Can't remember the last time I even saw a can of polish on the ship.

"You might say we're a little rough around the edges. The Marines we cart in and out of this sorry-ass country call us *pussies* because we don't see much action. Hell, what with all the crap they put up with, I suppose they got a right to bad mouth us. And we've been called a lot worse. However, we've seen our fair share of action. Been through a lot of tight places. *Nasty* comes in all shapes and sizes up and down the rivers.

"Most of the Navy looks down their noses at us because we don't clean up well. But that isn't our fault. There ain't enough gray paint in the world to cover up our rust. And as you can tell by our uniforms, the dress code on the *Hampshire County* is anything but regulation.

"To be blunt as burnt toast, when it comes to fighting ships of the line, you've hitched your wagon to a tail-end Charlie. We amphibs suck hind tit. Always have, always will. We're slow as molasses in January and easier to hit than the broadside of a barn. Half our equipment is down hard, and the other half has been patched up three times over."

Skip nodded slowly. Puffed out his cheeks. Blew out a lungful of air.

"As our new pork chop, you'll have to squeeze every nickel out of our budget. You'll be asked to find repair parts for equipment made by factories that went out of business twenty years ago. When you ask for more money to pay for the special tooling those parts require, the four-star banker types back in Washington will laugh in your face. Those desk jockeys couldn't care less about our dirty little ship and its dirty little problems.

"But make no mistake about it. Without the dirtbag gator Navy, nothing would get done over here. We're important. And don't let anyone tell you otherwise. So, if you don't mind rolling your sleeves up and generating some elbow grease now and then, you just might enjoy your tour with us."

Finished with his speech, he blew out yet another smoke ring. Watched for a few seconds as it rose to the ceiling. Then looked me straight in the eye.

"Okay, that's it for my sad tale of woe. How's that for a meet and greet?"

Stunned, I had to take a deep breath. Took another for good measure.

"Well, sir . . . I see sugarcoating isn't your style. But I appreciate your laying your cards on the table."

"Speaking of cards," said the skipper, "that brings me to the question of the day. Do you play bridge?"

"As in *I bid two spades*? Yes, sir, I do. I used to play a lot in college."

"Do you know Blackwood?"

"Better than Gerber."

"Great! Then you'll be my partner. I've been looking for a fourth."

And just like that, I was an official member of the wardroom bridge squad. A squad that would meet religiously after dinner every night while I was on board. On my way out the door, the skipper tossed me the CASREP (casualty report) list, supply's version of the walking wounded.

"That's your first order of business, Lar. It's what's hard down on the *Hampshire*. Some of it's been broke for six months and still waiting for repair parts. If they even exist. We got jury-rigs on board that would make Rube Goldberg blush. Last month, we had to fashion a makeshift sail to help us to the pier. Both engines crapped out, and if it hadn't been for a hefty tailwind, we'd still be floating around in the damn bay."

I took a quick scan of the two-page list. At supply corps school, they taught us if a ship our size had more than ten items on such a list, it was in dire shape.

"There has to be over a hundred items here!" I said, trying not to gasp. "How do *we* stay afloat?"

"By a wing and a prayer sometimes," said the skipper. "When we cast off three days from now, we'll be held together by good wishes and glue. But we'll manage." A quick knuckle rap on his wooden desktop. "God willing and the creek don't rise."

Words escaped me. I felt dizzy.

"One more thing," he added. "Ralph Hall, the lieutenant junior grade you're replacing, is being medevacked back to the States tomorrow night. Means your relieving process will be cut short. But don't worry. I don't put much stock in inventories."

Thank God for that. Counting all the supplies, food, money, accountable gear, and ship's store stock and balancing out the ledgers usually took a week of concerted, backbreaking work. I'd been given less than a day.

"What's wrong with Mr. Hall?" I had to ask.

"Migraines. Had 'em for six months. The galley fire probably pushed him over the edge."

Galley fire?

"What with it coming so soon after the explosion in the laundry."

Laundry explosion?

"Then again, it could have been his main storeroom. It has a tendency to flood in heavy seas."

Flood?

"Bad business, migraines," said the skipper. "Lights, sounds, even a slight breeze can be excruciating. My wife gets a few each year, but nowhere near as bad as Ralph's. He's been laid up in his bunk for three days now." Skip put a steady hand on my shoulder. Trotted out his most reassuring smile. "But I'm sure he'll perk up when he sees you."

———————

For a split second, I thought Ltjg Hall was going to kiss my feet. Now that I'd finally showed up, he could fly home.

"Thank God you're here!" he cried.

From his gaunt, hollow-eyed appearance, I could tell he was long overdue for the Freedom Bird. If his loose-fitting khakis were any indication, he must have lost fifty pounds during his tour. His face had a jaundiced hue, and his left eye sported a nasty tic. More bad omens. Was I destined to suffer a similar fate?

Chin up, Lindsey! said the optimist in me. *It's only your first day.*

Yeah, but look at this guy! countered the pessimist half. *He looks like death warmed over.*

With the end in sight, Ralph sucked it up and charged headlong into our whirlwind inventory. For ten straight hours, I followed him into this and that storeroom and then into the deepest, most inaccessible bowels of the ship, which would take me a week to find again.

We counted everything imaginable. Widgets, wadgets, nuts, bolts, thingamabobs, and bob-a-ma-things. We counted cans of corn, peas, lard, coffee, spaghetti sauce, succotash, and of course . . . beans. We counted powdered milk, powdered sugar, powdered eggs, and powdered powder. Salt, soup, and soap. We counted bags of potatoes, bags of flower, bags of fruit, bags of rice, and last but not definitely least, six burlap bags bursting with onions. Oh, yes, and in the freezer, we counted a hundred and ten pounds of rock-hard liver.

Done with all that, Ralph opened his safe and we counted money. A quick safe combination change, and it was *mine*, all mine! Over five hundred thousand dollars, to be exact. All those greenbacks dazzled me and my thin wallet.

Rich! I'm rich!

However, it all belonged to the government. And half of it was in the form of MPC (military payment currency), a cartoonish form of Monopoly money used in Vietnam to discourage black market misuse of dollars. Every so often, the Navy changed the series of the stuff. Added new colors and different serial numbers. Out with the old, in with the new; in the short period of one day, they'd render an entire set of currency worthless. They were supposed to be tightly kept secrets, but local venders had a sixth sense about when they were coming. As the change deadline approached, the Vietnamese scrambled to dump their old MPC for anything they could get.

An unscrupulous disbursing officer with brass balls and a fistful of dollars could make a fortune on the black market. With exchange rates soaring as high as twenty-to-one during the crossover periods, all he had to do was go out in town with greenbacks, exchange them at the outlandish rate, then pocket the difference. His books would balance, and he would walk away from Vietnam a rich man.

A wimp when it comes to taking chances with money, I quickly put such chicanery out of mind. No guts, no glory; I've never had brass anything. I do know, however, of at least one pork chop who succumbed to temptation and gave it a try. He's now in Portsmouth Prison serving five to ten.

THE RELIEVING PROCESS!

Those three words strike terror into the heart of supply officers everywhere. That's why I capitalized them. Given the amount of paperwork involved, it's comparable to a gigantic bowel movement. The outgoing pork chop is definitely *relieved*, but the new guy is anything but.

After the *process*, I signed on the dotted line. With a single stroke of the pen, I was on the hook to Uncle Sam for several million dollars in cash, stock, and equipment. Lose any of it and they would take it out of my salary (and my hide) for the next two hundred years. Before the ink dried, Lieutenant junior grade Ralph Hall was through the hatch, down the gangplank, and on his way to the airport. Leaving nothing in his wake but a vapor trail and a belated "Good luck to you, Lar!"

Given what I'd seen in the last two days, I couldn't blame him. Had I been in his shoes, I would have sprouted wings, too.

One of the ship's few perks was that officers had their own stateroom, so late that night, I lay awake listening to the sounds of water lapping against the ship's hull, contemplating my future. Since it was Sunday again, and with my stateroom catawampus to the galley, I opened my one porthole to dissipate the smell of liver and grilled onions wafting through officer country. As bad luck would have it, the ship was behind on meeting its quota, and some idiot had put them on the dinner menu. Namely me. Staring wide-eyed at the overhead, I pondered the past forty-eight hours and what I'd gotten myself into.

I was now in charge of feeding, paying, laundering, billeting, barbering, and procuring Snicker's bars for more than one hundred men. Providing repair parts for the antiquated equipment, they worked on ammunition for the World War II big guns they hopefully would never have to fire in anger. For a skinny kid not long out of college, I'd taken a big bite out of the responsibility pie. Hands laced behind my head, I let out a long, soft sigh.

"Way to go, Lindsey. You're in it up to your eyeballs this time."

Bottom line: I'd inherited a light-fingered workforce that quite possibly would get me thrown in jail; a galley with two cantankerous ovens that on occasion turned out nothing but fossilized carbon; a grill that refused to work on Tuesdays; three boilers that could produce anything but steam; a laundry with a leaky washer and an overpowered dryer that ran on two settings—*Burn* and *Scorch*; and two storerooms that flooded on a regular basis.

I had a throbbing headache and felt nauseous. We hadn't left the pier yet and I was already contemplating getting seasick. Just like the rapidly departed Ltjg Hall, my right eye had begun to twitch, and my pallor resembled the sheets beneath my sweating butt. Putting on the bravest front I could muster, I decided to count my blessings instead of sheep that night. Drifting off to a fitful sleep an hour later, I'd gotten to two.

First and foremost, I was still alive. Second, I hadn't developed a full-fledged migraine. Not yet, anyway.

———————

At the crack of dawn, a rolling thunder echoed down the passageway. With the timbre of Zeus and the power of Thor, it rattled the bulkheads.

"NOW REVEILLE! REVEILLE! HEAVE TO AND THRICE UP!

SWEEPERS, SWEEPERS! MAN YOUR BROOMS! THE SMOKING LAMP IS LIT IN ALL AUTHORIZED SPACES!"

Heave to? Thrice up? What the hell were they talking about?

But Zeus wasn't finished. Neither was Thor

"ALL HANDS WORKING PARTY REPORT TO THE MAIN DECK!"

Half awake, I scrabbled for my watch. Rubbing sleep out of my eyes, it took me a few seconds to focus.

"Five AM? You've got to be kidding!"

The hazy glow barely penetrating my porthole told me I'd been roused before the sun, a barbaric time for anyone to greet the day. Never a morning person, I do my best work after eight. And preferably after nine. People who spring from their warm beds bright-eyed and bushy-tailed should be hung up by their thumbs with piano wires. Or at least sterilized so they can't foist their sickness on the rest of the world. For at least a minute, my fogbound mind had trouble deciphering where the hell I was. Like a casaba melon dropped from a ten-story building, it eventually hit me.

Vietnam! In my stateroom. On an LST. Diesel oil and grilled onions.

Over the speaker, Zarathustra repeated himself. This time with more vigor.

"ALL HANDS WORKING PARTY TO THE MAIN DECK!"

Still dressed only in my skivvies, I staggered into the passageway. Sticking my head around the corner, I spied a chief heading aft. Chief Holms, the one and only chief onboard the Fat Lady.

"Uh . . . Chief?" I said, my throat raspy from not enough sleep. "All hands working party? Does that mean me?"

"All hands *means* all hands, sir. Better get a move on. Skipper's on his way topside."

I hadn't had breakfast and already they were putting me to work? I dressed in a fog, then stumbled down the gangplank with the rest of the crew to load provisions. From the bemused looks on their faces, I should have known something wasn't right. Blame it on sleep deprivation, I'd already passed five cases of canned beans down the line before I noticed I was the only officer on the pier. With an abundance of enlisted grins around me.

"Mr. Lindsey?" Lieutenant Davidson called down from the

quarterdeck. "It seems someone's pulling your leg. Officers and chiefs are excused from working parties."

My first day, and I'd been had. Shaking my head, I tipped my cap in the direction of Chief Holms and his ear-to-ear grin. My face a bright shade of red, I turned back to the skipper.

"Then perhaps I should head down to my office, sir," I said. "Where my talents will be better appreciated."

"Good idea," said the skipper, also grinning. "And if I were you, I'd be on the lookout for sea bats. They tend to swarm this time of year."

"Sea bats?"

"Ugly furry creatures with sharp teeth," he said. "They should be avoided at all costs. Nasty dispositions, and they tend to bite."

———————

My supply office turned out to be little more than a twelve-by-twelve cubicle. Less than six feet tall in most places. Since I'm a few inches over six feet, we didn't mesh all that well. Compounding the problem was the one-foot-wide iron beam directly above what I jokingly called my desk. Over the next few months, I couldn't count the number of times I bonked my head into that damn thing. Once so hard it required stitches.

The beam was a minor distraction compared to the temperature in the office. Located above the ship's boilers, the thermometer on the port wall pegged out at a hundred and twenty degrees. And it was always a *humid* one twenty. When the air conditioning went on the fritz, which was over half the time, it was worse than that.

The heat blast took my breath away. Sweating double time from every pore on my body, I maneuvered around the flesh-eating beam and plopped into my chair. Unbuttoning my shirt, I turned to Mantle. A requisition form was sticking to his shoulder.

"How can you work under these conditions," I said. Then pulled a form off my own forearm. "Everything sticks to you."

"You learn tricks of the trade after a while," said Mantle. "Like never hovering over a desk while you're sweating."

When I leaned forward, a DD-1250 (don't ask) glommed onto my right elbow.

"This will never do, Mantle. I feel like a six-foot sheet of fly paper. Pass me that towel over there. I have an idea."

Using three large rubber bands, I secured the towel around my forearm. Not only did it soak up my sweat but when I leaned forward again, nothing stuck to me.

"Not bad, sir," said Mantle. "That just might work. I'll round up some more towels for the rest of us."

"And see if you can scrounge up another fan. That dinky one on the wall isn't going to hack it." I glanced up at the standard issue wall clock next to it. "How long can you stand it down here in this heat?"

"Half an hour at most," said Mantle. "Any longer and we get light-headed. Start to see things."

"Thirty minutes is *way* too long. From here on, we'll be working fifteen minutes shifts. I can't have my people passing out."

As Mantle was leaving, he bumped into another storekeeper coming through the door. The infamous Markovich.

"You got your first new CASREP, sir," he said. "The vaps are down again."

One day in the hot seat and already our supply of fresh water was in jeopardy.

"Draft up a priority message," I said. "The sooner we go online, the sooner—"

"Already drafted and waiting for your signature, sir. As soon as we release it, I'll round up the boondockers. Looks to be a size nine this time."

Boondockers?

"What in the world are you talking about?"

"Standard procedure when the vaps go down," said Markovich. "Follow me. It's hard to explain."

One deck down, he led me into the wonderful world of water purification. The evaporators appeared to be a series of copper tubes connected to some kind of boiler apparatus. With a regulating device at one end that released a puff of steam every three seconds, the contraption looked suspiciously like a still. At the center of the regulating device was what seemed to be the sole of a boot.

"Is that a—?"

"From a size ten boot," said Markovich.

"One of Mantle's old ones, to be exact," added a skinny first-class boiler technician. Sporting a bushy beard that would have done Long John Silver proud, he extended a greasy hand.

"Name's Pappy. I'm in charge of this bilious bucket of bolts. I named her Daphne, after an old girlfriend who left me high and dry years ago. Infernal machine is older than me. And the main reason I drink too much. But she's my pride and joy. Without her, we'd all be drinking brine with our Scotch."

On cue, the *infernal machine* let out a resounding burp. Followed in short order by a wheeze, two clangs, a fart, then the closest thing to a death rattle I'd ever heard. Expecting her to blow any second, I ducked behind the nearest stanchion.

"Not to worry," said Pappy. "She's only completing her cycle. On a good day, and with all her parts, Daphne can churn out a hundred gallons an hour. Day like this, we have to make do with . . . maybe fifty. If we're lucky."

I watched as the evaporators began another cycle. As the pressure inside the boilers increased, Mantle's boot sole flexed upward until it touched a contact valve. With a steamy *whoosh,* the valve let loose, and the sole snapped back. The entire process took a little over a minute. It may have been non-regulation and awkward, but the thing worked. Two more clangs and Daphne started all over again.

"Reminds me of that old submarine movie," I said. "The one with Cary Grant and Tony Curtis where they paint the boat pink. They strapped a woman's girdle to some kind of pump."

Pappy grinned. Snapped his fingers.

"*OPERATION PETTICOAT!*" he said. "My favorite movie of all time! It's where I got the idea for the boot sole. Arthur O'Connell played the grizzled chief. On old tubs like the *Sea Tiger* and the *Hampshire County,* necessity is often the mother of invention."

"Um, Markovich said you need a size nine boot sole?" I said.

"This ten of Mantle's is a bit loose. Cuts down on our production. I thought we'd go with something tighter."

In the supply world, the customer is always right. Later that afternoon, Pappy decided a size nine and a half was a better fit. Optimum flexibility combined with maximum durability. Ramshackle as the device was, at least we'd have drinking water for the next few days. Fresh water showers? Not so much.

SIX
Batten Down the Hatches!

With Daphne's new size nine and a half boot sole locked firmly in place, the Fat Lady set sail the following morning, Ensign Lindsey not so firmly in charge of the ship's supply department. My first time at sea in anything larger than a rowboat, an electric spark shot up and down my spine as the ship made ready to depart. *Batten down the hatches, shiver me timbers,* or something like that. I was all eyes and ears as the sea detail turned to (went to) work.

"Let go the stern lines!" bellowed the skipper. "Starboard back one third!"

Churning up mud from the bottom, the ship's prop inched the fantail away from the pier until we were at a thirty-degree angle.

"Let go the bow lines! Port ahead one third!"

And as neat as you please, the bow began to swing out into the river.

"Starboard ahead one third!" Skip yelled. "Come right to one, two, zero degrees! Set the underway watch!"

Two minutes later, we were underway to Nha Trang, where we would take on lumber and rolling stock destined for a Marine base camp north of Bien Hoa. As part of a joint training program, we were also supposed to pick up four Vietnamese officers. After straightening out, we turned north out of the river mouth, chugging along at our standard snail's pace of eight knots.

Despite the calm seas, the ship immediately began to roll. Standing next to me on the flying bridge was Lieutenant junior grade Barry Kott, the ship's deck officer and weapon's guru. Two years younger than me and eight inches shorter, his nickname was "Popgun." Blond hair and blue eyes, Barry was a fun-loving beer drinker with a penchant for cheap cigars. He worked his ass off when onboard and partied even harder when he wasn't. After his first six-pack, he'd take on all comers. Including Marines twice his size. An observant sort, he noticed my greenish tint right away and turned to me with a knowing grin.

"Seasick already?" he said. "If you think this is bad, wait until we hit rough water."

"Yeah, I know," I said. "My man Mantle told me the Fat Lady is a real puke machine."

Barry took off his sweat-stained ball cap. Gave the brim a wipe. Looked out to sea.

"Actually . . . other than poor Timmy 'Buckets' Gable, not many of us ever upchuck. A steady rolling motion is what gives you the queasies. And the Fat Lady is anything but steady. There's no rhyme nor reason to the way she twists, turns, and slithers. Just when you think you've figured her out, BAM! She hits you with a new move. Took me forever to find my sea legs. First time out, I spent two whole days bouncing off the bulkheads."

He put his cap back on. Blurted a laugh.

"In *real* bad weather, she's like the roller coaster from Hell. Up, down, back, forth. You're forced to grab onto anything you can. Sometimes each other."

I raised both eyebrows. Let out a soft sigh.

"I guess I'll have to experience it for myself. Um, I haven't met Gable yet. Is he one of your men?"

"He's the communications officer. Ensign Timothy G. Gable.

Nicest guy you'd ever want to meet. Born in Lame Deer, Montana. Of all places."

"How come I've never seen him in the wardroom?"

"He's been seasick most of the time. Can't keep anything down. Poor bastard's lost thirty pounds since reporting on board. And that was only three months ago. He's got this inner-ear problem that affects his balance and upsets his stomach. The doc says it's chronic."

"So, what's he doing on a ship? Especially *this* ship."

Barry shrugged out a chuckle.

"Got me by the elbow."

———————

My first experience with Timmy Buckets was late the following night around 0100. I couldn't sleep and decided to take a walk on deck to catch a breath of fresh, onion-less air. I gravitated to the bridge where Timmy had emerged from his rack to stand JOOW duty (junior officer of the watch). Even in the dim light, I could see his green gills. Ltjg Hank Ayers had the senior watch (a.k.a. the conn) and was officially the one driving the ship. Nicknamed "Ears" because of how they protruded three inches away from his head, Hank was the ship's operations officer and was none too pleased with the purple bucket Timmy always carried around. Just in case. (That guy again!)

Timmy had the nasty habit of depositing his last meal into that bucket without warning. It was the reason everyone avoided him like the plague when the ship left port. He was a likeable sort, but at sea, you never knew what he might bring up.

Hank was standing on the flying bridge enjoying the cool night breeze wafting in off our starboard quarter. Timmy stood four feet to his right, his little purple bucket already three quarters full. And, unfortunately, upwind of Hank.

"Jesus, Timmy!" said Hank. "That puke pail of yours is foul. At least empty the damn thing once in a while."

Pale as curdled milk, Timmy nodded weakly.

"Yes, sir. Right away," he said." I'll toss it overboard."

Before Hank or I could stop him, Timmy heaved the contents of the purple bucket over the side. And into the wind. Which promptly sprayed the mess back into our faces. It's funny now, but back then, not so much. Trying to dig a piece of masticated carrot out of his hair, Hank's ears turned beet red.

"Goddamit, Ensign!" he yelled. "Get the hell off my bridge! And take that fucking bucket with you!"

"Sorry," said Timmy, head down as he trudged toward the forward ladder, ready to start on his second bucket.

I sailed on several ships during my stint in the Navy and I never saw a more nauseated human being. Timmy Buckets was friendly enough, but that night on the Fat Lady's bridge was the last time I ever stood downwind of the dude. A few months later, his detailer took pity on the eternally seasick Ensign Gable and transferred him to a desk job back in San Diego. The day he left the Fat Lady, Hank and I gave his purple bucket a fitting burial at sea. Once more into the wind. But this time, never to return.

———

Located two hundred miles north of Vung Tau as the crow flies, Nha Trang constituted a three day round trip for the Fat Lady. On the transit up the coast, mostly uneventful, Skipper Davidson decided to hold target practice. To my surprise, I was assigned duty as the forward fire director, a position that sounded, at least to me, more important than it was. Eager to try out the ship's big guns, I had to figure out how to strap myself into the fire director's oversized helmet, complete with a walkie-talkie thing and earphones. My job was to relay orders from the bridge to the gun tub. With only two orders to relay, I figured, how hard could it be? "Commence firing!" and "Cease firing!"—a trained kangaroo could handle that. And naïve fool that I was, I considered myself smarter than the average marsupial.

Standing behind my screw of stalwart gunners gave me chills to think that, at my command, those two big guns would soon roar to life, spitting fire at the distant horizon. Visions of manning the cannons on a four-masted man o' war swam through my head.

Argh! Give 'em a broadsides, mateys!

Truth be told, there were bigger guns in the fleet. Much bigger than anything the Fat Lady was packing. But to a guy who'd never shot off anything heftier than a BB gun, our twin forties looked like the guns of Navarone. Their shells alone weighed over two pounds each. With flared muzzles and a characteristic retort, they're hard to miss in any World War II flick. Old timers call them *bofors*. Brits call them *pom-poms*.

Ten miles offshore, the skipper slowed the ship to one third, and we put a boat in the water to tow a target. Since bofors aren't known for their accuracy, the boat driver let out a long, long, *very* long towline. He'd been through this routine before and wasn't about to take chances. A forty-millimeter shell can do mean things to a small boat. Sink it in a heartbeat.

Up first was a single-shot drill, to adjust for drift, wind, trajectory, and my bad eyesight. His forehead glued to an eyepiece, my head gunner shot a thumbs up in my direction, the universal *all systems go* sign. With his finger on the trigger, he had the target in his crosshairs.

"Forward gun manned and on target!" I shouted into my microphone.

"Very well," said a calm voice from the bridge. Unlike me, this wasn't his first time at the dance. "Commence firing."

Showtime!

"Fire one!" I bellowed. The correct command should have been a simple, if repetitive, "Commence firing!"

Fire one? Geez, Lindsey, this ain't no friggin' submarine. Get it right, will you!

The gun's report rattled through the soles of my feet, up my spine, and into my brain. My eyeballs congealed to the consistency of month-old pudding. My back fillings began to pulse. Cordite filled my nose. I was sure I'd gone deaf. Maybe blind.

A second later, our shell splashed down on the horizon. Closer to the tow boat than the target. Immediately, its driver began to wave a large white flag back and forth. Translation: "I'm not the target, assholes!"

Another order came from above.

"Right ten degrees," said Mr. Calm. "Elevate five." Short and to the point, even I understood.

"Aye, aye, sir," said I.

After my crew made their adjustments, I returned to the phone.

"On target," I said, my fingers crossed.

"Standby," said Mr. Calm.

Maybe they've decided to call the whole thing off, I thought. *Not waste any more ammunition.*

"Commence firing!" said the voice.

"F-Fire two," I said, repeating my first mistake. At that point, I wished I *really* was on a submarine.

The second big bang was even louder than the first. Now the tips of my fingers ached. My nose started to bleed, and I was sure I'd swallowed one of my fillings. My testicles throbbed, my asshole burned, and I was one-hundred-percent positive I wouldn't be able to have children.

Volleys three through ten went by in a numbing blur. Each banging away at my poor eardrums. Finally, the order I would have sold my soul for came down the line.

"Cease firing!"

Thank you, Jesus!

Before I could catch my breath, a second order soon followed. One that made my blood run cold.

"Prepare for rapid fire!"

Rapid fire? Oh, shit!

No doubt about it, I was going to die. My brain would explode like a stomped grape. I thought about abandoning ship, but the phone god spoke again.

"Commence firing!"

Those damn two words.

I don't remember passing on the order, but I must have, because all hell broke loose. They gave me these oversized earmuff thingies to wear, but it was like slapping a Band-Aid on a gut wound. The ensuing din lasted less than a minute, but it seemed like a year. When the smoke finally cleared, I had a ringing in my ears that wouldn't go away for two days. But wonder of wonders, we actually hit the target. Three whole times! For my gun crew, that was cause for celebration. Normally they didn't hit squat.

"Good job, Mr. Lindsey," said Chief Holms.

"What?" My ears were ringing so badly I couldn't hear a thing.

"Last time your guys didn't come anywhere near the target."

"Huh?"

"Not bad for a pork chop," said the chief. "You've got a sharpshooter's eye. Must have done some shooting as a kid."

"Huh? What?"

The next day, I discovered Holms had pulled my leg again. More embarrassed than offended, I confronted him after morning quarters, man to man. Or at least ensign to chief. After all, I supposedly outranked him.

"That bit about me having a sharpshooter's eye, Chief," I said. "You were bullshitting me, right?"

"Well, sir, I might have bent the truth a tad. Have to give you credit, though. You lasted longer than your predecessor. Mr. Hall bailed after the second volley."

"This fire director thing? A standing joke played on the new supply officer?'

The chief shifted his coffee cup to the other hand. Raised a slow eyebrow.

"Pretty much. Don't take it that hard, though. At least you made it through the entire shoot."

"I guess my real battle station is nowhere near a gun?"

The chief's grin widened.

"Nope. The skipper's got your actual general quarters assignment in his pocket."

"Captain Davidson was in on this little prank of yours?"

"He's the one who thought it up."

I had to laugh.

"I'm hoping this is the last of your jokes, Chief."

"At least until we cross the equator."

I'd heard about the King Neptune tradition, so I wasn't surprised. Actually, I was looking forward to the messy initiation. Sounded like fun.

"You aren't setting me up?" I asked. "Getting me to drop my guard until then?"

"I may be an old fart," said the chief, "but I ain't stupid. I got you twice. Three times would be gilding the lily. Besides, you're in charge of paying me. Come payday, you might forget to count. Take my word for it; the rest of my nasties are reserved for the crew."

"Good thinking," I said. "Nasties? What kind of nasties?"

The chief blew on his coffee. Took a sip as he looked out to sea.

"Simple stuff, mostly. The kinda things you can't pull on an officer. Like sending a rook seaman to the bilge racks for a jar of relative bearing grease."

"They fall for that?"

"Hell, one dim bulb spent half the morning rummaging around in the filth down there. The hangdog look on his face when he came back empty-handed was a thing of beauty. Then I sent him to the skipper for advice. Skip headed him all over the ship looking for a grease that doesn't exist."

"Captain Davidson is in on your pranks?"

"He's the biggest prankster on the ship. Laid a couple of doozies on me, and I'm supposed to be the old man of the ship."

"You ever lay one on *him?*" I asked.

"Hell, no! Would you? Playing tricks on your commanding officer is a good way to scuttle your career."

"Good point," I said. "Just for future reference, got any other nasty jokes in your arsenal of embarrassments?"

"A few tried-and-true standards. Like asking for fifty feet of waterline or a left-handed monkey wrench. Once I had a country boy from Alabama stand an underway mail watch at midnight. Told him to be on the lookout for the mail buoy as it bobbed by. He stood in the forward gun tub all night long, trussed up in a life jacket, holding a grappling hook. Poor bastard nearly froze his ass off."

I had to ask.

"You wouldn't happen to know what a sea bat is, would you, Chief?"

The chief laughed so hard coffee snorted out of his nose.

"Sea bats! Now there's a classic that hasn't been pulled off well in years!"

"I'm guessing there's probably no such critter," I said.

"Oh, they're real, all right. If you call a fake piece of fur real." The chief took off his cap to wipe his brow. "It's a takeoff on an old bait-and-switch routine. First, you cut a small flap into a cardboard box. Then you dangle a piece of fur from the flap, so your intended victim only gets a quick glance. 'What's in the box?' he most likely asks. 'A sea bat,' says you, placing the box down on the deck. 'Have a look,' you say. 'But be careful. Sea bats are known to bite.' When he bends over to take a gander, you clobber him in the butt with a broom. Or anything that's handy."

The prank reminded me of something SK3 Mantle told me last week.

"One of my men let me in on another of your tall tales, Chief. Something about a civilian sand crab losing his head on the Fat Lady. How his ghost roams the ship at night in search of it."

"That ain't no tall tale. It's the honest-to-God truth." The chief crossed himself. Took a deep breath. "During the ship's construction back in '43, a welder went missing. Last time anyone saw him, he was working on the bow doors. To this day, his body has never been found. Some say he got his head pinched off in one of the gears and it fell into a forward bilge compartment. One that got sealed up the next day. Legend has it, it's still there."

A faraway look on his face, the chief drained the last of his coffee in one large gulp. Sighed before continuing.

"On a calm night, when the sea quiets down to nothing, you can hear strange sounds coming from beneath the bilge plates down in the tank deck. Some say it's just the sea gods whispering about. But I know better. It's that dead welder searching for his head. Or someone else's head to replace it."

A big fan of Edgar Allan Poe, at first, I was mesmerized by the grisly tale. Grabbing hold of my better senses, I raised an eyebrow.

"That's a good one, Chief. Nice try, but I'm not buying it. Want to pull my other leg while you're at it?"

"I'm serious," said the chief. "Dead serious. Ask anyone on the ship, Captain included. Look it up in the ship's archives. That welder actually *was* beheaded. And his head is still missing. To this very day."

"If you say so."

I noticed we were heading into a fogbank. Thick and dark, it looked like a solid gray wall.

"What the hell is *that*?" I said.

The chief narrowed his eyes. Wiped out his coffee cup with a rag.

"Looks like a weather front to me. Fog can get pretty thick over a cool patch of water like the one we just entered. Happens all the time. Go forward and stand in the middle of the deck. It's a real hoot when we cut into the bank."

After listening to the chief's repertoire, you'd think I'd have known better. But I didn't. I was halfway down the main deck when our bow penetrated the fog bank. Only, it wasn't fog. It was water. A solid wall of water that broke over the deck with a thunderous roar. All I could do was turn and look back up at the chief, standing safely under cover on the bridge. He smiled at me, shrugged, and waved.

"Sorry, Mr. Lindsey, but I couldn't resist. Enjoy your shower."

That rain hit me like a ton of water balloons. So hard and heavy, it buckled my knees. For a few seconds, it was dark as night. I'd endured my share of downpours back in Ohio, but they were faucet drips compared to this.

Fearful of being washed overboard, I dropped to all fours and held on for dear life. In a minute, the sudden squall passed. The sun returned and the Fat Lady was still on course. But I looked like a drenched rat. Wiping off my glasses, I trudged back up to the bridge, leaving a trail of puddles in the passageway.

"You know that pay record of yours we were talking about, Chief," I said. Wringing out my ball cap. "Consider it lost. And if I were you, I'd watch what you eat the next few days. The cooks work for me, you know."

———————

That night, I was the talk of the ship. How I'd been "gotten good" by Chief Holms three times in one week. I *got* him back two days later, however. It's amazing what a laxative overdose in one's mashed potatoes will do to one's lower intestinal tract. Cleans out your pipes real quick—real messy. The chief was quickstepping it to the head all night long.

After that, we both called a truce. For the safety of all concerned.

SEVEN

The Nether Regions and One Hell of a Toothache!

"I don't give a shit about your damn supply regulations! And I sure as hell don't care how much the fucking thing costs!"

For a little guy, Ltjg William "Wild Bill" Morrison had the voice of a berserk foghorn. Not to mention a colorful vocabulary. I outweighed him by sixty pounds and was at least half a head taller, but that made no difference to the Fat Lady's irate engineering officer. He was nose to nose with me—actually nose to Adam's apple—and giving no quarter. His eyes blazed a flaming shade of red and steam hissed out of both ears.

"You supply pukes don't give a healthy crap about what life's like in the real world!" he bellowed. "All you care about is your goddamn rules and regulations! If you'd get off your paper-pushing asses once in a while and come down to the engine room, you'd see what real men have to live with!"

With that, he threw a crumpled requisition form into my face.

"And what's with the *Not Carried* shit!" he added. "We're asking for a critical repair part. One we use all the time! How come you dickwads can't get your shit together and stock the damn thing?"

By definition, supply officers and engineering types are supposed to hate each other. It's a cats and dogs thing. My predecessor had warned me about Wild Bill's volatile nature, that although his bark was bad enough, his bite was worse. He also told me if I valued my health, under no circumstances should I venture anywhere near the engine room. "Hell on earth," he called it.

As I smoothed out the crumpled form, I noticed from the use index that not only was the aforementioned repair part not stocked but more importantly, this was the first time it had officially been requisitioned.

"Calm down, Bill," I said. "According to our records, we're not authorized to carry this. As you can see by the form, there's been no demand registered from your department for over two years. Without any hits, there's no way we can ever bring it into stock. Have your people been submitting the proper 1250s to compile the projected usage data?"

I was on solid ground, but it was a mistake hitting a raging bull with facts imbedded in supply jargon. The large vein at Bill's temple began to throb. His eyes bulged out. Flames shot from his nostrils.

"Jesus Christ!" he shouted, spraying me with spittle. "Screw the damn 1250s!"

Clearly Wild Bill was not in the market for a lecture on how the Navy's supply system was supposed to work. "To hell with stocking procedures, *I want my damn part! And I want it NOW!*"

I had two options. I could launch a tirade of my own, match him spit for spit. Given how mad he was, that would have been pointless and probably painful. Or I could take the high road. Since I was the new kid of the block and not much of a spitter, I chose the latter. Turning the other cheek, I forced my best *the customer is always right* smile.

"Let me check into it, Bill. I'll see if we can come up with something. When you've got the time, I'd be happy to take a tour of your engineering spaces. To see how things operate around here."

That seemed to mollify him. For then, at least.

"Fine," said the spider to the fly. "I'll send one of my men around to fetch you this afternoon."

And with that, Bill stormed out.

Fetch?

I always thought the word was reserved for stray cattle. Maybe the family dog.

When I returned to my desk, SN Markovich looked at me as if I'd grown another head.

"You aren't really thinking of going down . . . *there,* are you, sir?" he asked. "*There*" sounded like a purgatory of some kind.

"Why not?" I said. "I might learn something. Maybe get a feel for the needs of our customers."

"Yeah, right," mumbled Kris. "The only thing you'll feel in the engine room is hot and filthy. But it's your funeral."

"It's *that* bad?" I asked.

Kris shrugged his best Alfred E. Neuman, *What, me worry*?

"As they say, nothing ventured, nothing gained. But if I were you, sir, I'd make sure my shots are up to date before going anywhere near the engine spaces. Snipes carry diseases, you know."

My people referred to the engineering department as *snipes,* not exactly a term of endearment. Engineers, in turn, referred to my people as *geeks, pukes,* or worse. Also without affection.

"First Chief Holms, now you," I said. "Is leg-pulling an Olympic event on the Fat Lady?"

Markovich had expressive eyebrows. He raised the right one ever so slowly.

"Don't say I didn't warn you, sir."

My men called our engine room *The Land Down Under.* "Snipes are like Morlocks," said my predecessor, referring to the 1960 sci-fi classic flick *The Time Machine* where Rod Taylor saves Yvette Mimieux and the Eloi from a band of subterranean monsters called Morlocks. According to Ltjg Hall, snipes were also beady-eyed creatures with pasty skin and sloped foreheads who lived in dank, forbidding places and never saw the light of day.

I thought he was joking. After lunch that day, I discovered he wasn't that far off the mark.

———————

"Are you ready for your tour, Mr. Lindsey?" said Pappy, my first-class EM friend in charge of the evaporators. "Mr. Morrison sent me to show you the way. Make sure you don't get lost."

I put down the report I was chicken scratching. After two hours of pencil pushing, I couldn't get the damn thing to balance.

"Ready as I'll ever be," I said. "I need a break from all this paperwork."

"Are you sure you want to go through with this, sir?" asked Pappy, a bemused look on his face. "Just between you, me, and that bulkhead over there, the engine room ain't a fit place for man nor beast. I never go down there unless I have to. And I'm a snipe."

"Are you trying to scare me off."

"Your funeral," he said. "But don't say I didn't warn you."

Words I'd heard somewhere before.

It took us twenty minutes to make our way down three decks, six passageways, four shafts, and one vertical, very slippery ladder into the nether regions of the ship. The temperature got hotter and more humid with each step. By the time Pappy and I reached the dreaded engine room, I was out of breath and yearning for the comparative *cool* of my office. From behind a latched door came a deep-throated rumble. A pulsing throb worked its way up from the deck into every bone in my body.

"Jesus, Pappy," I said, sweat now dripping from my nose, "is it always this hot down here? It's like a damn sauna."

"This is nothing," he said. "Wait until I open the hatch." He placed a gloved hand on the latch, hesitated. "Last chance to turn back. I could tell my boss you changed your mind. Got a sudden attack of sanity."

Taking the hottest deep breath of my life, I crossed myself. The intelligent half of me wanted to take Pappy's advice. Turn tail and run. I was curious about the engine room, but not *that* curious. On an antiquated bucket of rust, curiosity can kill more than cats.

"No, we've come this far," said my idiot half. "Might as well see it through."

When Pappy opened that hatch, a roar knocked me back two steps. I could count the heat waves bouncing off my chest. My glasses began to melt. I felt my nasal hairs singe when I sucked air in through my nose.

"Holy crap!" I gasped.

"I told you it was hot down here," said Pappy.

"Holy crap!" I said again. "How can anybody work in this heat? It's like Hell warmed over!"

Then the smell hit me. *Eau de* overly stressed motor oil. To keep my eyes from boiling, I squinted. On either side of a metal walkway lurked two diesel engines, the hearts of the ship, both rotating at idle. I could only imagine what they'd sound like kicked up to full speed.

All the pipes in the compartment leaked or oozed, covering every surface with a thin film of oil. Including all the Morlock snipes. Seeing my obvious distress, Wild Bill donned a sadistic grin.

"Welcome to my world, geek. I didn't think you'd have the balls to come."

"I don't anymore," I said. "My nuts shriveled to raisins the second Pappy opened that hatch. I'll never complain about the heat in my office again."

It was the first time I'd seen Wild Bill smile, which quickly morphed into an I-told-you-so smirk.

"Perhaps now you'll have a sympathetic ear next time I beg for a repair part."

We'd still be adversaries after that. It was the bestial nature of our relationship. But from that day forward, he and I had a mutual understanding. When Bill clapped a filthy hand on my shoulder, it left a black mark on my comparatively clean khaki shirt.

"Now that you're here," he said, "let me show you around."

In the next ten minutes—ten minutes was all I could take before passing out—I learned more than I ever wanted to know about diesel engines.

Do you know that diesels run without spark plugs?

I didn't.

———

At Nha Trang, I observed my first beaching operation. Five hundred yards from shore, Lieutenant Davidson slowed the ship to one third. At three hundred yards, he yelled, "Let go the stern anchor!" When the anchor flukes dug into the sand, we began to play out line, standard operating procedure for an LST. If the tide went out while we were conducting our business, we could winch in on the stern anchor to help retract us from the beach. Made perfect sense to me. But only after Barry Kott explained it to me three times.

After we beached—an antediluvian process similar to a giant whale sliding belly first into a sandbox—I watched "Popgun" work his magic. The way he directed traffic, packing the Fat Lady's tank deck to the overhead with gear and rolling stock boggled my mind. He must have played with blocks a lot as a toddler, because he used every inch available. When the loading was complete, a whistle sounded. We raised our ramp, closed the bow doors, then backed off the beach.

Start to finish, the entire operation took less than three hours, and before I could catch my breath, we were angling south out of Nha Trang harbor on our way back to Cat Lo. Gator sailors may not be much to look at come inspection time, always stinking of diesel oil and fried onions, but they can move cargo faster than any longshoreman alive.

The four RVN officers we picked up at Nha Trang were supposed to take part in the loading evolution, but they stayed in the background until it was over. Chain-smoking cigarettes and jabbering among themselves, they didn't want to get their uniforms dirty. We were told they were on a three-day training mission to learn sea navigation on a large vessel. *Just in case* America turned the ship over to them at war's end. If and when we ever left their country.

I thought I'd never see anyone more seasick than Timmy "Buckets," but I was proved wrong on our return transit. Within minutes of hitting open water, those four RVN officers were staggering across the main deck, urping nuoc mam anytime the ship rolled more than five degrees, a mere pittance for the Fat Lady. After the first hour, they retired to their bunks, not to be seen or heard from again until we reached Cat Lo. Whereas Timmy's hue was a pale white in rough seas, they quickly turned a bilious shade of green. Needless to say, they got in zilch training.

Our second night out, I got a chance to man my actual battle station. Much to my relief, it turned out to be nowhere near a big gun. For an hour, I was confined to a pitch-black cubicle not much larger than the width of my shoulders. My only company—an inanimate box containing the ship's CRYPTO equipment, a soon-to-be-obsolete encryption-decryption device. If the Fat Lady received an actual TOP SECRET message, something she never did my entire tour of duty, I was charged to pull these interlocking gears from the box and arrange them according to the current password sequence.

Since I wasn't authorized to view TOP SECRET messages (usually no CRYPTO gear officer was) the process had to be done in a lightless room, much like a photographer handling exposed film. I'd practiced for hours, so come drill time, I was confident I could slap those gears together in no time flat.

I spent the first ten minutes of the drill excited as hell, hands hovered over that CRYPTO box. Ready to decipher the all-important incoming secret message that would save the Fat Lady from certain destruction. After twenty minutes in the dark, my mind began to wander. Play tricks on me. All kinds of weird scenarios swam through my head, most the doomsday variety.

What if everyone on board gets killed? And I'm stuck down here in this three-by-three coffin?

I forgot to mention they locked me in. "For security reasons," according to the SECNAV manual on special transmissions. Just me, the CRYPTO gear, a .45-caliber pistol strapped to my hip, and my runaway imagination. Stale air, no light, tight space, and a loaded weapon within reach? Not a comforting situation, so the oddball scenarios kept coming. Fast and furious.

What if we get torpedoed and start to sink? Will anyone be able to get me out in time? For that matter, will anyone even remember I'm down here?

Despite the fact that Charlie had no navy, much less a submarine to launch a torpedo.

What if I suffer a heart attack? Who would know? I'd expire in the dark!

Not likely, considering my age and good health.

What if I have to pee?

Now *that* was a real problem.

"Should have gone before you got in the car," my mother used to say.

As soon as the word *pee* popped into my head, my bladder filled to overflowing. Next time I'd bring an empty jar with me. One with a large mouth.

Eventually I got bored. The drill could go on all day. What was I going to do for the duration? Play I spy with myself in the dark?

I spy something . . . black. No challenge there.

To pass the time, I flipped on the light switch for a second. Lo and behold, I made a startling discovery.

As dilated as my pupils were, I found I had taken a perfect picture of my surroundings in negative relief on my retinas. The detail was amazing. No matter which way I turned my head, the snapshot remained for at least five seconds. When it faded away, all I had to do was flip the light switch on and off again. And *voilà!* Another eyeball Polaroid.

This tomfoolery kept me occupied for all of five minutes. After that, boredom overtook me again and I fell sound asleep. What all good CRYPTO officers aren't supposed to do, nine out of ten do anyway.

I don't how many minutes or hours passed in the pitch. Finally, a knock at the door jarred me awake. Apparently, the drill was over.

"How'd you do in there, Mr. Lindsey?" said the messenger of the watch dangling a set of keys. Thank God he hadn't lost them.

"Piece of cake," I said, doing my best to sound alert, and trying to hide the fact that I'd fallen asleep at the switch.

The messenger donned a slow grin.

"Don't forget your pillow next time, Mr. Lindsey. Makes nap time a lot easier."

———————

Through no fault of my own, that very same night, the radio shack declared war on me. Not on my department or any of my men, just me. I'd just come down from chatting with the dog watch (nothing to do with canines) and was in my bunk when this sudden searing pain shot across my jaw. The mother of all toothaches, it felt as if my fillings were boiling over. Jerking upright, I banged my head into the overhead hard enough to draw blood.

"What the—"

Another shooting pain bent me double. A woodpecker had

invaded my skull and was trying to bore his way out. I saw stars. Felt sick to my stomach. Still in my skivvies, I staggered down the hallway in my bare feet into the empty wardroom. No relief there, my jaw was now giving birth to twins.

I wobbled out the port hatch and onto the main deck. Outside in the fresh air, the pain eased a bit. The throbbing was still there, just not as intense. So I kept on walking. Strange, the farther away I got from officer's country, the better I felt. Halfway to the bow, the pain was gone entirely.

What the hell is going on? I asked myself.

Figuring it must have been something I ate, I shrugged it off and started back to my stateroom. Within a few steps, the pain began to return. By the time I reached the wardroom, it was back full force. At the ladder leading to the radio shack, the pain increased to seeing God proportions. The cause of my pain seemed to be emanating from up there. By the time I reached the fourth rung, I was seeing whole galaxies of pulsating stars. I pounded on the radio shack door with both fists.

"Whatever you're doing in there, for God's sake, STOP IT!" I yelled. "It's killing me!"

The first-class radioman on duty opened the door to find the ship's half-naked supply officer collapsed in the passageway, holding his jaw, and babbling in tongues. He quickly twisted a dial on the console to his right, and just like that, the pain stopped. Now a puddle of relief on the deck, I would have kissed him on the lips if I'd had the strength to stand.

A one-in-a-million chance occurrence, the radio shack had been transmitting evening message traffic on a frequency that homed in on the density of my larger back fillings. In effect, it turned me into a human radio. With a proper set of woofers, I could have broadcast rock 'n' roll to the rest of the crew. The radioman offered me a hand up.

"Sorry about that, Mr. Lindsey. Same thing happened to a chief on my last ship. You're lucky. Back then, it took the ship's dentist three days to figure out what was bugging him."

"Apology accepted," I said. "You couldn't have known. But please, I beg you. Forget that frequency."

He scribbled something into his logbook, then taped a note above the radio dial.

"Already taken care of, sir. We'll never use it again. You have my word."

A month later, however, an apprentice radioman accidentally dialed in the forbidden frequency. I was in the wardroom when the pain sledgehammered me. Bending double, I spit a mouthful of spaghetti across the table into Hank's face.

The following day, I *accidentally* lost that apprentice's pay record. That was the last time the radio shack came anywhere near that demon frequency. What goes around comes around. Screw with a pork chop's teeth and he's likely to screw with your wallet. For the rest of my time onboard, I had no dental problems. I take that back. I did come down with one troublesome cavity. But I blame that on my love of chocolate.

Humongous Vietnam creepy-crawly next to author's big toe.

EIGHT
Rocket Alley, a Bonehead Mistake, and Kissing Your Sister!

In three short weeks, the Fat Lady made seven runs down six tributaries. All to and from places I couldn't begin to pronounce. Only a month in-country, and for me, the Vietnamese language had blurred into something akin to a children's song.

Ding dang, Dong tem. Bing bang, nuoc mam.

We'd moved tons of "don't know what" to "don't know where." Most destinations being wide bends in muddy rivers where the ship could snuggle up to unload its cargo. Sweaty little places slapped together as an afterthought. Places that would be stripped bare ten seconds after the Americans left for good.

We also made four transits of Rocket Alley, a narrow, twisting three-mile stretch of a lower river delta where Charlie ambushed anything that floated by. Empty or not. Never major attacks, they'd lob a few mortar rounds at us, fire several AK-47 bursts in our general direction, then beat feet. Just to be annoying and let us and the rest of the world know they were still out there. We, in turn, would return their fire a thousand-fold. Just to let *them* know we had more bullets—a lot more.

Rocket Alley was a major free fire zone, so we would blast away at both shorelines with enough firepower to level Sheboygan. If we'd had a kitchen sink on board, we would have thrown it at the enemy. After only a month, American ships had turned the alley into a vast no-man's-land. Something akin to the devastated landscape between trenches in World War I.

For at least two miles inland, there wasn't a hint of green on either side of the river. No trees, no vegetation, hardly a blade of grass. The entire area had been cropped, shorn, weed-whacked, flambéed, mulched, tilled, stripped, scorched, and parboiled into a dull shade of pockmarked brown. With the smell and consistency of a spoiled diaper.

Our third transit found us headed for Binh Thuy (pronounced *bin-two-ee*) about twenty miles upstream from Rocket Alley. The crew was at battle stations, all eyes trained on the *Zone* coming up, when the skipper yelled his first orders.

"Full speed ahead! Commence firing!"

During these passages, every man not on watch was issued a weapon of some sort and assigned a position behind the sandbags lining our decks. Yours truly included. Our only orders—shoot anything that moved. And most things that didn't. That included birds, bugs, snakes, shadows, and ripples in the water. A ripple might mean a sapper with a satchel charge strapped to his back was headed our way. As slow as the Fat Lady was, we weren't about to take chances. Swimming with the current, even a fair-to-middling swimmer had no trouble catching us. Even if he was cradling a bomb.

Upon hearing the order, I hunkered behind the third sandbag to the left of the flying bridge. My weapon of choice—a snappy little carbine. Shorter and lighter than its bigger and more popular M-16 cousin, a carbine used a smaller caliber bullet and didn't make as much noise. An important consideration for my sensitive ears. It also didn't kick as hard. Equally important to my bony shoulders.

In the twenty minutes it took us to steam through Rocket Alley, I fired thirty-four clips of ammunition. At fifteen rounds a clip, I accounted for over five hundred bullets all by my lonesome. And I was a slowpoke. The guys on either side of me fired twice as fast—and also hit nothing.

To my knowledge, no one has ever calculated the ratio of shells fired in Vietnam, us to them. A hundred thousand to one? Maybe a million to one? The figure is too staggering to contemplate. If sheer fire power is any indication, however, we should have won the war many times over. Sadly, in a war, it's not how much you shoot that's relevant; it's how much you hit. And I'm fairly confident *that* ratio wasn't in our favor. When it came down to bang for the buck, Charlie had us beat hands down.

Finally, the captain ordered, "Cease firing!"

Transit over, we all sighed with relief, safely behind our sandbags. Most lit cigarettes. As the smoke on shore began to clear, we took the opportunity to evaluate our handiwork. We had fertilized both riverbanks with another ton of lead, but the devastated landscape looked much the same. The phrase *redundant destruction* popped into my head. Along with *flogging a dead horse* and *sledgehammering a mosquito*. We sure showed that inanimate stretch of bullet-ridden mud who was boss.

"Secure from general quarters!" Skip ordered.

As the crew and I were stretching and scratching, a spent bullet clanged off the superstructure ten feet above me. Someone, or something, had actually returned fire on us. A lookout in the forward gun tub sounded off.

"Sniper! Mound off the starboard quarter! One-thirty degrees! At a thousand yards!"

A thousand yards is a hell of a reach for an AK-47. For our twin forties, it's a walk in the park. Normally Charlie wasn't that stupid.

"Forward gun tub," said the captain. "Fire at will! Let's shake up the bastard!"

Our gunners took two volleys to draw a bead on the mound where the hapless sniper was hiding. A two-pound projectile packs a hell of a wallop, and twenty shell bursts later, the mound was leveled flat. For a fifty-yard radius, nothing remained but a huge brown cloud drifting away with the wind.

"Cease fire!" ordered the captain. "That should toast his buns."

Hoping to catch a glimpse of our vanquished foe, or at least pieces of him, binoculars all over the ship trained on the ill-fated spot. We all thought nothing could have survived such a barrage. I was about to turn away when I noticed a slight movement under a large clump of dirt. Up jumped a hatless, weaponless pair of shredded black pajamas caked with mud. Shell shocked and probably deaf, the poor guy just stood there staring blankly at the huge gray ship heading slowly up the river. When I focused my binoculars on his head, I could read the expression on his face—*what the hell was I thinking?*

Coming to his senses, he dropped his plastic bottle of nuoc mam and took off for the distant tree line, waving his arms like a banshee. Knowing they couldn't draw a bead on him in time, the forward gun tub just laughed. That was one VC who would think twice about shooting at another LST.

———————

After dinner that night, just before we made Binh Thuy, Barry and I were standing on the bridge, watching the sunset's parade of changing colors. Brilliant oranges through blushing pinks, finally into royal purples. Despite where we were, and what was happening all around us, the war hadn't dulled Mother Nature's artistic talents. Reflecting on our transit through Rocket Alley, I had a disturbing thought.

"Uh, Barry? What would have happened back there if we took a serious rocket hit to our tank deck?"

"Highly unlikely," said Barry. "These old *T*'s were built to protect their innards. The tank deck is protected on both sides by two separate compartments running the entire length of the ship. A rocket would have no trouble penetrating our outer hull, but it would explode in the first compartment. And if not the first, definitely the second. A bigger worry would be a mortar. Given the difficult angle, and with the Fat Lady on the move, the odds of that happening are at least a thousand to one."

"What if Charlie got lucky and dropped one through the main loading hatch? That's a pretty large opening."

"Four hundred square feet, to be exact." Barry scratched his neck. Let out a slow whistle. "Not much of a target for a mortar man. But I suppose it could happen."

"What are we carrying down there, anyway?" I asked. Barry looked right, then left, to make sure we were alone.

"Can you keep a secret?"

"Of course," I said. "My lips are sealed."

"It's a hush-hush shipment of special ammunition. Do you know what phosphorescent shells are?"

"Only that they make a hell of a racket and throw off enough light to illuminate a dozen football fields."

"That ain't the half of it. They also carry their own oxidizing agent and fuel. In many ways, they're worse than napalm. Once they go off, they can't be extinguished. Get a fragment on you and it'll burn into your flesh. Won't stop till it comes out the other side. Same thing with metal. Even underwater."

I looked down at the deck. Those shells were no more than twenty feet below my feet. Swallowing hard, I shook my head.

"Just how much of that stuff is down there?"

"About a hundred tons worth."

My turn to let out a slow whistle.

"Would a single mortar be enough to set all that off?"

"Big time."

"Would it sink the ship?"

"Sink it?" said Barry. "Hell, there would be nothing left of the Fat Lady but metal shavings. And as for flesh-and-blood idiots like you and me, the word *vaporized* comes to mind."

Eyes wide, I turned toward shore to watch the last traces of purple fade to gray over the jungle.

"Thanks for the encouraging thought, Bar. You sure know how to ruin a perfectly good sunset."

That night, I couldn't keep my mind on Skip's bridge game. He and I were down two rubbers and doing poorly in the third. I'd even trumped my partner's ace, something I hadn't done since high school. We were losing a five spades bid when Ensign Gable, the JOOW, knocked on the bulkhead. Without his purple bucket, thank goodness.

"Sorry to disturb you, sir," he said. "But this priority message came in over the wire."

"No problem, Timmy," said the captain, raising an accusing eyebrow my way. "The way this game's been going, I need a break."

He donned his glasses to read the message. Running a hand through his hair, he groaned softly.

"Oh, great! When it rains, it pours."

"Bad news?" I asked.

"In spades. We've been ordered to hightail it back down the river to Cat Lo as soon as we unload at Binh Thuy. Headquarters wants us to load up with fuel, then haul ass up the Bassac to some dink water base called Dong Tam. The Marines up there are about to run out of fuel, and we've been commandeered as a tanker."

Dong Tam? I thought. *Sounds like a Scottish penis beanie.*

Two more worry lines on his face, the captain turned back to Timmy.

"Tell them we're on our way. And order up flank speed."

"Aye, aye, sir!"

Staring at the bad news message, the skipper lit up his umpteenth cigarette of the evening. Leaning back, he laced his fingers behind his head to blow out a smoke ring. After a few seconds, he sat up straight. Looked me in the eye.

"Okay. Where were we? If I'm not mistaken, five spades is the bid. Thanks to you."

We were in for a rough trip. Even at flank speed, a tricky business on the rivers, it meant a two-day hardship was in store. No rest for the wicked; it entailed another fun transit of Rocket Alley followed by two sleepless nights. Always a pragmatist, the captain knew he couldn't do anything about it now. Bridge on the other hand. . .

———

By the time we reached Dong Tam, the crew had been at general quarters for forty-eight hours straight. Since time was of the essence, we had to chance steaming up the Bassac at low tide. Scraping the bottom frequently, our wake turned to mud. If we ran aground, we'd become sitting ducks. Our nerves frazzled; when we rounded that final bend to Dong Tam, we were not a bunch of happy campers. As we were lining up for our beach approach, we received another priority message. Even more of bombshell than the first, it stretched the captain's neck chords tighter than violin strings.

"Goddamnit! Some shitass Marine stepped on his crank! Talk about a bonehead mistake!"

The oil Dong Tam needed wasn't the kind we had in our tanks. We'd busted our balls and made the trip for nothing. Loosely translated, the message said, "Oops. Sorry about that."

I'd never seen the skipper that upset. Not angry upset. Full-blown, *Stand by for a ram,* MAD!

"Lar," he growled through clenched teeth. "Grab your hat. We're going to pay the CO of this goddam pissant base a visit!"

I couldn't imagine why he'd want a supply type to tag along. But with his eyes spouting molten fire, I wasn't about to question his logic.

"Right away, sir!"

As soon as the Fat Lady's ramp hit the beach, we were off and running. By the time I got to the Jeep, Skip had Susie in first gear. I didn't think it was possible to burn rubber on sand, but he managed to. I'd never seen a human jaw tighter in my life.

As we were barreling through the jungle, I couldn't get that one nagging thought out of my mind.

Why in the world does he want ME along?

=====

The man in charge of the "Goddam pissant" base turned out to be a Marine major, with a second lieutenant flunky running interference in his outer office. The lowly gofer didn't stand a chance. Skip steamrolled him like a two-hundred-pound angry bowling ball.

"Out of my way, sonny! It's your boss I'm after, not you!"

With me at his heels, he barged into the major's ramshackle office.

"You stupid prick!" bellowed the captain, spraying globs of spit in the process. "What kind of shitty operation are you running?"

For added emphasis, he threw his hat at the startled major, narrowly missing his right ear. It crashed into a picture on the far wall, shattering the glass. Skip was halfway across the major's desk when it dawned on me why he'd brought me along. As the tallest officer on the ship, with maybe the longest arms, I was there to hold him back. By pure luck, I was able to grab his belt just before he launched himself. I'm no lightweight, but he dragged me halfway across the desk. The major, a clone of our captain, same barrel chest, same square jaw, bit through his cigar.

"Who the hell are you?" he roared, matching Skip spittle for spittle. Two peas in a pod, he had the same gravelly voice. "Get your fucking ass out of my fucking office!"

I'd been thrust into a hard place between two angry rocks. From the looks in their eyes, World War III was about to break out. Semper fi versus anchors away. And the way the spit was flying, it wouldn't be pretty.

"We came all this fucking way for nothing!" Skip said, with me still holding onto his belt. "Two fucking days, my crew sweated their asses off to get your precious fuel oil up here. Then you jerkwads have the balls to tell us "Never mind. It was all a mistake." I oughta punch your fucking lights out!"

Unable to reach the major with me still attached, he slammed his fist into the desk instead. So hard, I heard a crack.

"Hold on, asshole!" said the major. "What the fuck are you talking about? What goddamn oil?"

"The goddamn oil you asked us for!"

"*Us!* Who the hell is '*Us*'?"

"Me, that's who! Lieutenant Richard P. Davidson and a crew of a hundred plus exhausted sailors on the USS *Hampshire County*! LST-819! The big, ugly gray ship parked on your damn beach ready to unload all the fucking oil you no longer fucking need!"

"I didn't order any fucking oil! Not from you! Not from anybody!"

For several heartbeats, the two stood there glaring at each other, horns locked like a pair of rutting bulls. With confusion slowly replacing belligerence in their eyes, I hoped bloodshed might be averted.

"Well, somebody must have placed that order," I said, my one and only contribution to the potential brouhaha.

"Do you have a copy of the message?" asked the major.

"Just so happens, I do," Skip said. He pulled a crumbled piece of paper from his pocket. Handed it over. After scanning it quickly, the major shook his head.

"I never released this." Then he yelled through the door. "Lieutenant! Get your butt in here!"

I have to give the major credit. When it comes to ass chewing, I rank him right up there with the best. Patton himself couldn't have done better. When that gofer second-string limped out of the office, he carried his gonads in one hand and two pounds of his right butt cheek in the other. A lowly ensign myself, I was embarrassed to witness the slaughter of a fellow shavetail. While the major was in the field, apparently the poor guy had misinterpreted a crisis situation and acted in his stead.

"Sorry about that, Rich," said the major. Now it was *Rich*. "My man took too much initiative while I was away and didn't bother to do his homework. Mea culpa for letting this happen under my watch. You have my solemn word it'll never happen again."

Given his pound of flesh, Skip cooled down. He climbed down from the desk. Retrieved his hat.

"Impressive," he said, "the way you dressed your man down. A first-class ass chewing; he'll limp for a week."

"Two, if I have my way. He's a good kid, really," said the major. "Little rough around the edges, though. Doesn't stop to think sometimes. You know how it is with greenhorns."

"Tell me about it." Skip laid a hand on my shoulder. Broke out a grin. "Just so happens I'm breaking in one myself." Turning to me, "You can let go of my belt now, Lar."

"Yes, sir," I said.

Crisis averted, the three of us trotted off to the officer's hut to get rip-roaring drunk. Actually, only Skip and the major got drunk. As a teetotaler, I'd been assigned as the designated driver, a role I was to assume for the rest of my tour.

After a steak and beer cookout on the beach for the crew of the *Hampshire County*—compliments of the major—the Fat Lady returned to business as usual. Up and down the Mekong River. Picking up this, dropping off that, our working credo once again was *We Deliver*.

During the next month we made so many river transits, I began to recognize some of the peasants who stopped working in their rice paddies to wave at the big ugly gray ship stinking up the air and scaring away the fish. When I think back on it, maybe they weren't waves. And they might not have been all that friendly.

———————

We were tied up to the fuel pier at Cat Lo, a Friday, I think. Then again, it could have been Saturday. After a while, what you called a day didn't matter. I knew it wasn't a Sunday, however, because meatloaf wasn't on the menu, and we always had meatloaf on Sundays. That or, God forbid, liver and onions. Whatever day it was, it was late in the evening, just after sunset, and half the crew was off clubbing it up in Vung Tau, with little on their minds but cheap drinks and even cheaper women. Not necessarily in that order. Hank "Ears" and I were stuck onboard with the duty, a condition that bothered Hank more than me. That man dearly loved his beer. We were standing on the flying bridge, shooting the breeze, when I noticed another *T* heading for our pier. Coming from the north, she was probably returning from a run to Danang.

"That looks like the *Luzerne County*," I said, recognizing her hull number. Sister ships, our paths crossed often in the delta. *Luzerne* was just as slow, just as old and stinky as us. Maybe not quite so ugly.

"She's riding high in the water, so she must be empty," said Hank. "Probably wants to tie up alongside us to take on fuel."

"I'll have the watch drop some fenders and stand by to secure lines," said I.

Four months on board and I was beginning to sound like an old salt. My cap was now beyond filthy, and my gold band had turned a disgusting shade of lime green. It may not have been in Lieutenant Davidson's league grunge-wise, but it was getting there. As the *Luzerne* made her approach, I noticed something wasn't quite right.

"That's an odd angle she's taking, Hank. Captain Davidson would never bring the Fat Lady in so steep."

Hank snapped a pair of binoculars to his eyes.

"Different strokes for different folks. Every captain has his own style. Uh, oh. She's coming in on one screw. And having trouble with her rudder."

Just then, the *Luzerne* belched a big black cloud of smoke from her port vent. She was now only two hundred yards away and closing fast. As if an LST could do anything *fast*.

"Oh, shit!" said Hank. "There goes her other screw! We're in for it now. Better alert the captain, Lar. He'll want to see this."

Unfortunately, Skip was in the shower when we took the broadside. The collision made a lot of noise and rattled the entire ship, but as crunches go, it wasn't that bad. Sort of like two giant tortoises making love.

Skip was dressed only in a towel and flip-flops, shampoo suds dripping from his hair, when he stormed onto the bridge.

"What the hell was that?" Then he saw the *Luzerne* nuzzled up to our port side at a crooked angle. "Oh, no! Not again!" As if it happened every other day.

Apparently, it wasn't the first time we'd been *kissed* by our sister ship. Leaning over the side to assess the damage, Skip lost his towel. Not a pretty sight.

"How'd it happen this time, Hank?" he asked.

"She lost both of her screws, Cap'n. And I'm pretty sure her rudder jammed."

"That would do it, all right." Skip pulled at his neck. Let out a slow breath as he retrieved his towel. "They must have run into trouble up the coast. Maybe even a mine."

At that point, the *Luzerne*'s captain appeared on his flying bridge, a wry grin on his face. Looking over at Lieutenant Davidson, he gave a *shit happens* shrug. Standing no more than twenty feet from the three of us, he didn't have to raise his voice.

"We gotta stop meeting like this, Rich. Our wives are gonna get suspicious."

At least the man had a sense of humor.

"You got that right, Karl. Some days, you get the elevator; other days, you get the shaft."

"We took a rocket hit just south of the inlet. Damaged our rudder and bent the shaft on our port prop. Then the starboard engine crapped out on our approach. Talk about your double doses of rotten luck."

I couldn't believe how calm the two were. As if they were old friends discussing the weather. Or they'd been involved in a minor fender-bender on Main Street. If it had been *my* ship, I'd have been sweating bullets. In the spit and polish fleet of battlewagons and destroyers, careers got flushed down the toilet for much less. Running into another vessel, especially to one tied to a dock, did not look good on a CO's fitness report. But this was the down-and-dirty gator Navy. LSTs ran aground all the time. It's why they were built. Who cared if they ran into each other now and then?

"Headquarters ain't gonna be too happy," Skip said. "What with this coming so soon after the last time. Although I can't remember who ran into whom back then."

"Neither can I," laughed the *Luzerne* captain. "We must be getting old. Screw 'em if they can't take a joke. I won't tell if you won't.

Hell, what's one more dent on these rust buckets? Stingy bastards. Headquarters doesn't give us enough money to keep a rowboat afloat, much less these pieces of shit."

"Roger that. Got much damage over there, Karl?"

"Nothing I can't live with. How about you, Rich?"

"Looks like you bent two stanchions and buckled a few plates, but we'll survive. Any dessert left over from dinner?"

"Just so happens, my stews have half a pan of cherry cobbler waiting in the wardroom pantry."

"My favorite. Got any fresh milk to go with that?"

"A couple gallons worth."

"Great! As soon as I get dressed, I'll be right over."

And that was that for the big collision. It says a lot for your state of mind when all your troubles can be washed away by a slice of cherry cobbler and a glass of cold milk. I guess the two skippers had bigger fish to fry than worrying about a dumbass report to headquarters. In the scheme of things, a couple of bent stanchions and a buckled deck plate or two didn't amount to a hill of beans in Vietnam. Even I, the guy in charge of keeping track of the *beans*, wasn't counting.

Where our sister ship "kissed" us. Note the dent in our side.

NINE
Oh, Boy! Bangkok!

The following morning brought more bad news for Lieutenant Davidson. It found him in the wardroom as we were all eating breakfast. It came in the form of Chief Holms.

"Sorry to disturb your meal, Cap'n," said the chief. "But I thought you'd want to know right away. Looks like the *Luzerne* caused more damage than we thought."

Skip set down his fork. Looked up at the ceiling. Rolling his eyes, he lit up another cigarette. His third of the morning.

"Okay, Chief," he said. "Lay your tale of woe on me."

"We can patch most of the dents. But one is close to the waterline and stretches across two compartments. I'm afraid it could endanger our watertight integrity. If we encounter rough seas, it just might—"

Skip let out a slow groan.

"That's a kick in the teeth so early in the morning."

When it comes to water, a *lack of integrity* could sink the ship.

It's what did the *Titanic* in. Along with an ill-placed iceberg. Icebergs didn't frequent Vietnam, but there was an abundance of ill will in-country that could do just as much damage.

"I'm afraid there's more, sir," added the chief. "I hate to add insult to injury, but the shock of the collision must have sprung the gear mechanism in our starboard bow door."

"You mean it's stuck?"

"Not quite. Opening is no problem. We just won't be able to close it again."

That was also not good news. Underway, an open-door policy was a one-way ticket to the bottom for any LST. About as practical as a screen door on a submarine.

Skip pushed his eggs from one side of the plate to the other. He blew out a smoke ring as he scratched his head. Less than an hour old and already the day had turned to crap.

"An LST that can't close its doors is pretty much useless, Chief. On top of that, you're telling me we could sink if we take a serious hit?"

"Like a rock, sir."

"Ain't that a bitch! Any other choice tidbits you want to drop on me? One of our screws fell off? The crane toppled overboard? Maybe the ship's laundry exploded? Again."

Skip leaned back, lacing his hands behind his head, mulling what to do next. Actually, there was very little he could do. What Rocket Alley had failed to do, the *Luzerne County* had accomplished in a single nudge. We were officially out of commission. An LST that can't haul cargo is just a floating rust barge. And now there was some serious doubts as to the floating part.

Watching Skip's wheels turn, I munched on a piece of toast. A few of my fellow officers half-heartedly picked at their omelets. Someone on the other side of the table coughed.

"What if we—" ventured Wild Bill. Then he fell silent. Like the rest of us, he could come up with nothing.

Me? I was just the lowly supply officer. When it came to running a ship, I barely knew port from starboard. Fore from aft. So, I buttered another piece of toast and kept my mouth shut. Knowing he was out of options, after a few seconds, Lieutenant Davidson sighed.

"Hate to say it, gentlemen, but it looks as if we're in for a long haul back to Guam. It's the nearest repair facility that can handle our problem. A cantankerous bow door is serious. We can latch it down for the trip, but if we can't lower it, we're pretty much useless."

This brought a chorus of groans from the wardroom. Me included. Our homeport of Guam wasn't exactly the garden spot of the South Pacific. Three thousand miles to the east of Cat Lo, it presented a tedious twelve-day transit. One way. Headwinds and rough seas could easily extend it to two weeks. Fourteen straight days at sea wallowing around in a skittish old tub was not an appealing prospect.

"At least some of us will get to see our families again," Skip said, trying to accentuate the positive, but failing miserably.

See our families again meant him, Chief Holms, and Wild Bill Morrison, the only ones who'd spring big bucks to drag their families to the island. And I do mean *drag*. Guam is far from a tourist attraction.

"Not much we can do at this point," he continued. "I'll ask headquarters for permission to set sail for Guam right away. They'll piss and moan, maybe throw a hissy fit or two, but I'm sure they'll okay it. They have no choice in the matter. I should get their response sometime this afternoon, but hold off on telling the crew until it's official. No sense in spoiling their breakfasts too."

Butting out his cigarette, he reached for his third helping of eggs. One thing about the captain, he loved his scrambled eggs. With shredded cheddar mixed in. "Cheesy cackle fruit," he called them.

"Well, don't just sit there, guys," he said. "Your breakfast is getting cold. Dig in. No sense in crying over spilt milk."

As usual, he was right. Headquarters' approval arrived just before dinner. But attached was a short caveat. And for once, it turned out to be *good* news. Prior to the cooks serving up our liver and onion, Skip called for an all hands meeting on the main deck to spread the word.

"Men, you'll be happy to learn we've been ordered back to Guam for repairs."

A smattering of moans rippled through the crowd. Someone in the back muttered, "There goes our combat pay."

But the Skip wasn't finished.

"Before we head to Guam, we've been ordered to pick up a

repaired admiral's gig and deliver it to the battleship *New Jersey* on our way out."

The moans subsided somewhat only to be replaced by looks of *Big deal, so what?*

"Now, here's the good part. The gig is currently located in Bangkok, and we're authorized five days of port liberty after we load her up."

Out with the moans. In with the cheers.

Bangkok! Every red-blooded sailor's wet dream! Comparing the naughty delights of Vung Tau to Bangkok was like comparing hamburger to filet mignon. A Ford to a Ferrari. I'd heard stories about Thailand's capital city. Beautiful women as far as the eye could see. Beautiful, *willing* women, the ugliest of whom was drop-dead gorgeous. For tired, overworked, underappreciated sailors, it was the best news possible.

The following day, the crew perked up, smiled again. Everyone was civil to each other, even geeks and snipes. Laughter returned to the mess deck. The crew stopped complaining about the food, a big plus for me. That evening, as we sailed out of Cat Lo's harbor, every jacktar onboard had a spring in his step. Instead of turning north up toward the delta as we usually did, we headed south toward the gulf of Thailand and Bangkok. With all that good Thai beer, incredibly hot, scorch-your-innards Thai food and, of course, knock-'em-dead Thai women. That night when we hit our racks, more than sugarplums danced in our heads.

The main topic of conversation on the ship for the next few days was how fantastic Thai women were. "Did you know that nine out of the last ten Miss Worlds came from Thailand?" Things like that. In the heart of every sailor on the Fat Lady, far away from wives and girlfriends, hope had once again sprung eternal.

––––––––––––––

On our second night out, Barry and I took an after-dinner stroll on the main deck to walk off a double helping each of spaghetti and meatballs. As usual, we ended up in the forward gun tub to watch the sunset. Barry lit a cigar. I leaned back against the forty mount to gather my thoughts.

"Ever been to Bangkok, Barry?" I asked. "Is it as great as they say it is?"

He popped me two thumbs up.

"Better than great. It's jam-packed with the most amazing women God ever put on this planet. With more favorable approaches to sex than American women. To them, making love is like scratching an itch. Last time I was there, this tall brunette turned me inside out. Damn near killed me. Thought I'd died and gone to heaven."

His grossly stained coffee cup in hand, up strolled Chief Holms, grinning. Never having seen him without that cup, I was beginning to think it was a flesh-and-blood appendage.

"I heard what you said, Lieutenant. My last Thai lady had a set of legs that wouldn't quit. Reached all the way to the ground, they did. The way she wrapped those beauties around me! Best sex I ever had."

"Wait a minute, Chief," I said. "You're a happily married man. At least so you've told me."

"What's that got to do with the price of beans?"

"What about your wife back home?" I asked.

"What about her? It's a matter of physical adjustment. She's there. I'm here. It ain't natural for a man to do without. It's a proven medical fact that long dry spells can give you a heart attack. Ask any doctor."

"What if your one and only ever found out?"

"Oh, she knows. For the most part. We got this arrangement. She don't ask and I don't tell."

Having drained the last of his coffee, the chief wiped out the cup with a rag.

"It's the unwritten code of WESTPAC," he said. "A tour of duty out here can stretch to well over a year. That's a long time to do without a little, let's say, diversion. Smart wives realize this and turn the other cheek. As long as we don't broadcast it or bring back any nasty critters, they're good with it. Those who aren't turn into ex-wives *real* quick."

"I'm glad I'm not married," I said. "Don't think I could look my wife in the eye."

"You get used to it," said the chief. "I been married for fifteen wonderful years, and in all that time, I only slipped up once."

"Just once?"

"I said the wrong name at the wrong time. If you catch my drift."

"What happened?"

"Those dry spells I mentioned?" The chief laughed as he thought back on it. "Had to remodel the kitchen and paint the house before I could wiggle my way back into my wife's good graces. Took me two whole months to pay the piper."

"Serves you right," I said over a grin. "She probably should have asked for a new car to boot."

"Who says she didn't?"

After a good laugh, the three of us settled back to enjoy the sunset. With the stars twinkling on one by one, Barry tossed his cigar overboard. Then crossed his arms.

"First order of business when we get to Bangkok will be to get our boy Timmy laid," he said.

I thought I'd heard wrong.

"Wait a minute," I said. "Are you telling me he's still a virgin? From what the chief here just told us, there's no such thing in WESTPAC."

"Dude's a died-in-the-wool cherry boy," said the chief.

"How can you be sure?"

"Look at the guy," said Barry. "It's written all over his face. If Timmy's ever had a woman, I'll eat my hat. Hell, I'd even eat the skipper's hat. And I wouldn't touch that flea-infested thing with salad tongs."

I still couldn't believe it.

"What about all the time he's spent in Vung Tau? Surely Timmy's had his chances."

"The ship's usually in and out and he's always been too seasick. It'll be different when we get to Bangkok. We'll have five whole days to pop his cherry." Barry leaned forward on a railing, looked out to sea. "The chief and I came up with a plan. The Continental Emporium won't fail us. Timmy may hit the beach a virgin, but he'll set sail a full-fledged man."

"Continental Emporium?"

"World famous combination dance club and massage parlor. You can get anything your heart desires there."

"Sounds like a glorified cat house," I said.

"But a high-class cat house," said Barry. "Several notches above what Vung Tau has to offer. Much cleaner, too. The girls line up behind this one-way mirror and you take your pick. Like an all-you-can-eat buffet."

Barry extended his hand in my direction.

"You in with us?"

Not about to miss out on the fun, I shook it.

"What can I do?"

"Just watch and enjoy. And maybe cart us back to the ship if we get falling-down drunk."

"Gotcha," I said, "I'm your man."

Our plan was simple; get Timmy drunk enough to forget about being seasick. Once he saw all those beautiful woman in Bangkok, nature would take its course. By the time Chief Holms, Barry, Hank, and me got him to the Continental Emporium, deep in the heart of the Pat Pong district, he was feeling no pain. And nowhere near seasick. Standing in front of that one-way mirror, he was like a kid in a candy shop. Dressed in terry cloth short-shorts and skin-tight T-shirts, over a hundred breathtakingly beautiful women lounged around on twenty overstuffed couches watching Bonanza reruns on TV or reading movie fan magazines. With most of my blood rushing from my head to my nether regions, I had to sit. Barry may even have drooled.

"I'll take number six!" said Timmy. "No, number thirty! Scratch that, make it twenty-two!"

Decisions, decisions, a goofy smile spread as he mulled over the delicious choices arrayed before him.

"Hell, I'll take all three!"

"Careful, tiger," said Barry. "This is your first day in the big leagues. Don't bite off more than you can chew and whiff your first time at bat. Those are real women in there. Experienced women with real needs. For starters, maybe you should pick just one. See how it goes."

"Then twenty-two it is," said Timmy, going for his own age.

The concierge announced Timmy's choice into a microphone and Miss Twenty-Two put aside her magazine, adjusted her camel toe, then walked through the door.

"Hello," she said to Timmy. "My name Kamlang," displaying a pouty mouthful of perfectly white teeth. "But you can call me Kam."

The five bedazzled Americans in the room had to remember to breathe; Kam was that captivating. Timmy just stood there, too terrified to move.

"Ma-Ma-My name is—" he finally managed.

"Timmy. His name is Timmy," said the chief. "Take it easy on our boy, Kam. This is his first time, uh, here." Wink, wink.

"I see," grinned Kam. "Then I treat him special. Give him number one massage."

Taking Timmy's hand in hers, she gave a little bow. This one was a keeper.

"You come with me, Mr. Timmy," she said. "No be nervous. As American commercial on TV say, 'You in good hands now.'"

She led him into one of the side rooms. After they were gone, Barry turned to me.

"Damn! I was going to pick Kam for myself. I hope she's not too much for Timmy. A woman like that might tear him a new one."

"What are you, his mother?" I provoked. "This was your idea, remember? I'm sure Timmy can handle himself."

"Yeah. But can he handle all *that?*"

Consensus was to hold off on making our choices, *just in case* something went wrong in *there*. Sure enough, strange sounds began to drift out of Timmy's room. Strange, embarrassing sounds.

"What you do?" asked Kam. "It not go that way." Then a giggle. "Here, me help." Another giggle. "Much better now. Nice and easy. We do this together."

We all felt bad for Timmy. His first time at the plate and he was taking one high and tight. Maybe we should have given him pointers. Learning to ride a bicycle can be difficult. Especially the first time out. In sex, as in life, the road to success is not always an easy one. Lot of bumps and turns along the way.

"I should have written out some notes for him to study," I said. As if I were an expert on the matter.

Kam soon stopped her coaching. Then started to moan. Softly at first, then growing ever louder. Within a few minutes, she was screaming her head off. Half in English, half in Thai. And she wasn't calling for help. Barry nearly swallowed his cigar.

"Sounds like they're making a porn film in there! What the hell is she doing to him?"

"From the sounds of it," I said, "the better question is what's *he* doing to *her*? Maybe *we* should be the ones taking notes."

Kam was now grunting out phrases entirely in her own language. Although I couldn't understand any of the words, I had a good idea what they meant. Mixed in with several *Oh, God*s must have been a string of *Yes, Yes*ses.

Except for the three-ring circus taking place in Timmy's room, all activity in the Continental Emporium ceased. The girls in the viewing room stopped watching TV. The magazine readers lost their places. And all eyes turned toward the sounds of passion throbbing through Timmy's door.

My mouth dryer than a panhandle sandstorm, I downed my Diet Pepsi in one gulp. Barry's chin fell to his chest. Hank's ears turned a dark shade of maroon. And for the only time I can remember, Chief Holms had an unhinged look on his face.

Grunts, groans, moans, yelps, squeals, rasps, and gasps of all kinds echoed around us. All that was missing was a brass band. The sounds of sex grew louder and louder, finally reaching a fevered pitch. One last female shriek and it was over. Not so much with a bang, but a whimper.

The four of us stared at each other in stunned disbelief. Was that really *our* Timmy "Buckets" in there? Doing who knows what to that poor girl? A subdued yet dreamy voice drifted from the room. Kam's.

"Ooooo . . . you were so beeg!"

The appropriate thing to say given her profession? A client cooing to her high rolling *farang* customer? I don't think so. Barry lit up another cigar.

"Holy crap! I guess we underestimated Timmy."

"Or at least sold him short," I said.

"Hot damn!" said the chief. "Now it's my turn! Time to get busy."

After picking Miss Eighteen, he had his pants and skivvies off halfway to his room. I couldn't help but notice something strange on his bare ass.

"Uh, Chief?" I said. "Why do you have two *W*s tattooed on your butt cheeks?"

Pulling up his shirt, he bent over to moon me. In that position, his backside spelled out "Wow."

"Any further questions?" he asked.

"Nope. That about covers it," I said. "Enjoy yourself in there."

"I plan to," said the chief.

And he was gone.

When Timmy walked out of his room, arm in arm with Kam, he was greeted by a standing ovation from everyone in the building. And by three officers from the *Hampshire County*, each with a long-stemmed cherry clenched in his teeth. We'd brought them along, *just in case,* to commemorate the occasion.

Pork chop ensign and his pubescent Fu Manchu moustache.

The myopic pork chop doesn't hit the broadside of a barnacle.

TEN
Payback for a Spit-and-Polish Battleship!

Timmy "Buckets" may have lost his virginity in Bangkok, but someone else brought back a few unwanted six-legged *souvenirs* to the ship. Unfortunately for most of the crew, it turned out to be one of my men, SN Henry Grant, the Fat Lady's laundryman. Since Grant oversaw washing the crew's clothes and bedding, he promptly spread the nasty little buggers to everyone onboard. Including me.

Two days after loading the admiral's gig onto our main deck, we were five hundred miles at sea, on our way back to Guam, when a persistent crotch itch struck. When I pulled down my drawers to check it out, I noticed a large freckle that hadn't been there before. When the freckle moved, I freaked out and made a beeline for sick bay.

"What the hell is that?" I asked the ship's corpsman.

"It looks like you caught the crabs too, Mr. Lindsey," said the doc. "The entire crew's come down with them."

"Crabs? But how? The Continental was immaculate. Had a clean bill of health."

"Your laundryman must have frequented a seedier establishment to get his jollies. He's infected the whole ship."

"Just by doing our laundry?"

"Crabs love the heat. All it takes is one load and they're everywhere." Doc reached into one of his cabinets to pull out a small tube. "This ointment should do the trick. Put a dab down there in the evening before you go to bed and another in the morning. Three days and your *freckles* will be gone."

I turned the tube over to read the label.

"Does this stuff work?"

"Sure does. We never leave port without an ample supply on board. We go through three cartons of the stuff every WESTPAC cruise."

By the time we reached Guam, "Grant's Revenge" as it came to be known, was nothing but an unpleasant memory. For that first week underway, however, SN Grant was persona non grata and wisely made himself scarce.

After our attack of pubic lice, I was standing on the fantail early one morning, watching several bottlenose dolphins fishtail through our prop wash. They like to jump a ship's bow wake, but the Fat Lady moved so slow, all she could muster up front was lackluster foam. I had completed an inventory of the dry foods storeroom and was getting a much-needed breath of fresh air. As Barry strolled up, something big and black shot across the sky. Rocket fast, it sounded like a runaway freight train. Blown away, I watched it all the way to the horizon.

"What the hell was *that*?" I asked.

Barry looked down at his watch.

"The *New Jersey*'s open for business early," he said. "Usually they don't let loose before noon. That was a shell from one of its big guns. Probably a test for their targeting radar."

"You can actually *see* the shell?"

"Their sixteen inchers weigh over a thousand pounds each. And they're visible in flight to the naked eye."

Another shell screamed across the heavens, headed in the same direction. I looked to the far horizon.

"We're ten miles from shore," I said. "And the *New Jersey* isn't even in sight."

"Boggles the mind, doesn't it?" said Barry. "What's more amazing, she's probably shooting at something ten miles inland."

"She can reach that far?"

"You have to remember, it's one *big* gun. And they carry nine of them."

I let out a slow whistle.

"Must be one hell of a ship."

"Over twice our length and three times as fast," said Barry. "With four screws at full speed, she can do thirty knots into a stiff wind. Hell, her anchor alone would sink us. When she pulls up to the pumps, she sucks down two and a half million gallons of high test. Her engines make ours look like lawn mowers."

"Powerful, eh?"

"Over two hundred thousand horses' worth," said Barry.

Yet another shell shot across the sky. Followed in quick succession by three more.

Barry lit his first cigar of the day. Blew out a thin stream of smoke, then nodded in the direction of Vietnam.

"Looks like they found the range. I'd hate to be on the business end of one of those babies. Makes molehills out of mountains in no time flat."

I almost blurted out a *WOW!* Thanks to Chief Holm's butt tattoo, however, I was reluctant to use the word ever again.

"Amazing!" I said instead.

Twenty minutes later, the mighty battleship finally appeared on the eastern horizon. A small dot at first, then growing ever larger. And larger. As she continued to launch volley after volley at an unseen target, I could see smoke and fire belching from her three massive gun turrets.

Approaching her at our mundane eight knots, the great ship loomed out of the sea, like a gigantic fire-breathing whale. When we were a thousand yards from her, she called a temporary halt to her barrage. As we tied up aft of her bow, she blotted out the sun. Wallowing in the overhang of her main deck, the tip of our radio mast barely came to her gunnels. Looking up at that massive hulk of gray metal above us, we felt like a dinghy tied up to the *Queen Mary*.

The USS *New Jersey* was everything we weren't. Sleek, graceful, awe-inspiring, powerful, swift, heroic, regulation, and most of all, clean. We were dirt. She was gold. And from the looks her crew gave us, everyman onboard her knew it.

While we were leaving the combat zone, I had radioed ahead to transfer my MPC so I had official business with *Jersey*'s disbursing officer. Other than our skipper, I was the only person invited to set foot on the historic battleship's polished wooden decks. And Skipper Davidson wisely declined.

"Their invite was a courtesy thing," he said. "I'm a lowly lieutenant and *Jersey*'s skipper is a four-striper with one foot in admiral's britches. *Way* out of my league. My unpolished boondockers aren't up for it."

From the looks I got when I crossed their quarterdeck, you would have thought I was a leper. My uniform was a bit shabby and frayed around the edges, but four months of hot, sweaty, backbreaking work up and down brown water rivers will do that to a set of threads.

"Whose navy is *that* guy with?" I overheard a second-class signalman say.

"That's an LST sailor," said his buddy. "You know, a Salvation Army reject."

Their disbursing officer (his only duty) met me in the wardroom, at least thirty times the size of the Fat Lady's. Also a mere ensign, he couldn't believe I was the sole pork chop on my ship.

"There's only *one* of you?" he asked.

"Just me, myself, and I," I replied. "How many supply officers do you have on the *Jersey*?

"Ten, by my last count. A full commander, a lieutenant commander, three lieutenants, four ensigns, and a chief warrant officer."

"We've only got ten officers on our entire ship," I said. "Total."

"Our wardroom seats a hundred at one setting. And our crew measures over sixteen hundred strong."

"That's a small city!" I said. "How do you get to know everybody?"

"You don't. This morning, I ate breakfast across from a junior grade I'd never seen before."

"Isn't that kind of depressing?" I asked.

"You think this is bad? Try an aircraft carrier. The bigger ones bunk down over four thousand men. And that's not counting when their air wing is on board."

The ensign was a likable enough sort, but strictly regulation. Right down to his immaculately shined shoes. Unlike mine, which were a mass of scuffs, you could see your face in them. After we finished our money exchange, he took a deep breath and opened up a bit.

"What's it like?" he asked, a look halfway between curiosity and envy on his face. "Being your own boss, I mean? Are you really in charge of everything?"

"The whole nine yards," I said, surprised at how satisfying that sounded. "Now and then, I even get a chance to drive the ship."

"Lucky dog! They don't allow any of us chops anywhere near the bridge. Day after day of nothing but the four walls of my disbursing office. I can't remember the last time I saw the sun. If I never see another pay record, it'll be too soon. Have you seen any *real* action?"

I told him what it was like going up and down the rivers, embellishing this, exaggerating that. As all gator sailors tend to do. When I finished my dog and pony, I felt world's better about my lot in life. And despite my grossly unpolished shoes, I walked a little bit taller heading back to my ship.

While I was gone, the admiral's gig had been off-loaded and the Fat Lady was standing by to cast off. As we pulled away, I noticed a large canvas bag dripping fluids dangling from the *New Jersey's* forward anchor. Right above where we'd been tied up. Chief Holms stood at the railing, staring up at it with a satisfied smirk on his face.

"Uh, Chief?" I said. "You wouldn't happen to know anything about that bag up there, would you?"

"Good riddance to bad rubbish," he said. "That'll teach those battlewagon pussies to bad mouth us."

While I was sequestered down in the disbursing office, some insults had been hurled the Fat Lady's way by the *New Jersey's* crew. Things like, "That looks like a rusted turd someone forgot to flush." Or "Does that piece of crap actually float?"

"What's in the bag?" I asked.

"Yesterday's garbage," said the chief. "Mostly liver and onions left over from lunch. I hope you don't mind, but I asked the cooks to save some for me. In this heat, it should start to stink real quick.

It'll probably take those *Jersey* pukes all day to figure out where the stench is coming from."

I had to laugh.

"That's a terrible waste of good garbage, Chief. For a quicker and higher quality stink, you should have flushed out the heads. Then the *Jersey* really would have smelled like shit."

Chief Holms snapped his fingers.

"Damn! Wish I would have thought of that. I like the way you think, Mr. Lindsey. You're even sneakier than me."

Bone-dry empty in the heavy seas this side of the San Bernardino Strait, the Fat Lady was being tossed around like a frenetic cork. After careening from bulkhead to bulkhead for two straight days, the frazzled crew was back to snapping at each other. An exhausting routine, with all that up-and-down, back-and-forth motion, you couldn't eat or drink without making a mess of your uniform. Taking a crap was even more of a challenge, an ordeal that nine times out of ten ended up with you soiling yourself. You couldn't even shower. On the third day, we all stunk worse than last week's garbage.

At night, no matter how I wedged myself into my bunk, my innards kept sloshing around. With my stomach gurgling like a half-filled water balloon, it was impossible to sleep. Counting sheep, eating cookies with warm milk, reading a boring paperback, even balancing one of my tedious ledgers—nothing worked.

After catching catnaps whenever we could, the crew looked like the walking dead. Their eyes sunken and at half-mast, my men stumbled about in a sullen stupor. On our way to Bangkok, both the wardroom and the mess deck had been abuzz with laughter and high hopes. Now all we did was chew and swallow. We spoke in clipped phrases. And only when we had to. Most times, we merely grunted.

With the good times of Thailand in our distant wake, Wild Bill and I were back to our dog and cat ways. He called me "Dickhead." I called him "Asswipe." Said even worse things behind each other's backs. The caldron came to a boil on one afternoon the first week out. I was down in my office sweating out another OPTAR report. Literally sweating since, once again, the air conditioning had crapped out. That's when SK3 Mantle hit me with the bad news.

"Mr. Lindsey? We got a problem in the repair parts storeroom. A *big* problem."

I wiped sweat from my eyes with a toweled forearm. Leaned back to take a deep breath. Drained the last of my Diet Pepsi. It was going to be one of those days.

"Okay, lay it on me."

"Words won't do it justice, sir. You'll have to see it for yourself."

"The damn storeroom didn't go all laundry on us and explode, did it?" I asked.

"I'm afraid it's worse."

That didn't sound good.

Mantle took me on a circuitous route that led to a hatch we'd never used before. It was on the deck of my men's living compartment.

"The storeroom is just below us, sir," he said.

That also didn't sound good.

"Why did we come this way?" I asked.

"When I open the hatch, you'll see," he said. Then handed me a flashlight. "You'll need this."

When he un-dogged the latches, I found myself staring at my own face, reflecting back from a dark shiny surface. Oil. Black Gold. Texas Tea! The primordial ooze had reached three quarters up the bulkhead to submerge all five shelves in our storeroom.

"Holy Crap!" I said. That's fuel oil down there, Mantle!!"

"That it is, sir. Lots of it. Five and a half feet deep, by my best guess."

"What's it doing in our storeroom?" I asked.

"Got me by the elbow, sir."

That phrase was beginning to annoy me. I was hearing it *way* too often. When I was in high school, my mother, the English teacher, told me that swearing was the strongest thing a weak man could say. I think Mark Twain said it first. Staring down at all that blackness, I forgot her good advice and let loose a string of expletives that would have made Satan blush.

"Wait a minute!" I said. "Didn't we take on fuel yesterday?"

"That we did, sir."

"That tears it! Goddamn snipes! Get me a bucket, Mantle. We're going to pay Mr. Morrison and his band of Morlocks a surprise visit."

By the time we reached the engineering office, I had worked

myself into a lather. Hopping mad? You bet! So, I growled at the first snipe I ran across.

"Where's your fucking boss?"

Pappy, the evaporator man, backed away with his hands up. Nodded toward the far side of the compartment where Wild Bill was hunched over a control panel wearing a confused look.

"These dials can't be right," Bill said to one of his equally confused petty officers. "We couldn't have burned that much fuel in less than a day. Have you taken a manual reading?"

His man rapped on the glass.

"Twice, sir. And the readings are accurate. We're down six thousand gallons."

"Damn it! That means we have a leak somewhere. A big one."

"I checked our wake, Lieutenant. We aren't trailing a slick."

"Then where in the hell did all that fuel go?"

That was my cue.

"Missing some oil, are you, Mr. Morrison?" I said, tapping him on the shoulder. As he was turning around, I emptied the contents on my bucket down the front of his shirt. About two quarts worth of fuel oil. "Here's some of it back. The rest is safe and sound down in my goddam repair parts storeroom!"

Shouting at someone nicknamed *Wild* Bill probably wasn't a smart move. Neither was dousing him in his own oil. But I was fighting mad. And now, so was he.

Slipping and sliding around in all that oil, neither of us got in much of a blow. A few shoves and we were flat on our backs on the deck grappling like third graders. Looking back on the encounter, I'm thoroughly ashamed of myself. And, I'm sure, so is Bill. We both reacted badly. *Behavior unbecoming an officer* would have been the opening charge at our court martial.

We soon realized neither one of us was landing punches, so we stopped flailing away. I grabbed him by the shirt. He grabbed me by mine. Our grips locked, we rose nose to nose, our legs skittery. It was a miracle we didn't break our fool necks.

To the captain! The thought came to us simultaneously. *I'm gonna tell!*

Holding tight to each other, the four-legged, third grader trundled off to see Skip. Our captain, in his infinite wisdom, would settle this.

Down the corridor, up two ladders, and through the hatchway into officer's country, I'm sure half the crew saw us bouncing from bulkhead to bulkhead, jawing incoherent curses at each other. Leaving an oily slime in our wake, we were pinballing down officer country when Skip came out of his sea cabin. Spying us, he stopped dead in his tracks. Then rolled his eyes.

"What the hell?"

"Captain!" we said as one. "He—"

Before either of us could state his case, our boss raised a hand. Shook his head.

"Stop! I don't think I want to hear this. Come back when you've both cooled off. And only after you've cleaned up."

Smart man that he was, Skip then slammed the door on us. It was the reason he was the ship's captain and we were junior officers who apparently had yet to finish the third grade.

With the wind taken out of both of our sails, Wild Bill and I stood there for a solid minute, eyes blinking, dripping oil on the deck, Bill still holding on to me and me onto him. Feeling like a pair of idiots, we finally let go of each other.

"Do you know how ridiculous we must look?" said Bill.

"Like a couple of bratty kids," said I. "No wonder Skip told us to take a hike."

Bill looked down at his ruined uniform. Then over at mine.

"I wouldn't have given us the time of day either."

I reached out to flick the only clean spot on his chest.

"Hate to bring it up, Bill," I said. "But that shirt of yours won't pass inspection. Even on the Fat Lady. And there isn't a chance in hell my laundry is ever going to get it clean again. Seaman Grant, even on his best days, won't come close."

Bill gave a tug at my oil-soaked sleeve.

"You forget, Lar," he laughed. "The laundry's been down for a week. Besides, look who's talking. That isn't your best bib and tucker. Your shirt's dirtier than mine."

"*Bib and tucker?*" I said with a grin. "Who the hell talks like that?"

"Hey, give me a break. That's the way we speak in the Midwest."

Calling a truce, we put our heads together to solve our problem. Later that day, Bill had his men rig up a system of hoses and set up a siphoning station to pump out the wayward oil. He even dispatched a working party to help clean up the mess in my storeroom.

Working party? Why the Navy refers to such dirty details as *parties* is beyond me. Parties are fun and frivolity. Work is just plain work.

"We have a bigger problem," I said to Bill. "The oil dissolved all the labels in that storeroom. My men don't know a wobble from a widget. Without labels, they won't be able to identify anything."

Wild Bill may have been a hothead at times, but he also had a quick mind. It took him all of five seconds to come up with a solution. A damn good one, too.

"My men know what parts they're looking for. I'll have them accompany your SKs to the storeroom to help find them."

It worked like a charm. In the next few weeks, my men learned something about engineering and his men picked up a few pointers about supply. Scratch my back, I'll scratch yours; Bill's idea was a win-win. One we implemented on a permanent basis.

Mr. Morrison and I would still have *heated disagreements* now and then (being at odds would always be part of our job descriptions), but after the *Great Oil Spill of '69*, we stopped calling each other names. At least we toned it down a notch. "Dickhead" and "Asswipe" morphed to a more civilized "Jerk" and "Idiot." With an occasional "Moron" thrown in for good measure.

The Admiral's gig on its way to the *USS New Jersey.*

ELEVEN

Juan G. Tern and Susie. May She Rest in Peace!

My first major discipline problem came to a head four days after the oily storeroom incident. I was never an in-your-face officer when dealing with my men. Call me soft, but I think reason and logic should come before threats and shouting. Fear and broken eardrums motivates on a short-term basis, but in the long run, the effects can be counterproductive. Yell too loud and too often, and the *yellee* soon tunes out the *yeller.*

But I was at my wit's end with this second-class cook of mine. How he made second class was beyond me. CS2 Durton was his name, and nothing I tried worked on the guy. Lectures, training sessions, motivational discussions, heart-to-heart talks, it was like preaching to a brick wall. I felt like burning every psych book I'd ever read and punching his lights out. In the end, I gave up and resorted to a threat. If he didn't *straighten up and fly right* (a common expression in the military), I promised to hit him *where it hurts*. In the pocketbook.

"Look, CS2 Durton," I said, no nonsense in my voice, "I'll make it simple. I'm giving you one month to square yourself away. If I don't see any improvement, I'm going to bust your sorry ass down to third class. *Comprende?*"

"Yes, sir," he said, behind a thinly veiled smirk. "I understand."

But I knew he didn't.

The last straw came a week later. I was outside the galley, inspecting an oven vent for grease buildup. After releasing the screen trap, I stuck my head inside for a better look. Because I'm tall, I was able to see all the way into the galley. I spied Durton standing in one corner by himself, preparing mashed potatoes for dinner in our giant mixer. He had his back to me. To my horror, he zipped down his dungarees and took a whiz into the mixer.

With a gag, I bumped my head on the vent. Jerked back. Out in the fresh air again, I took a few seconds to calm down. I love mashed potatoes. Always take second helpings. My first impulse was to confront Durton on the spot. Catch him with his pants down, so to speak. Then drag him down to the tank deck and beat the crap out of him. The US Navy, however, takes a dim view of pork chops who beat up one of their cooks. Even if that cook is pissing on the food. There's no menu for that.

I thought of Chief Holms, our old man of the sea. Theoretically, chiefs aren't supposed to lay a hand on the crew either. Sometimes, however, they *bend the rules* when no one is looking. I caught up to the chief on the fantail while he was taking a smoke break. Coffee cup in hand, of course.

"Chief?" I said, "I've got a delicate problem on my hands. Something I hope might be right up your alley. One of my men is in dire need of some, let's just say, *serious redirection.*"

"That's what I'm here for, sir. Your skinny second-class cook giving you trouble again?"

"You know about Durton?"

"Word gets around. Bad apples always rise to the surface. What's he done this time?"

"He contaminated some of the food."

"Contaminated?"

"I caught him pissing in the mashed potatoes."

"Son of a bitch! I love mashed potatoes."

"So did I. But not anymore."

With a disgusted scowl, he asked, "What will you do to the creep?"

"Kick him out of the galley, of course. Then bust him down to third class. If I had my druthers, he'd scrub decks for the rest of the deployment. With his own toothbrush. I'd really like to plant my size elevens up his sorry ass. Of course, with this bar on my collar, I can't."

"Say no more, Mr. Lindsey. I'll have a little *talk* with your wayward cook."

"I don't want you to get in any trouble. He's not worth it."

"No problem," said the chief. "We won't lay a hand on him."

We? I thought.

Looking out to sea, Chief Holms took a long drag on his cigarette. Then blew it out slowly.

"In the old Navy," he continued, "*we* didn't have problems like this. We had special ways of dealing with incorrigibles. *Rocks and shoals*, we called it. It may have not been pretty, and nine times out of ten, it involved some pain, but it worked. Basically, if a man went to captain's mast without a few bruises, he hadn't been properly *counseled*, if you catch my drift. Nowadays, you can't look cross-eyed at a scum sucker without getting dragged up on charges. But we still have our ways.

We, again.

"What's your plan?" I asked.

The chief's devilish grin was a thing of beauty.

"Less said, the better."

Not sure I wanted to know what he meant by that. I nodded slowly.

"Then I'll leave my problem in your capable hands."

"Consider it solved."

The following morning at quarters Durton, the pissing cook stood tall in a set of fresh dungarees, the first I'd ever seen on him. His hair was neatly combed, his nails were dirt free, and he even smelled clean. I don't know what a GI shower entails (I was later told it has something to do with a bristle brush), but it left him with a well-scrubbed sheen. I'd never seen a human being in a redder set of skin. Whatever the chief and his friends did, Durton never came close to *contaminating* the mashed potatoes again. Or anything else, for that matter.

———

Twenty-four hours after the chief's *intervention*, Durton's color was slowly returning to normal, and we were two days from Guam. Skip and I were standing on the bridge, basking in the glow of our dinner bridge victory as we savored the cool evening breeze wafting off our starboard quarter. Drifting across the deck was the smell of land, a welcome aroma after three dreary weeks at sea. A harvest moon hung low along with a canopy of twinkling stars. A calm sea cradled the ship as she plodded along at her steady, if unremarkable, pace. The salt spray and metronomic throb of her engines combined to make both of us drowsy. That, and the second helpings of meat loaf we'd both devoured at dinner. As usual, the topic gravitated to bridge.

"I prefer Blackwood to Gerber," Skip said. "Much more dependable, don't you think, Lar?"

Having no preference either way, I could only agree. Lieutenant Davidson was head and shoulders the better bridge player. And I wasn't half bad.

"Right you are, sir," I said.

That settled, we both watched a shooting star stream across the heavens. An unwritten rule of the sea, you could never be *friends* with your captain. Impractical at times and awkward at others, it wasn't in the cards. As steady bridge partners, however, he often confided in me. After the star plummeted beneath the western horizon, he sighed.

"From here, it's just a straight shot *home*," he said, the word not setting right with him. "Home," he repeated. "As if anyone could call Guam home."

"At least you'll get to see your wife and daughter again," I said.

"There is that," he said. "But my family reunion comes at a price. To get this command, I had to sign on for four years. Not two, like the rest of the crew. Headquarters likes to hold on to their skippers as long as they can. Can't really blame them, though. Makes for better continuity, I guess. The extension was the only way I could get them to ship my family over."

"Sounds like they have you by the short hairs."

"Tell me about it. It was hard on my wife relocating halfway around the world, but I needed the command to further my career. Bless her heart, Laura never complains. As always, she just packs up and goes wherever the Navy sends us. I don't know what she sees in an old fart like me, but she's stayed with me through thick and mostly thin. Even after dragging her to some of the god-awfulest places on Earth. Life's hard on a Navy wife, having to pull up roots every few years. And I couldn't ask for a better daughter than Becky. Hasn't given me a lick of trouble."

Skip let out another sigh, this one longer than the last.

"Of course, now that she's turning fourteen, that may change. She's at the age where she's beginning to notice boys. And what's worse, as pretty as she is, the boys are beginning to notice her. Big time."

"Sounds like a few more gray hairs might be headed your way," I said.

"You got that right."

Thinning his lips, the skipper pulled at his neck. Then looked out to sea.

"Why do little girls have to grow up, anyway?" he said. "Why can't they stay all sugar and spice? At least into their twenties."

From that, I knew his daughter was strictly off limits to the crew. And any other red-blooded male in Guam. Remembering what I was like as a teenager, I couldn't fault the man.

He lit up his second cigarette. Took time to blow out another smoke ring. Enjoying a second helping of easy silence, we both leaned on the railing to watch a school of porpoises at our wake, moonlight reflecting off their smooth skin. Several minutes passed, then surprise of surprises, Lieutenant Davidson spouted verse.

"*The sea awaits . . . Silent, strong, vast in her power . . . A woman always, she cast a bewitching spell . . . Her call must be answered . . . as sailors, we surrender. To her bosom, we are borne . . . come the tide, we are gone. . . "*

You could have knocked me over with a feather. Our grizzled

commanding officer—the same man who almost decapitated a Marine major with his cap—quoting poetry?

"I never heard those lines before," I said. "They're good, real good. Who wrote them?"

"Believe it or not, I did."

Now I was *really* impressed. Not exactly poet laureate stuff, it was a damn sight better than anything I'd ever come up with.

"You're a man of many talents, Skipper."

"But alas, a master of none. Other than this ship, of course."

With the crew standing mostly tall at quarters the following morning, the forward lookout spotted something strange off our port side. A quarter of a mile out, a large bird flew erratically and parallel to our course. Head hanging down, it seemed to be struggling to keep above the waves. In my binoculars, I saw it was a mottled tern and that the poor creature was exhausted. Unlike seagulls and pelicans, terns are not seagoing types. If he set down in the water, he'd probably drown. Standing next to me, Barry saw him too.

"We're three hundred miles from land," he said. "What the devil is he doing way out here?"

"My guess is he got blown off course by the trade winds," I said. "He's probably looking for a place to land."

"Could be. But the poor guy's headed out to sea. And from the looks of him, he's not going to last much longer."

"I don't think he sees us," I said.

Barry lowered his binoculars. Turned toward the bridge. Called out an order.

"Give me a loud single blast!"

The tern heard our ship's horn and made an immediate sharp left to head straight for us. Alerted by the blast, a crowd soon gathered along the port side to root him on. Head-on like he now was, I gauged his wingspan to be about four feet. Pretty large for a tern. Flying only a few inches above the surface, now and then, one of his wing tips slapped water. A few times, he dipped below a rolling swell and disappeared from sight, only to rise a few seconds later.

At two hundred yards out, I could tell he wasn't going to clear the Fat Lady's side. From his vantage point, our main deck must have looked higher than Mt. Everest. Ever so slowly, using the last of his strength, he began to gain altitude. Five feet, then ten feet above the waves. Finally fifteen. But that was it. He could go no higher.

"Stand by that horn!" yelled Barry. "On my signal! Long and hard!" To the crowd on deck, "Lower the safety lines!"

Just when it looked like the tern would crash into us, he gave the order.

"NOW!"

Like a peal of thunder from Olympus, on high, the Fat Lady's blast juiced the last ounce of strength out of that exhausted bird. Two quick strokes propelled him up and over our gunnels with no more than an inch to spare. Landing wheels up and wings out, he skidded to a twisting stop on his belly. Too tired to stand or fold his wings, he lay there panting. Come hell or more high water, he wasn't going to budge from that spot. He didn't even object when our concerned crew gathered around.

That's it for me, boys, his eyes seemed to say. *Do with me what you will, but I've flown my last mile. From here on, this dirty bird is walking.*

He didn't even fuss when Chief Holms gently picked him up.

From that moment on, that wrong-way tern was the ship's pampered pet. The crew held a contest at lunch to name him. First prize—weekend liberty when we hit port. Second prize—two weekend liberties. As I said, there isn't much to do in Guam. Pappy the evaporator man garnered the honor with "Juan G. Tern," the *G* standing for *Good.* As in *one good turn* deserves another. Clever!

The deck apes made a nest for Juan out of a shipping crate, complete with padded perch, and attached it to the starboard flying bridge so the watch could keep an eye on him. However, Juan spent most of his time strutting around on the ship's compass, happy as a clam, watching us go about our business. The polished brass seemed to fascinate him, and he used it as a mirror to preen himself. For some reason, he fancied the captain's bridge chair as a personal litter box. To keep the skipper from catching wind, as soon as Juan made a *deposit*, the messenger of the watch was there with a rag to wipe it up.

For two days and three nights, Juan ate like a king. Every man onboard slipped him something from the galley at least once. My cooks being the worst offenders. His favorite delicacy turned out to be pieces of boiled chicken. No one had the heart to tell him it was a distant relative of his. By the time we reached Guam, that well-fed tern looked like a feathered beach ball with legs. He was no birdbrain; Juan knew he'd glommed on to a good thing, and not once did he try to fly away. Not even after we tied up to the pier.

During our entire stay in Guam, whenever anyone went ashore, the first salute was of course for the ensign flag. But the second was always for Juan G. Tern. After a few times, he caught on to the ritual, and if you forgot to render him his honors, he'd puff out his feathers, clack his bill twice, and give you a dirty bird look. A friendly reminder he was due a salute.

———

After three plus weeks at sea, from a distance, Guam looked good. At least through your binoculars. Protected by a coral reef and flanked by a jutting rock precipice called Lover's Leap, Agana, was the largest city on the island, a travel brochure approximating an idyllic curved bay, white sands, and majestic palm trees swaying in the tropical breeze; it listed things you'd think tourists would pay thousands of dollars to visit—if it weren't for the fact that there was little else to do on the always hot and humid island. Making our harbor approach, I thought I heard strains of Enzio Pinza singing "Some Enchanted Evening" from *South Pacific*. Then again, it may have been Rossano Brazzi. When it comes to that musical, I always confuse the two.

Wearing our dress uniforms, which may have been white at one time but were now a pale yellow, Skip, Barry, and I stood on the starboard flying bridge taking in the sights. Most of the crew were lined up at attention on the main deck *manning the rails,* a Navy tradition when returning to home port. It was intended to dress up the ship, or in our case, make it more presentable. After so many months in 'Nam, however, it was like trying to lipstick a pig.

Although most of us had no loved ones waiting on the pier, it was still a homecoming of sorts. At least for the next few weeks no one would be shooting at us. Best of all, tied up to the dock, we would be assured constant air conditioning. Glorious, blessed air conditioning!

Shielding his eyes from the sun, Lieutenant Davidson scanned the beach.

"I wonder what surprise Laura has waiting for us," he said. "Last time, she strung this humongous banner across the bluff overlooking the bay. Damn thing must have been a hundred feet long and six feet high. Said 'Welcome back *Hampshire County*! Glad to have you home!' in green, fluorescent letters. You could see that thing two miles out to sea."

"Sounds as if your wife goes all out," I said.

"That ain't the half of it," Skip said. "Mrs. Davidson is one of a kind. The world's best cook, she'll fatten up that skinny ass of yours in no time. And she knows more dirty jokes than Chief Holms. Better ones, too."

A prideful smile edged onto the skipper's face.

"Laura let's 'em rip in mixed company," he said. "Runs rings around me when it comes to cussing."

Just then, the bluff came into view. Camped on top was a full brass brand in garish purple and gold uniforms, flanked by thirty or so cheerleaders. Out front stood a diminutive blond woman wearing a drum major's hat, a baton in her right hand. On her cue, the band struck up a tune. For a second, I thought Skip was going to cry.

"How about that," he said. "In all this heat, she got the high school band to dress up for us."

"What's that they're playing?" I asked.

"The University of Missouri fight song. My alma mater. Go Mizzou!" Skip wiped at an eye. "She's outdone herself this time."

When the band transitioned into "Anchors Aweigh," fireworks shot out over the cliff, exploding into red, white, and blue streamers.

"Nice touch," Skip said, his voice cracking.

The band shouted, "Go Navy!" Tucked their instruments under one arm, and on Mrs. Davidson's command, saluted us.

I know it may sound corny, but I got all misty. And so did the skipper and Barry. Hardened warriors home from the front? A full minute had to pass before any of us could speak. Finally, Skip nodded toward the bluff.

"Think *that* was something? Wait until you see the spread she's laid out for us tonight."

"Us?" I said. "You mean we're invited?"

"Hell, yes. The whole damn ship. Make sure you bring your appetite. *Who-can-eat-the-most* is a tradition at our house. A Davidson homecoming challenge."

Thoughts and questions popped into my mind. *If it were my wife who had waited all these many months for my return, she sure as hell wouldn't welcome a hundred freeloaders into our home. Especially not my first night back.*

"It's been over eight months since you've, um, seen your wife," I said. "Don't you want to be alone? Spend some *quality time* together? Or whatever it is married couples do."

"We save the *whatevering* for the second night, Lar. Let the boiler build up a full head of steam. If you know what I mean."

"You're a better man than I, Skip. I couldn't wait that long."

"Anticipation is half the fun. Like Christmas Eve when you were a kid."

———————

After we tied up and went through the rigmarole of greeting the muckety-mucks from squadron headquarters, Lieutenant Davidson ordered Susie, our over-the-hill Dodge pickup, to be set on the pier. Since his wife never met him at the dock (in deference to the geographic bachelors and single men onboard) as the ship's designated driver, I was to ferry him home, then bring Susie back. Skip smiled a thumbs-up to the crane operator.

"Be quick with that lift," he said. "I got places to go. People to see."

In the months we'd been gone, we hadn't had an accident with the crane. The deck crew, consummate professionals that they were, hadn't dropped a single pallet. Hadn't broken so much as one egg. Until today. How that truck slipped out of its sling is still a mystery. But slip it did. From a height of about thirty feet above the pier, Susie twisted suddenly to the right, her nose tilting down. There she dangled for all of ten seconds, Skip and I holding our collective breaths.

The crane operator tried to compensate for the slippage, but that only compounded the problem. As if contemplating a swan dive, Susie shuddered once. Then with a grinding snap of chains, she pitched forward to crash nose first onto the dock. The only bright spot was that no one was hurt. The fall not only crinkled her hood and dislodged the engine but it also twisted the frame. As old as she was, all the king's horses and all the king's men wouldn't have helped.

Pin-drop silence, almost funereal, reigned on the pier. It was as if we'd witnessed the passing of an old friend. Every man onboard the Fat Lady had ridden in that old pickup at one time or another in various stages of sobriety. Susie had been our landline, our supply vehicle, our taxicab, and all around good-gal reminder of that special set of wheels we had waiting for us back home. To see her rendered into a pile of junk was more than some of us could handle. Barry let out a soft moan. Chief Holms may have whimpered. After a long sigh, Skip removed his cap, wiped his brow, then looked up at the sun.

"Well, at least she's on the pier. I asked for quick and I guess I got quick. My fault for rushing things."

I could tell it bothered him inside. A lot. But he wasn't about to let an accident spoil the crew's homecoming.

"Better give Public Works a call, Lar. Tell them we've had a misadventure of sorts. Maybe they can rustle us up another vehicle."

And he left it at that.

———

A few days later, the ship's resident mechanic pronounced last rites over Susie. "Sorry, Captain, but I'm afraid Susie here has motored her last mile. There's nothing I can do for her." She was lifted back onboard and shrouded with a tarp. Just before we went into drydock, she was buried at sea with full honors in one of the most moving ceremonies I ever attended. A week later, headquarters replaced Susie with a newer old truck, a reconditioned Ford with half as many miles on her. But it wasn't the same.

———

That first night, the entire crew descended on the Davidsons'. And then some. Skip was a popular figure on the island, and half of Guam showed up to eat, drink, and help cook local delicacies in six huge outdoor ovens they'd helped set up in his backyard.

Guamanians are gracious, fun-loving people who live to eat and party. They'll celebrate anything at the drop of a hat; even the Skip's grungy mess and the return of the Fat Lady fit the bill nicely.

Most of them brought exotic dishes I'd never heard of. All of them unpronounceable, sinfully fattening, and beyond delicious.

Well over five hundred people must have passed through the Davidsons' front door that night, and not one of them went away hungry. I never saw so much food in one place. Personally, I stopped counting after my tenth lumpia. My caloric intake that night surged well beyond gluttony levels, and for the next month, I never went near a scale.

As bad luck would have it, however, our third night back coincided with Guam's annual termite mating swarm, a nocturnal event of Biblical proportions. During the night, the air gets so thick with horny insects, it's impossible to breathe. As soon as the males finish copulating, they roll over and die, resulting in billions of dead bugs on the highways. Come morning, thousands of hungry frogs hit the roads in droves, lapping up all the dead bugs. Add moving cars to the mix and you've got tons of flattened amphibians. Two hours in the hot sun turns them into crispy critters local kids pry up and sail. They call them Frisbee frogs. Swear to God.

Juan G. Tern

Susie, after the fall... All the king's horses and all the king's men.

TWELVE
Skip and Go Naked!

The ship spent most of her time in Guam swarmed by a horde of cvilian sand crabs (dock workers). With their acetylene torches going full blast around the clock, they quickly straightened out our damaged hull plates and welded into place three new support stations. However, they had a devil of a time with our dyspeptic bow doors. While they scratched their heads, Skipper Davidson implemented a generous liberty policy and encouraged the crew to see the sights of Guam. What little there were.

We all went on endless hikes (locals called them *boonie stomps*) to Talafofo Falls, to a World War II tank farm in the middle of the island, and to the jungle cliffs at the northern tip of the island. A few hardy souls even dived to the wreck of a Japanese zero, complete with a fake skeleton in its cockpit, half a mile off a southern beach. Not to be outdone, one sunny afternoon, Barry and I snorkeled out to the shark pits of Agana Harbor, so named for all the WWII bomb craters that attracted hordes of blue tips.

Our excursion ended abruptly when numb-nuts Barry got trigger happy and shot off his speargun into an unsuspecting hammerhead. It was like ringing the dinner bell for every shark in the bay. A long-time scuba diver would never do anything that stupid intentionally. I hadn't been in the middle of a shark feeding frenzy before, and never will again. Fortunate to scramble out of the water with all my appendages still attached, I suggested to Barry that the next time we went diving, he leave the damn speargun at home.

Speaking of idiots, two weeks later, Hank and Barry combined their IQs to come up with something even more stupid. On a poorly thought-out whim, they decided to take on the local watering hole. As officers' clubs go, Guam's Pump Room wasn't much. The menu was limited, the food so-so, and the décor reeked of early American trailer trash. The place even smelled bad. But the Sump Pump, as it came to be known, was famous throughout the Western Pacific for one unique and very powerful drink. Devised by one of their demented bartenders, an ornery cuss who'd been there since prohibition, the drink was called a *Skip and Go Naked*. Aptly named, it could put hair on a bald man's butt.

Served in a tall glass, the *Naked* consisted of six shots of six different rums hand ladled carefully into layers, each layer dusted with powdered sugar. Sucked through two straws to keep the rums from mingling prematurely, each *Naked* was topped off by a two-beer chaser. The Pump Room was so proud of their demonic concoction, they offered a hundred-dollar prize to any fool who could polish off three in less than an hour. Along with an engraved plaque to commemorate the insanity. Followed up with a quick ambulance ride to the hospital to have your stomach pumped.

As a teetotaler, I wasn't sure, but it seemed to me that the alcoholic content of eighteen shots of rum and six cans of beer was on the wrong side of lethal. In the twelve years the drink had been around, no one came close to mastering the *Skip and Go Naked*. Much less walk away with all their faculties. Undaunted by this ominous fact, one night, Hank and Barry, both awesome drinkers in their own right (or mind), decided to answer the challenge. Despite serious misgivings, I agreed to drive them to and from the Pump Room.

Maybe pick up the pieces if any were left. Their brilliant strategy was to gobble down a cheeseburger between each drink.

"To dilute the effects of the booze," said Hank.

"And soak up the beer," added Barry.

"Not to rain on your parade," I said, "but there must be some reason nobody's come close to claiming that hundred dollars."

As with all self-proclaimed drinkers, my words fell on deaf ears. Hell bent for leather, they vowed to win that plaque for the Fat Lady.

"Have some faith in us," said Barry. "You've seen us in action. You know what we can do."

"Yeah," said Hank. "Unlike you, Lar, *we* can handle our liquor."

I raised both hands in defeat.

"Okay. But don't say I didn't warn you."

"It's in the bag," said Barry.

"Piece of cake," said Hank. "That plaque'll look great on the wardroom wall."

So, against my better judgment, about 2200 hours one balmy Friday, I drove my two overconfident alkie friends up the long hill to the Pump Room.

The night started out innocently enough, with Hank and Barry downing half a cheeseburger each to pave the way for the boozy main course. Barry had his with cheese and lettuce. Hank opted for ketchup only. Lots of ketchup. As soon as they finished their appetizers, the bartender set two *Skip and Go Naked*s in front of them.

"Good luck, boys," he said, a wicked gleam in his eye. "May God have mercy on your souls."

Barry eyed his tall glass as it dripped beads of moisture onto the table.

"This doesn't look so scary," he said.

"It's a lot smaller than I thought it would be," said Hank.

But those glasses looked huge to me. As colorful as a rainbow, and brimming with ninety-proof rum, they would have knocked me on my ass after one sip. Even the twin straws sticking out of them looked nasty. Like double barreled shotguns ready to blow your brains out.

Taking a deep breath, Hank mustered up the courage to go first.

"Over the lips, under the gums, look out stomach, here she comes!"

And to the cheers of fifty or so onlookers, they were both off. Word had spread. People are curious when at the expense of others. They tend to gather around train wrecks and car accidents. And this was a disaster in a tall glass waiting to happen.

I have to give those two baboons credit. They started off strong, like a pair of gung-ho Marines charging up an enemy beachhead. Matching each other swallow for swallow, in less than five minutes, they downed the first three levels of rum, sugar and all. Without any effects. Their eyes remained focused, their speech clear. They were even making jokes about how they would spend the hundred dollars and where they were going to mount the plaque in our wardroom.

"Easy peezy," said Hank.

"No sweat," said Barry.

Ten minutes later, *Naked 1* was in the record books. Batman and Robin were even ahead of schedule. After three quick bites of hamburger and a rousing chorus of "Anchors Aweigh," they started in on *Naked 2*.

Halfway through, they both slowed. At the thirty-minute mark, they hit the wall. The dreaded *wall*. Their spines turned to rubber, and they began to slouch. Beads of perspiration appeared on their foreheads. And just like that, the piece of cake turned to concrete. They even had trouble finding the straws with their mouths. Barry let out a loud burp. Hank farted. Then vice versa. And everyone in the room knew the *Naked* was about to chalk up two more victims.

Trying his best to rally, Barry took another bite of his burger. Then made a face.

"Yuck! Who *bissed* on my *purger*?" he said. "This tastes like dap *crog*!" Another burp. Then a giggle. "I mean dog crap."

"Easy for you to say," laughed Hank, his eyes going in and out of focus. He picked up his ketchup-drenched burger. Brought it to within an inch of his face. Studied it closely for a few seconds.

"This thing's all covered with blood," he wailed. "All right! Which one of you bastards shot my burger?"

His eyes still swimming, he pulled out what was left of the meat patty and snuggled it next to his cheek. As if it were a pet gerbil.

"You killed my burger!" he moaned to no one in particular. "It was my bestest friend in the whole wide world. And you *shot* it!"

And he was dead serious.

With a bemused expression, Barry took one long last sip of his drink. Then with a roll of his eyes, he slithered down his chair and under the table. He never actually passed out, but for the rest of the evening, Lieutenant Kott carried on a serious conversation with the floor. In a language not of this earth. Speaking in tongues, some people call it.

Undaunted by his fallen comrade, Hank pushed on. He finished off *Naked 2* and was a swallow into his third beer when he jerked upright in his chair, as if someone hit him in the face with a ball bat. That, or he'd been introduced to God. Wide-eyed and no longer sure what year it was, he tried to stand. But his legs wouldn't cooperate.

"I . . . I think I'm gonna—"

And then he did. All over the table. And on Barry, under the table.

"Whoop-sa daisy," said Hank, sporting the biggest shit-eating grin I'd ever seen. "Me do a bad thing."

I'd never seen anyone fall like that. Hank didn't so much hit the floor as corkscrew himself into it. Arms and legs akimbo, like overcooked spaghetti, he collapsed in on himself, a hundred and fifty pounds of tepid Jell-O. Fortunately, you can't hurt Jell-O, so he came out of it without a scratch. Although he did ruin a perfectly good set of khakis in the process.

Final score of the evening: *Skip and Go Naked*—2, *Hampshire Idiots*—0.

There was no hundred-dollar prize awarded that night. No impressive wall plaque hanging in the Fat Lady's wardroom. The next day, however, the two great pretenders woke to the mother of all hangovers. For me, that was satisfaction enough. I, of course, had been stuck with the backbreaking task of manhandling two sloppy drunks into a truck bed and driving them back to the ship. That, however, turned out to be the least of my worries.

In the middle of the night, Hank came down with a serious case of the munchies. No surprise since he'd deposited his breakfast, lunch, and dinner on the Pump Room floor. Uncertain of where he was, he staggered into the wardroom pantry where the first thing edible to blur his vision was a newly decorated cake. A cake destined for Skip's birthday the next day. In no condition to quibble about knives, plates, or forks, he gouged out a huge chunk of cake with his bare hand, crammed it into his mouth, then wandered back to his bunk, where he promptly passed out for the second time that night.

I discovered the mess early the following morning and followed the trail of cake crumbs to Hank's stateroom. I found the culprit fast asleep making disgusting gurgling sounds, his face covered with frosting and crumbs. Normally, I'm a forgiving sort. But not this time. My stewards spent a lot of time decorating that cake.

It was probably mean of me, mushing the rest of Skip's cake into Hank's face while he slept. And I suppose, in his drunken stupor, he could have suffocated. He didn't, but it would have served him right. A befuddled Hank approached me hat in hand just before lunch, a sheepish look on his face. It had taken him that long to wake up.

"Uh, Lar?" he said. "I don't know how they got there, but there's cake crumbs all over my bunk."

I dabbed some frosting from his nose.

"That's strange," I said. "And there seems to be some crumbs in your hair, too."

Big sigh from Hank.

"Last thing I remember is getting attacked by this giant bloody hamburger. Man! What a nightmare!"

I fought for a straight face.

"Maybe you ate something that didn't agree with you," I said. "There's a broom in the gear locker. Dump the crumbs in the garbage after you change your sheets."

"Thanks, I will." Hank turned, then stopped halfway out the door. "Um, I didn't do anything stupid last night, did I?"

"You might say that. But don't worry. I won't tell."

Barry also had a surprise waiting. When I returned to my stateroom after making my early rounds, I found him leaning over my bunk, his head back and eyes closed, taking the world's longest piss on my mattress. The officer's head was one door down and he'd come up one door short.

"Never again," he muttered to the overhead.

Finally, he zipped up, then reached out to flush. Frustrated in that, he wobbled past me without a word, his eyes at half-mast and as red as the rising sun. From his pained look, I could tell he was in a world of hurt. His hangover would linger well into the night and through most of the next day.

To make sure the two realized the error of their ways, I had the galley cook up a double order of liver and onions that evening. With an order of fried fish on the side. I also propped open the door to officer's country to let the aroma drift into their staterooms. Hank and Barry were double timing it to the head all night long. Six trips for Ears; seven for Popgun. I kept track. On Barry's first dash, I switched mattresses with him.

———

After two long weeks in home port, the entire crew came down with island fever. As I said, at eight miles wide and thirty-six miles long, there wasn't much to do in Guam. Not a bad place for a weekend visit, but it wasn't Hawaii. When that third Monday rolled around, most of us were ready to put to sea again. Even if it meant heading back to Vietnam. Which of course, it did. Two days before we were scheduled to weigh anchor SK3, Mantle knocked on my stateroom curtain with a clouded expression.

"Can I talk to you for a minute, Mr. Lindsey. Man to man?"

I set aside the ledger I'd been working on, pulled over a chair. One of the first things I learned as an officer was *man to man* meant trouble.

"Have a seat, Mickey. What's your problem?"

When he sat, I noticed he was missing his new teeth. One of my pet projects in port had been getting a complete set of dentures made for him. Mantle's parents were dirt poor, and until he joined the Navy, he'd never been to a dentist. By age eighteen, he'd lost most of his teeth and was terrified of needles and drills. It had taken some serious coaxing on my part to convince him to go to the base dental clinic.

"You might as well take advantage of your dental benefits while you can," I had said. "In the civilian world, it'll cost you an arm and a leg to fix just one tooth. The Navy can make you a whole new mouthful for free."

I even promised to go with him. Which I did. And the base dentist did a bang-up job. Mantle's gleaming white teeth fit perfectly and worked even better. He no longer had to gum his food. His new chompers filled in his smile nicely, made him look years younger. For the first few days, he smiled at everyone just to show them off.

"Where are your teeth?" I asked. "Forget to put them in this morning?"

Mantle's face fell to the floor so fast I thought I heard a thud.

"No, sir. And that's only the first of my problems."

"What happened?"

"Like an idiot, I went out and got drunk last night. Tied a doozy on at the enlisted club. I was woozy when I got back and collapsed on my bunk with my clothes on. Forgot to take out my teeth. Usually, I put them in a glass of water before I switch off my bunk light. But this time, I passed out as soon as my head hit the pillow."

Mantle sucked in a deep breath. Thumped a knuckle to his head.

"What a pinhead! I should have known better. Sure as shooting, in the middle of the night, up came dinner. I barely made it to the head in time to upchuck everything. Including my new teeth. Before I realized what happened, I flushed them away."

A pitiful look, I thought Mantle was going to cry.

"I'm sorry I let you down, Mr. Lindsey," he said. "After all the trouble you went to for me."

I felt bad for him. He really loved those teeth. My kinder half wanted to console him, say "It's not the end of the world, Mantle." The officer in me, however, wanted to kick him in the slats for being so careless.

"It's not the smartest thing you've ever done, Mantle," I said. "I can't say I'm not disappointed. The Navy went to a lot of trouble making you those teeth. And in one week, you puke them away? By all rights, I should put you on report for destroying government property."

Mantle's head couldn't have hung any lower.

"However," I continued. "Since we're headed back to the combat zone soon, maybe I can convince the clinic to make you another set of dentures. For insurance purposes. I'm pretty sure they retain all their teeth molds for over a year, so it shouldn't be too much trouble. I play racquetball with one of the dentists, and he owes me a favor. I'll ask him for a rush job."

"You'd do that for me?" asked Mantle.

"On one condition."

"Name it."

"No more getting drunk and flushing your teeth down a commode."

Mantle's right hand shot to his heart. Made a crossing motion. "You have my word."

"Okay," I said, "you mentioned losing your teeth was your *first* problem. What's the second? Is it also alcohol related?"

"Afraid so. And it's a big one."

Mantle's lips tightened, and one by one, he slowly unbuttoned his shirt to reveal the world's ugliest tattoo.

"I don't know where or when I got this last night," he said, "but it won't wash off. And I tried hard. Even used a bristle brush."

I tilted my head to the right for a better look. Then back to the left.

"What's it supposed to be?" I asked.

"An American bald eagle," said Mantle.

Trying for a better perspective, I leaned back.

"An American *eagle,* you say? Sorry, Mantle, but it looks more like a pregnant vulture than an eagle."

Whatever it was stretched across Mantle's chest, armpit to armpit, navel to neck, in a typical screaming eagle pose. Or in this case, screaming vulture.

"What's in its claws?" I asked.

"They're supposed to be arrows," he said.

"Arrows? Arrows don't bend like that. They look like bananas with feathers."

"I must have been lying down when the tattoo guy put them in."

"Didn't he compensate for the curve of your belly? No offense, but you aren't the skinniest guy on the ship."

"I guess he wasn't very good with the needle."

"I guess not. What color scheme was he trying for?"

"I think I asked for red, white, and blue. Going for a flag thing."

"Well, that may be red, or at least a pinkish red, but your white is more beige than white. And if that's blue on your chest, I'll eat my hat."

Another sigh from Mantle.

"It *does l*ook kinda green, doesn't it?"

"The Irish will love you come St. Paddy's Day."

"What am I gonna do? I can't go home like this."

"Sorry, Mantle. Other than never taking off your shirt in public, I can't think of a thing. I suppose a tattoo that size can be removed, but it'll probably take weeks. And it'll be painful coming off. More painful than going on. If I were you, I'd wait until I get back to the States. I wouldn't trust the butcher who did this to grind off anything this large."

"My parents are going to kill me."

"With good reason," I grinned. "That's one nasty looking piece of art you've got on your chest. But look on the bright side. At least it doesn't say *Mom*."

Or WOW, I thought.

The ship's big guns devouring a shave-tail ensign.

Catching twenty winks where you can.

THIRTEEN
Back to 'Nam.

The following day, a toothless SK3 Mantle sucked it up and was back at what he did best—scrounging. I was on the pier overseeing the pre-deployment loading of provisions when he pulled up in the ship's new old truck, its bed piled high with gear. To my right, our head stew burner was in an animated conversation with a local grocer. The cursing phase of the transaction had just begun.

"These are beets!" shouted my cook. "No one on the ship will eat these things! I ordered beans. *B-E-A-N-S!* There's an *N* at the end of the damn word! Not a *T!*"

"Your *Ns* look like *Ts*," said the grocer.

"Are you blind? It's not even close!"

Figuring they could handle it by themselves, I turned my attention to the overloaded pickup.

"Looks like you had another successful run, Mantle. What did you '*requisition*' for us this time?"

Requisition was our code word for *stealing. Appropriation, confiscation, donation,* and *conscription* were also part of the vernacular. *Thievery, hustling,* and *piracy* also fit the bill.

"I hit the jackpot this time," said Mantle. "My best haul ever. Made out like a bandit."

Which, of course, was exactly true.

I noticed he was wearing a clean set of pressed dungarees, with the name *Oznot* on its shirt pocket. Perched atop his head was a crisp new ball cap, with USS *New Jersey* embroidered across the front.

"I see you chose an appropriate *donor.*"

"Payback's a bitch," said Mantle. "This'll teach those battlewagon bums to bad mouth the Fat Lady."

I pointed at his shirt pocket.

"What's with the name?"

"Oznot? That's my special touch. It's an in-joke the *Jersey* won't get."

I didn't get it either.

"In-joke?"

"Remember that *Ulysses* movie they showed on the mess deck last week? The one starring Kirk Douglas?"

"Great action flick," I said. "Enjoyed it immensely."

"The scene with the cyclops got me thinking. After blinding him with a burning stick, Ulysses told the monster his name was *Nobody.*"

"Yeah, I remember. Pretty clever. What's that got to do with Oznot?"

"Well, when cyclop's family asked him who attacked him, he said, 'No Man did this to me.'"

I still didn't get it.

"So," continued Mantle, "when I typed up the bogus requisitions for all this stuff, I put down the name *David Oznot* for good measure. *OZ. NOT.* As in *doesn't exist.*"

The light bulb went on and I broke out laughing.

"Good one," I said. "I'd love to see that snooty commander's face when the paperwork hits his desk. *"We didn't order any of this crap! And who the hell is this guy Oznot?"*

Among other things, sitting in the back of the truck was a new soft ice cream machine. One that could kick out three flavors by the gallon. A big favorite of chocolate in any form, Skip was so pleased with Mantle's acquisition, he put him in for the Navy Achievement Medal, the highest award a supply puke could hope to achieve. Although it never came through, probably because the Skipper couldn't mention Mickey's underhanded operation, it was still a great honor.

On that positive note, we headed back to Vietnam the following morning.

Guam now many miles in our wake, we were headed for the northern part of South Vietnam where most of the heavy fighting was. Our orders, vague as always, stated we were to *assist* in the relocation of several Marine units from Danang to Okinawa. As usual, it meant hauling all their rolling stock and gear. Tons and tons of it. Only, this time, we'd have passengers. A contingent of leathernecks was assigned to ride with us, ostensibly to protect their valuable equipment from the light-fingered squids on that old floating turd of a rust bucket. I can't say I blamed them.

With no replacement parts available anywhere in the world, Guam's shipyard had patched up our bow doors as best they could by stringing a series of cables and pulleys along both gunnels to the stern anchor windlass. A jury-rig of unsightly proportions, at least we could close our doors again (albeit at a snail's pace).

On our final load out in Guam, three hulking bulldozers, a dozen Jeeps, ten pickups, and mounds of construction gear had been crammed into our tank deck. Afterwards, ten deuce and a halves (two and a half ton trucks) were driven up to the main deck and chained down to our grappling eyelets. We were to drop off the entire cargo at Danang for a detachment of Seabees on Monkey Mountain before picking up our first load of Marines. With their high-backed canvas coverings, and being tightened down with turn-buckled grips to keep them from bouncing on their springs, those big trucks looked like green water buffaloes squatting to take a dump. Barry and I were on the flying bridge as we pulled out of Agana Harbor. Both of us cast a dubious glance at the verdant *herd*.

"I've got a bad feeling about those trucks," said Barry. "In rough seas, it won't take much to pop them loose. For the Seabees' sake, I hope to God we don't run into a serious storm."

"What's the weather forecast?" I asked.

"Hank tells me we'll be skirting north of a high pressure front all the way to 'Nam. With head winds from the south. The balloon watchers say we shouldn't have a problem if we keep a hairy eyeball on the barometer. That a storm is unlikely." Barry shook his head. Grimaced. "My gut, however, tells me we're in for a gully-whumper. No matter what course we take. If a sudden monsoon swoops down on us, we'd be looking at thirty-degree rolls. No way in hell those trucks could survive that."

"Did you warn headquarters?"

"Sure did," said Barry. "Even talked to the chief of staff, Commander Hubbard, personally. Dude sloughed me off. Gave me that you're-only-a-junior-officer look he's famous for. Told me they'd already taken the possibility into account. His very words. Said those trucks were badly needed in-country and that it was a chance he was willing to take."

Barry looked out to sea. Snorted.

"No skin off my nose. Orders are orders. I'll bet you a ten spot every one of those trucks will be on the sea bottom before the week is out."

Knowing the odds, and that the weather forecast was in my favor, I extended my hand to shake on it.

"I'll take that bet!"

———————

Three days later, the *unlikely* hit us with a fury. Barry and I were once again standing on the flying bridge when the storm clobbered us. This time, we had to hold on for dear life. Driving wind whipped the waves into a nasty shade of mean. Fifteen footers thumped into our starboard quarter, and the rain pelted horizontally into our faces. Other than building an ark, there was little anyone could do to help those deuce and a halves. If any of their chains snapped, it would slice a man clean in half, so no one could go near them. With bated breath and our hands tied, Barry and I could do nothing but cross our fingers. Watch and wait for the inevitable.

"Which one do you think will break free first?" asked Barry. "My money's on the closest one, starboard side. Leaning to the right like that, she's not long for this world."

The ship snapped into a thirty-degree roll and all ten trucks jerked back and forth, straining at their tethers like giant beetles ready to take flight. We both knew it was only a matter of time.

"I fancy the second one on the left," I said. "She looks like a jumper to me."

"Add another ten to our bet?" asked Barry.

"You got it."

No sooner had the deal been made than Barry's truck popped its chains. Skittering across the deck like a scalded cat, it pinballed into my truck, then backed over the side taking thirty feet of safety line with it. Landing flat on its back in the water, in three seconds, it was engulfed by a towering wave and plummeted into the briny depths below.

Super impressed, I let out a long, slow whistle.

"Man! That sank like a friggin' rock!"

"They always do," said Barry. "That's why they're called *two-ton* trucks. They aren't made to float."

Just then, the truck I'd betted on broke free. After sliding across the deck, it corkscrewed over the side like an Olympic diver going for the gold. Because it hit nose first on entry, I gave it an 8.0 for style points. Not enough to earn gold or silver, but well within reach of a bronze. Of course, eight eager competitors were still on deck, waiting their turn.

"Day late and a dollar short," I said, handing over my ten dollars.

"Whoops! There goes another one," said Barry.

"And another," I said as a fourth truck followed suit. "Won't be long now. Culling time, the herd has started a conga line."

Like lemmings hell bent for their own destruction, within minutes, trucks five, six, seven, eight, and nine bounced in orderly fashion over the side. Number six took out a stanchion in the process, the one we'd repaired in Guam. Number nine saved its vengeance for one of our five life rafts, smashing it to smithereens.

Of our original ten green *buffaloes*, only one remained. The last survivor was chained down aft of the bow gun tub. For five minutes, Barry and I watched that valiant truck battle the hungry elements. Protected somewhat from the howling winds, it had a slight advantage over its dearly departed sisters.

Exhibiting the carburetor of a champion, number ten put up

one hell of a fight, clutching onto her chains for all she was worth. With hope in my heart, I thought she might be able to weather the storm. But alas, it was not meant to be. A sudden bow crash from a huge wave did number ten in. Wrenching free with a startling crack, she tipped over onto her side. Wheels spinning uselessly in the air, she slid down the full length of the deck, emitting a metal-to-metal screech as she sideslipped toward us. Crashing into the wheelhouse with a dull thud, she shattered two portholes before slithering backward. She finally came to rest on the starboard gunnels, her two back wheels teetering precariously over the side.

For a heart-stopping few seconds, that valiant truck hovered there, trying to catch one last look at life above the bounding main. *Goodbye, cruel world,* she seemed to say. Then with a final shudder, almost a salute, number ten gave up the ghost and joined her sisterhood on the bottom.

And just like that, the main deck massacre ended. Too stunned to speak, Barry and I could only gape at where the herd of trucks used to be.

"That was quite a show," said Barry at last.

"I can't believe it," I said. "Twenty minutes and they're all gone. Four hundred thousand bucks' worth of equipment down the drain."

"Literally," said Barry.

"Commander Hubbard is going to be royally pissed when he finds out his cupboard is bare," I said.

"That's one message I'll enjoy drafting," grinned Barry. "I wonder what's the proper way for a *junior officer* to tell a senior commander 'I told you so.'"

I had to laugh.

"How about starting off with a healthy *neener-neener*?"

"Sounds good to me," said Barry. "I may even capitalize it."

———————

Adding to the carnage topside, the smaller vehicles stowed below got banged around pretty bad. Most of them had to be towed off when we landed. Several were salvage jobs destined for the scrap heap. Broken glass from shattered headlights, windows, and mirrors was everywhere on the tank deck. Any cargo stored in them was a total write off. To say the Seabees were upset would be a monstrous understatement. Watching their junk being off-loaded, their commanding officer turned two shades of purple.

"You lost *all* our trucks!" he shouted at Barry in a Louisiana drawl. "Fuck me, Shorty Dawson!"

I later learned Shorty Dawson was an old-time lineman for the New Orleans Saints.

"Every last one of them, sorry to say, sir," said Barry. "I warned them about the bad weather, but they didn't listen to me."

"Them? Who the hell is THEM?"

"Our headquarters, sir. To be specific, Commander Hubbard, our squadron's chief of staff. That's *Hubbard,* with two Bs. He can be reached via COMPHIBPAC in Guam. I have the exact address, if you need it."

Popgun may have been only a *junior officer,* but he had his ways. Headquarters would get an earful from one pissed off Seabee.

While we were unloading the wreck of the Hesperus at Danang, a refrigerated truck pulled up. Recognizing the pork chop insignia on my collar, its Vietnamese driver walked over, invoice in hand.

"Got load of numba one steaks in back," he said in strained English. "For transfer to battleship name of *New Jersey.* Boss say you sign for them."

"Steaks? I don't know anything about any—"

"I'll take care of that, sir," said Mantle, strolling up in his *Oznot* uniform. Without his new teeth and supporting a suspicious looking moustache, he snapped off a salute. Something he didn't do often.

"Name's Oznot," he said, pointing to his shirt pocket for the benefit of the driver. "I'm with the *Jersey's* shore detachment. I've been ordered to accompany this shipment out to Yankee station. To make sure it gets there untouched."

I fought off a grin.

"Ah," I said. "You battlewagon boys don't trust us lowly gator slobs? Very well, *Oznot,* carry on."

After Mantle signed for the steaks, and while they were being safely transferred to our freezer, I pulled him aside.

"What's with the fake moustache? You look like an extra in a porn flick."

"It's a disguise, sir. So the driver can't identify me later. In my line of work, you can't be too careful."

"You arranged all this?"

"Did it before we left Guam."

"Five hundred pounds of filet mignon? The *New Jersey* is going to be royally pissed. Again."

"And rightfully so," grinned Mantle.

"Too many times to the same well and someone will get suspicious," I said.

"I've got one more trick up my sleeve. But that's all. I promise," said Mantle.

"I shudder to think what that demented brain of yours will come up with."

"It's already in the works. Next time we make port I'm gonna—"

"No, don't tell me," I said. "It's safer for all concerned."

Mantle's prideful smile was beyond photogenic.

"A wise choice, Mr. Lindsey."

"Now, go put your teeth back in," I said. "And get rid of that stupid cookie duster. You look ridiculous."

———

After the off-load, we anchored in the middle of Danang harbor. Being so close to the Ho Chi Minh trail, security in the north was much tighter than it had been in the south. A week didn't go by that a ship wasn't booby trapped. Sappers loved to float magnetic *packages* down the river. Packages that exploded when they came in contact with a metal hull. To guard against such attacks, ships in the harbor were directed to install flood lights and post armed guards throughout the night. Ordered to shoot anything floating on the surface, their M-16s barked from dusk to dawn.

The incessant rifle fire made for sleepless nights in Danang. If Vung Tau was the R & R capital of Vietnam, Danang was pain-in-the-ass central. Unlike Vung Tau, Charlie never partied in Danang. Instead, they left special *gifts* lying around. Gifts that went BOOM when you came anywhere near them. So, nobody objected when the captain implemented a sundown curfew.

Trucks destined for Davy Jones' locker.

FOURTEEN
Call it . . . Macaroni?

Twenty-four hours after the Seabees off-loaded their trashed cargo, a surprise MPC series change came in over the wire. The news— as welcome to the indigenous population as a root canal without Novocain—spread like wildfire throughout Danang. A wailing gnashing of teeth rose from the city, all of it coming from distraught vendors. And who could blame them? They were about to lose a bundle during the transition. I had to drop everything, gather up all the ship's funny money—close to $200,000— and hightail it up to the top of Monkey Mountain, the site of the local disbursing office. DK3 Wendell, my one and only disbursing clerk, was equally unhinged.

"Why couldn't the powers that be hold off until after payday, Mr. Lindsey? Far be it for a lowly third class to complain, but it would save us a ton of heartburn. In just two days, we wouldn't have so much money to count. The Navy seems to go out of their way to generate superfluous paperwork."

I had to agree.

"Always have, probably always will," I said.

Thomas Hawthorne Wendell had a sensitive mind that housed an IQ higher than mine. Well-read with a clap trap mind and a degree in art appreciation from Slippery Rock State University, his vocabulary put every officers' on board to shame. He also had a way with numbers, a talent that kept me out of jail on more than one occasion. He should have been an officer, but a stint in the Peace Corps did him in, an unjustified disqualification in my book. In deference, I respectfully nicknamed him Wilkie, after the 1940 liberal Republican candidate whom he looked a little bit like.

"Waiting until after payday make too much sense," I added. "And Washington never lets something so mundane like common sense clog up the wheels of progress."

"Point well taken, sir."

The two of us packed up all our Military Payment Currency and jumped in the ship's new old, and still unnamed, truck. Wendell, with an unloaded .45-caliber pistol stuffed into his holster, sat in the driver's seat. A pacifist at heart, he had a fear of loaded guns. When I slid into the passenger side, I had my trusty carbine clutched in my right hand. With only one bullet in the clip, it would have done me little good if we ran into trouble. I'd forgotten to reload after our last sandbag shoot-out. In my left hand was a leather pouch full of Monopoly money. Dressed in ill-fitting flak jackets, threadbare uniforms, and crumpled ball caps, the two of us looked like refugees from a Goodwill outlet. With only one bullet between us, we were pretty much defenseless.

"What a beautiful day to count fake money," said Wendell, dripping sarcasm as he started up the truck. "My fingers are a tingle with anticipation."

My man had a droll sense of humor. Most of the time, I appreciated it. At that particular moment, not so much.

I shook my head. Pointed toward Monkey Mountain.

"Onward and upward," I said.

Despite what most people think, counting money is not all fun and games. And when it's someone else's—government money for which you're personally accountable for and can't spend—it's zip, squat, diddley fun. After counting out eighty thousand dollars' worth of one-dollar bills, you forget if seven comes after six. Never famous for accuracy or speed, I've been known to miscount on more than one occasion. Needless to say, I would make a lousy bank teller.

To keep our minds from the impending *count*, on the way to Monkey Mountain, we chatted about this, that, and nothing. As we were passing China Beach (yes, there actually is such a place, one that in no way resembles the old TV series), Wendell waxed poetic about modern artistic expressionism. As usual, I had trouble keeping up. With my knowledge of art limited to dogs playing cards on velvet, the only things I remembered was that Picasso's first name was Pablo and one of Dali's more famous works featured something that looked like a melted pocket watch.

When we came to a deserted stretch in the road, something went *bang* on our right side and the truck lurched to the left. Wendell yanked the wheel back to the right, and we shot nose first into a ditch. Only his quick reactions kept the truck from going belly up.

"What the hell was that?" he yelled.

"Sniper!" was all I could think of. "Let's get out of the truck!"

Like a pair of scalded cats, we tumbled headfirst into the ditch. He from his side, me from mine. Heads down, we scrabbled on our bellies to seek cover behind the nearest embankment. Wendell, clutching his unloaded pistol in front of him. Me, leveling my one-shot carbine at the nearest tree.

"Where is the damn sniper?" I asked, my head on a swivel.

"I can't see anyone!" said Wendell.

I don't know it it's possible for a human being to dig a hole with his belly button, but the two of us gave it the old college try. Unlike John Wayne, who would have charged out from behind that embankment, guns blazing, we decided our best course of non-action was to lay low and keep our heads down. If that sniper wanted our truck, he could have it. He could also take the MPC. Which I left sitting behind the passenger seat.

Your money or your life? I never gave it a single thought.

After an hour of crouching and cringing (in real time, it was more like five minutes), we decided to chance one eyeball each. Peering over that mound of dirt, the first thing that greeted us was the sight of our truck stuck nose-first in the far side of the ditch. With its back right tire shredded. There wasn't a solitary soul within three hundred yards of us. We hadn't been sniped, attacked, or bombed. Or even waved at. Way, way down the road was a peasant herding his team of oxen along, paying the two crazy Americans no mind.

We'd suffered a blowout. An ordinary, happens-every-day, no-big-deal flat tire. Rolling over onto our backs, we both sighed with relief. And watched the clouds go by overhead. The one on the right looked something like a chicken trying to fly. Wendell said it looked more like a profile of Van Gogh. After a few seconds, he let out an embarrassed chuckle, then rose to his feet.

"Much ado about nothing, I guess," he said. Then dusted himself off.

"Yeah, somewhat akin to a fool," I said, butchering what little Shakespeare I knew. "The less said about this unfortunate incident, the better."

"Agreed," said Wendell.

Kapow!

I don't know what caused my carbine to go off like that. Maybe I jarred the trigger when I crooked it across my arm. Thank goodness it wasn't pointing at anyone. But it sure scared the hell out of the only two people around. And maybe that peasant three football fields away.

From high in a palm tree fifty yards to our right came this pitiful squawk. Then a large black bird plummeted to the ground. Followed by a dozen or so fluttering feathers. My errant single bullet had drilled an unsuspecting crow, maybe a raven, that had been catching a bird nap amongst the fronds. My first and only real combat action in 'Nam, I'd capped an innocent bird. Me! A dues-paying member of the SPCA.

Ever so slowly, we walked over for a closer look. Fortunately for the raven, it had been a clean kill, straight through the heart. At least the poor creature hadn't suffered. When Wendell hit me with a wry look, I knew what was coming.

"Don't say it," I warned him.

But of course, he ignored me.

"*Nevermore*," he said with a grin.

With a shake of my head, I bent to pick up one of my victim's feathers. After turning it over a few times, I stuck it in my cap. It would stay there for the rest of my time in Vietnam. To this day, that cap, complete with a black tail feather, hangs on my wall. (I've included a picture of said cap with feather as verification.)

Wendell took a step back to assess the new addition to my chapeau.

"I like it," he said, a tilt to his head. "Adds a bit of much needed flair. Maybe some panache. You should call it *Macaroni*."

"Macaroni?"

"As in Yankee Doodle."

I had to groan.

"There's nothing like a good joke," I said. "And *that* was definitely *nothing* like a good joke. For that, you can change the damn tire all by your lonesome."

"Me and my big mouth," said Wendell.

But of course, I had to help. Barely a hundred and ten pounds soaking wet, and skinny as a No. 2 pencil, Wendell wasn't the strongest sailor on the Fat Lady. Or the most mechanically inclined. He could quote Shakespeare well enough, and was an expert at balancing the books, but he didn't know the business end of a tire iron.

———————

The MPC exchange took us less than an hour. But it seemed like three days. After signing on the dotted line, I was standing outside the disbursing office, taking a well-earned breather, looking down on the sprawling settlement of Danang. From that height, I could see the entire city, and miles down the coast. Across the way, a helicopter hovering over Freedom Hill Beach caught my attention. The local disbursing officer, a young lieutenant, walked up to offer me a cigarette.

"No, thanks, I don't smoke," I said. Then pointed toward the beach. "Those are strange markings on that chopper."

"That's a ROK gunship," he said. "As in, Republic of Korea. They're bad ass dudes. Nobody messes with them."

Before I could ask why, what looked like a sandbag with legs tumbled out of the helicopter.

"Did you see that?" I asked. "Something fell out of their starboard door!"

"Not something. Some*one*. Looks like they're interrogating prisoners again."

"But they're at least three hundred feet up. How could they—"

"They *don't* survive. That first step is a real eye-opener," said the lieutenant. A smirk inched up as he lit up his cigarette. "That's how the ROKs work. Say what you want about their tactics; they always mean business."

"A fall from that height would kill anyone," I said.

"At least it has in the past," said the lieutenant.

I couldn't believe his cavalier attitude. Then again, he'd been in Vietnam much longer than me. And seen a hell of a lot more.

"Isn't that against the Geneva Convention?" I asked.

"I'm not sure Korea ever signed it. Different strokes for different folks, I guess."

A second *sandbag* tumbled out of the helicopter. Gobsmacked, I watched it all the way down, until it exploded in a fine pink mist on the beach. Turning away, I had trouble breathing.

"How does *that* get anyone to talk?" I asked.

"That particular prisoner never talked," said the lieutenant, "but I'm sure it got the next guy in line's undivided attention. The ROKs line up eight or nine prisoners with their arms tied behind their backs, then bring them up to the door one at a time. After placing a gun to his head, they ask a question. If he doesn't answer quick enough, they give him the boot. If they're feeling charitable, they shoot him between the eyes before kicking him out. If not, they let gravity do their dirty work. Poor bastard has about two seconds to contemplate the folly of silence before hitting the ground."

"Man, that's brutal!"

"Brutal, but effective," said the lieutenant. "As they say, war is hell."

I let out a slow whistle.

"I'd hate to have the ROKs for an enemy."

"You and me both," said the lieutenant. "Whenever we have a life-and-death question to ask a prisoner, we turn him over to the Koreans. Nine times out of ten, they come up with the information we need."

Before I could get my next question out, six more *sandbags* plummeted from the chopper, one right after the other.

"What the hell is happening now?" I asked.

"Someone talked," replied the lieutenant.

My throat tightened up.

"What do you mean?"

"The Koreans don't care much for keeping prisoners around. So, they tend to *clean house* after a successful interrogation."

"You can't be serious."

"Dead serious. They've been in Vietnam almost as long as we have and have yet to keep a single prisoner longer than a day. They don't even have a holding compound."

I shot him a sarcastic glance.

"Yeah, right! America doesn't permit savagery from their allies."

"Dream on, big guy," said the lieutenant. "The ROKs make Lieutenant Calley and the My Lai massacre look like a two Band-Aid boo-boo. About a year ago, it got so bad, some reporter from the *Times* made a big stink about their take-no-quarter policy. A New York congressmen followed suit with a speech about the deplorable inhumanity of the Koreans. A week later, the president issued a cease and desist and the ROKs dutifully captured and detained twenty-three prisoners the very next day. Got front page coverage in the *Stars and Stripes.* Even made a few headlines back in the States. For a while, everything was hunky-dory. A month passed and all the high-horsers went back to sleep."

"My gut tells me that's not the end of the story," I said.

"Give that man a cigar. Two months after the press release, a small two-line notice came out on the back page of the *Stars and Stripes.* It stated simply that the Koreans had shot twenty-three prisoners trying to escape. No muss, no fuss."

"'Trying to *escape*?'"

"That was the official release."

"And you believed it?"

"Not a word. The ROKs got tired of feeding those extra mouths. The Koreans give no quarter and expect none. In a way, I respect them for it. I know Charlie does."

"What about the locals?" I asked.

"They're scared to death of them, too. The Koreans go out on patrols just like the Americans. A few weeks back, one of their patrols got ambushed, their location given away by a VC sympathetic village. The very next day, the ROKs killed every man, woman, child, and dog in that village. Cut off their heads and put them on stakes. No more ambushes."

The lieutenant took another drag on his cigarette. Raised an eyebrow.

"Sometimes it pays to advertise."

I felt weak in the knees, sick to my stomach. Sitting safe and sound at night on the Fat Lady, for the most part, I'd been protected from the realities of war. The lieutenant's sobering tale made me aware of just how fortunate I was to be stationed on a heavily armed ship.

"I'm glad I'm not Korean," I said. "My conscience couldn't live with that way of life."

"I hear what you're saying," said the lieutenant, "but being the baddest dude on the block has its advantages. Suppose you had to pick which squad you went out with on night patrol. An American squad that had a good chance of getting ambushed? Or the Koreans? Who the enemy avoids like the plague? Me? I'll take the ROKs in a heartbeat. If we ever turned this fucking war over to the Koreans and let them fight it their way, it would be over in a few months. Maybe weeks."

I could see his point. On our way back to the ship, Wendell and I counted our blessings instead of money.

That night, I had a nightmare that I was buried up to my neck on a deserted beach. Sandbags with legs were raining down from the sky, kicking and screaming as they came. As they burst around me, the sand began to pile up, higher and higher, until it reached my lips. Drowning in all that sand, I woke with a start. My sheets were sweat-soaked and my mouth dry as cotton. After guzzling two glasses of water, I kissed the deck beneath my feet.

Thank God for the Fat Lady.

———

SN Markovich caught up to me after quarters.

"Mr. Lindsey? Hate to bother you, but I need some high-powered help. I've got this special deal in the works on base."

"Special deal? What kind of deal?"

I'd heard his song-and-dance routine before. Markovich was

just as sneaky as SK3 Mantle when it came to scrounging, only not quite as good at it. Sometimes he got caught. Whereas I would follow Mantle's lead anywhere, with Markovich, it paid to ask a few questions first.

"It's perfectly legal," he said. "And strictly by the books. Sort of. But it requires some delicate coordination."

"What kind of coordination?"

"Refrigerated transportation. I have a buddy who works in Danang's frozen food warehouse, and he told me a hundred cases of Dixie Cup sundaes earmarked for the officers' club at China Beach came in yesterday. He's arranged for an *accidental breakdown* of one of his freezer units so he can survey the shipment. He's going to send half to his barracks and the other half to us as a personal favor. He owes me big time for our last liberty together."

Ice cream sundaes? I was onboard in a flash.

"Great! The crew will love it!"

You couldn't get sent to jail for *appropriating* ice cream. Especially not sundaes that, according to the books, had already melted. Allegedly.

"There's just one thing," said Markovich. "My friend can arrange to have the *surveyed* cases put on pallets, but somehow, we've got to get it from his warehouse to the ship. And the warehouse is located fifteen miles from the nearest pier."

"No problem," I said. "I'm sure Mantle can rustle up a freezer truck. He's done it before. I'll have Chief Holms pack one of our LCVPs with ice for transport out to the ship. As long as we have someone standing by on the crane to load the pallets, melting should be kept to a minimum. Even in this heat."

"That would be great! Thanks, Mr. Lindsey."

And with a newfound spring in my step, I headed down to my office, satisfied I'd put into motion a sting operation of my own. At least I'd picked up the ball and run a few yards with it. I'd been onboard six months, but I still had a lot to learn about playing the artful dodger. Compared to Mantle, I was second-rate when it came to being devious. And always would be.

That afternoon, I dropped Mickey off at the motor pool to *arrange* for our refrigerated transportation. Then hustled over to China Beach to run an errand for Skip. If all went well, we were to meet at the gate out front in an hour, then proceed in tandem to the warehouse to pick up our sundaes.

I could almost taste the chocolate.

———————

It took Mantle longer than expected to work his black magic, so he was running late. Parked off to the side of the road outside China Beach, I passed the time by watching the mass of humanity flowing by. Bicycles, mopeds, jitneys, wagons, ox carts, push carts, hand carts, and a zillion pedestrians, it was a multi-colored feast for the eyes. Along with a cacophony of sounds to my ears.

In the short span of ten minutes, I bore witness to every item man had ever made or sold. Balanced on peasants' heads, pulled along in carts, strapped to the back of vehicles or animals and hanging off the sides, the shopping list would have done Walmart proud. Whatever you could eat, drink, wear, throw, ride, watch, sniff, smoke, pinch, poke, or listen to was in that parade. I even saw a three-bulb pole lamp identical to the one my parents had when I was in the first grade back in Ohio. Same ugly lime-green shades, same bulbous shape.

Drowsy from the heat, my thoughts began to wander. I was about to doze off when I caught the strains of a familiar tune in the distance. The one I'd heard from my first day in-country. Every sailor, soldier, and Marine in Vietnam knew the words to the classic by heart.

We got to get out of this place . . . If it's the last thing we ever do. . .

We got to get out of this place . . . Cause, girl, there's a better place for me and you. . .

And it was getting louder.

It came from a distant American truck convoy down the street, headed in my direction. To warn the locals and give them a chance to get out of the way, our convoys took to blasting rock 'n' roll from a pair of attached speakers at full volume. Usually, it worked. This time, however, only half of the traffic meandered to one side, most of them not even bothering to look up. The other half continued to go about its business, ignoring the noisy metal monsters bearing down on them.

It's just the obnoxious Americans again. No big deal. They won't run us over.

And, of course, they didn't. When the convoy reached my

bottleneck curve, it slowed to a grinding five miles per hour and settled in with the rest of traffic. After downshifting to first gear, the lead driver leaned back and pulled out a pack of Marlboros.

Smoke 'em if you got 'em!

I watched the convoy slowly disappear around the bend, its idling big trucks following the peasants, like dung beetles following ants.

Nice to see people can still get along, I thought, my eyes drooping back to half-mast. *Even in a war.*

Five minutes into my catnap, I was roused by another distant tune, one I had trouble placing.

Waltzing Matilda? I thought.

Like Moses parting the Red Sea, that song worked miracles on the crowd. Anything on two legs or four immediately dived for cover. One second it was rush hour on the freeway. The next, high noon in Dodge City. This time, it wasn't an American convoy that was bearing down on me and my truck. Had he still been alive, even Gary Cooper would have taken to higher ground.

I'd heard the Australians were a boisterous lot, a fun-loving bunch with eccentric ways. But I'd never seen any of them up close and personal. Painted a drab orange, their trucks were huge, much larger than ours. Their monstrous tires made them look like two story buildings on wheels. Whereas the Americans had slowed to a pedestrian five miles per hour, the Aussies maintained their pace, a blustery thirty miles per hour that was raising a cloud of dust.

Bolted to the top of each truck cab was a 50-caliber machine-gun mount, manned by a soldier wearing drab orange goggles. Looking like an apparition from a science fiction movie, they terrified the local peasants. And scared the piss out of me. Just as the Vietnamese knew the Americans would stop, they also knew the Australians wouldn't.

The Aussie-lead truck made a slight miscalculation and came into the curve too fast. Swinging wide, its driver plowed into the half dozen or so shacks close to the road, wiping out their front porches. Not bothering to slow down, he sounded two ear-splitting blasts on his horn and continued on his merry way, leaving a shower of plywood splinters and shredded tin fluttering in his wake.

Chin on my chest, my immediate concern was for the mass of humanity that must have been squashed flat in all those shacks. But amazingly, nobody died. In fact, as far as I could tell, no one suffered so much as a scratch. When the Aussies were long gone, people reappeared out of the woodwork. Or what was left of the woodwork. A few tentative faces poked out of windows that used to look out on porches. After a wave of fist shakings at the unholy demons from Down Under, and a string of babbled curses, the villagers promptly went about the business of reconstruction.

I later learned such demolition derbies were commonplace. That within a day, the porches would be rebuilt, and things would go back to normal.

As they say in the real estate world, *Location! Location! Location!*

———————

Mantle finally showed up in his *appropriated* refrigerator truck, and we headed out to pick up our sundaes. Transfer of *melted* Dixie cups made, we hauled ass down to the pier where Markovich was waiting with our LCVP, loaded down with every ice cube the Fat Lady could generate, about five hundred pounds worth. After loading our two pallets (we paid the Vietnamese crane operator two cartons of American cigarettes to *look the other way* when it came to the paperwork), we headed out to the ship. Using our walkie-talkies, we alerted our own crane operator to stand by, that we were on the way. The three of us then settled back to enjoy the boat ride, pat ourselves on the back, and count our mouth-watering chickens.

Before they hatched.

When we pulled alongside the Fat Lady, a sling already hung over the side. Time being of the essence when it comes to melting ice cream, consensus was to lift both pallets in tandem on a single platform. An all-hands working party stood by to manhandle our precious cargo to the freezer as soon as it hit the deck.

Everything was going like clockwork. Thinking about all the chocolate sundaes they'd soon enjoy, the crew was already salivating. Rough calculation—every man on board was in line for at least ten. Most would have no trouble packing away that much ice cream in one sitting. I knew I wouldn't.

I don't know what caused the safety latch on that hook to slip, but slip it did. Maybe it was payback for all the tricks we'd pulled on the *New Jersey*. Maybe it was just rotten luck. But twenty feet above the water, the load broke free with a snap that could be heard all over the ship. Like a chocolate covered piñata, both pallets split apart when they hit the water, scattering our Dixie Cups across the surface in the process. Since the pH factor of Danang's harbor was akin to your average septic tank, our sundaes were instantly rendered unfit for human consumption.

When that line broke, we all gasped in unison. Like most disasters, what followed happened in slow motion. But there was nothing anyone could do. We just stood there with our mouths open, watching our special treats float away with the current. Although it wasn't his fault—I made a special point of letting everyone know it wasn't—for the rest of the week, no one talked to that crane operator.

That night, as I tossed and turned in my bunk, dreaming of frozen delights never meant to be, I was serenaded by a strange symphony. Sounds of rifle fire began to echo across the bay. Followed by quick muffled explosions. One after the other, the sequence repeated itself for at least an hour.

Other ships in the area were shooting our Dixie Cups as they floated by. To them, they must have looked like satchel charges. The *chocolate sundae massacre* lasted well past midnight, until the last of the wayward cups had been properly dispatched.

I may have spent more disheartening nights in Vietnam, but I can't remember a single one.

Ltig Lindsey and his trusty crow-killing carbine.

My *Hampshire County* ball cap fifty years later. Note the unlucky crow's feather (Macaroni) is still attached.

FIFTEEN
Who Dropped the Damn Anchor?

Falling on the first full moon of January, *Tet* is the Vietnamese version of New Year's Eve. In the twentieth century, it had never been a good day for the French, the Americans, the Australians, Koreans, or anyone else in the country not wearing black pajamas. In 1968, the Viet Cong kicked off the new year by taking the fight to the streets of South Vietnam's cities. A loud and messy business, urban warfare rang up horrific casualties on both sides. The daily death counts sparked a plethora of stateside protests. Congress spouted off with comments like "We may be winning the war on the battlefield, but we're losing it here at home on the college campuses and in our streets."

Self-appointed political experts claimed such dissidence was the Viet Cong's objective in the first place. And they could have been right. Without Tet, 1968 there might never have been a Kent State in 1970.

The following year, two days prior to January 1969's first moon, the Fat Lady was ramp down on Danang's crumbling LST beach. We were finishing up another rush job, loading lumber destined for Cua Viet, a muck-hole gathering of tin huts more than a hundred miles up the coast. Since it was close to Tet, we were on high alert, in a hurry to put to sea and avoid the holiday altogether. The enemy, however, threw us a curve ball and came calling early that year. Charlie liked to mix things up now and then.

Skip and I were on the bridge watching Hank and Barry handle the final stages of our onload. All things considered, it had been a good day. The load had gone well and only a few more pallets of lumber remained on the beach. For once, we were ahead of schedule. Or so we thought.

The sun had already set and the lights glimmering across the bay from Monkey Mountain cast a shimmer across the water. Overhead, dozens of illumination flares added a festive air to the night. Their billowed white parachutes seemed almost peaceful—if you forgot their sole purpose was to point out someone hiding in the bushes who wanted to kill you.

"Nice night," Skip said. "Wind's coming from the south, so the sea should be smooth as glass."

"I hope so," I said. "Maybe we'll finally be able to—"

A huge explosion to my right cut me off. Its shock wave rattled the entire ship. Blew both our ball caps off our heads. In the distance, a fireball engulfed what used to be one of the Navy's four monster fuel tanks. The heat blast was so intense, anyone facing starboard had their eyebrows singed off. Mine wouldn't grow back for a month.

"What the hell was that?" Skip shouted.

"Must have been an accident at the fuel tanks," I said. "Maybe a leak of some kind."

Then came the mortar whumps. In rapid succession, three rounds landed in the complex to our left. Much too close for comfort. Two more blew up a maintenance shed to our right.

"Accident my ass!" Skip belowed. "We're under fucking attack! All hands to general quarters! Set the sea detail! Prepare to retract! Engine room, stand by for full speed! We've gotta haul ass. Now!"

"What about the onload?" I asked.

"Screw the onload!"

Like bees rushing back to an endangered hive, the shore detail scrambled up the ramp, Hank and Barry directing traffic. Cua Viet would have to be content with the lumber we had onboard. The rest, they could order from the local hardware store. When another shell exploded fifty yards to our left, the entire bridge ducked.

"They're walking their mortars in on us!" Skip said.

Lying flat on the deck, I nodded in agreement.

"Loosen all lines!" he ordered. "Engines back full! Draw tight on the stern anchor!"

With a sucking shudder, we were off the beach, our ramp only halfway up, doors still wide open like a hungry baleen whale. We left our two forklifts high and dry on the sand with their engines running. Given the circumstances, it was the best we could do. As soon as we had enough water beneath our keel, Skip barked out more orders.

"Starboard back full! Port ahead full!"

The Fat Lady groaned in protest, and we churned up a muddy froth as we turned. She hadn't been built to accommodate such quick actions. After the longest three minutes of my life, our bow finally pointed seaward. Thankfully, the doors had started to close.

"All ahead flank!" roared Skip.

With a twisting rumble, the ship jolted forward. Not so much with a jolt—more like a nudge. As slow as the Fat Lady was, she never did anything with a jolt.

Five knots...

Seven knots...

Nine knots...

It took time to crank the Fat Lady up to speed, what little of it there was.

Chaos continued to rein onshore. Around the fuel piers, all hell was heading west and crooked. In the confusion, bursts of haphazard gunfire broke out as trigger happy sentries everywhere fired at anything that moved. Maybe even at each other. In less than a minute, the number of flares in the sky increased tenfold to light up the sky bright as day. And make us an even better target.

Sounding like the world's largest buzz saw on steroids, directly ahead of us, Puff the Magic Dragon made a strafing run at the base of Freedom Hill. Also nicknamed "Spooky," Puff was actually a lumbering AC-47 cargo plane with a double rack of eight Gatling guns mounted on one side. With her ungodly firing rate, she was able to plant a bullet in every square foot of land. Every fifth shell was a tracer, and from behind my sandbag, it looked like Puff was emitting a solid beam of light. As she flew overhead, she spit forth thousands of scalding hot spent casings. Everyone beneath her path scrambled for cover. Including friendlies.

Finished with her first run, Puff banked sharply to the left, then made another attack, mowing Freedom Hill the other way.

"Damn!" said Skip. "I'm glad that *futher mucker* is on our side."

"You and me both," I agreed, my face still planted to the deck.

Something tugged at our stern so hard we both lurched forward. I caught the chart table leg a few grateful inches below the family jewels. Thumping into the ship's brass compass, the skipper let out a groan.

"Damn it! What now?"

Ten. . .

Seven. . .

Five knots. . .

We were slowing!

Skip pounded on the voice tube. Almost broke it in half.

"Engine room! What the hell? I didn't order a speed change!"

Confusion from the engine room.

"I don't know, sir," came the nervous reply. "It's not us. We didn't touch a thing. The ship is shaking something fierce, but according to our dials, we're still rung up at *all ahead flank*."

"Then why are we stopping?"

A shout from the starboard watch. "Captain! We've dropped the stern anchor!"

"WHAT?"

Every head on the bridge swiveled aft. Sure enough, our stern anchor line trailed off at a flat angle, tight as a drum snare. I gasped. Skip swore.

"Shit! No wonder we're slowing down! We're dredging up half the bay behind us!"

He attacked the voice tube again.

"All back full! And don't spare the horses!"

Not the order any of us wanted to hear. I couldn't believe our bad luck.

"We're headed . . . *back*, Captain?" I asked.

"Talk about major screw up!" he said. "We've got to back down and pick up our goddam anchor! At this rate, we won't make it out of Danang in one piece."

Every cloud has a silver lining. Ours that night turned out to be that capricious stern anchor. No one knew how it dropped like that. Or why it picked that moment to malfunction. Perhaps a gear slipped. Maybe the shelling jarred it loose. But just as we started to back down, a waterspout erupted ten feet ahead of our bow. Had we continued on course, we would have taken a mortar round amidships.

The captain's eyes went wide and white. His chin dropped three inches. None of us said a word.

"Talk about blind luck!" he said finally. "There but for the grace of a damn anchor." He crossed himself. Looked to the heavens. "Thank you, Lord. We owe you one."

"I think I messed my pants," I said. "That, or I've had another religious experience."

With the stern anchor safely back on board, the captain barked out another order.

"Engine room, all ahead flank! Give me all she's got! Times two!"

Dodging two other ships headed for who knows where, it became a race to see who could get to safe waters first. The farther away from Danang the better. When we cleared that first harbor buoy, everyone breathed easier. From there, it was a straight shot to the open sea.

"Lights off the port bow!" shouted the forward lookout. "Constant bearing, decreasing range!"

In layman's terms, that meant we were about to collide with something.

Skip snatched up a pair of binoculars.

"Oh, crap! It's the *Luzerne County* again. Look like she's taken a hit. All that smoke means she's lost an engine. Maybe her rudder. Helmsman! Come left twenty degrees!"

The helmsman responded immediately, then asked, "Why isn't she heading out to sea like the rest of us, sir?"

The same stupid question had popped into my head.

"Their CO's trying to beach her. To keep the channel free. Without a rudder and at half power, that's what I would do."

"And I thought *we* were the ones in deep kimchi," I said. "Can we do anything to help them?"

"I'm afraid not. No sense in putting both of us in harm's way. Steady as she goes, helmsman."

Angling left to avoid the crippled *Luzerne*, we watched with bated breath as she slowed to one third speed, then plowed into the shore, demolishing three small fishing boats and a ramshackle pier in the process.

"Locals ain't gonna be too happy about that," I said, mostly to myself.

Skip scanned the crash site for a few seconds, then lowered his binoculars. Shook his head.

"Poor Karl can't catch a break," he said. "First, he runs into us, and now this. But he did the only thing he could. Smart thinking, beaching himself at the White Elephant like that. It's the safest spot in the bay."

"Why's that?" I asked.

"The Elephant's owned by a powerful drug lord. Richest man in three provinces. He's got big time connections everywhere in this damned country. Nobody, the VC included, wants to get on his bad side. The last thing Charlie would do is drop a mortar round anywhere near his complex."

When I looked back at Danang, I saw fires had broken out everywhere—except at the White Elephant. It was as if a protective bubble had been erected over the place.

"Karl may be an unlucky cuss, but he's not stupid."

Turning to his right, the captain gave another order.

"Come right ten degrees to a heading of One, Three, Zero."

Winded from their mad dash off the beach, Hank and Barry were just entering the bridge when a series of even larger explosions rocked our port quarter. Off the fantail, two giant fireballs collided in the sky, like a pair of Titans fighting for air space. Rocket trails crisscrossed the sky. From a distance, Danang looked like any big American city on the Fourth of July.

"Jesus H. Christ!" said Barry. "They must have hit the ammo dump."

Awed by the conflagration in our wake, for the next ten minutes, the three of us watched in silence. By the Grace of God and our quick-thinking captain, and more than our fair share of luck, we finally made it safely to open seas. In times of war, however, you can't rely on rabbits' feet and lucky charms to survive. When your tit's in a wringer, you'd better lay your odds on something more powerful than luck.

After taking a deep breath, Barry broke the silence.

"What do we do now, Skipper?" he asked.

"We head for Cua Viet. Not much else we can do. We sure as hell aren't going back to Danang. Helmsman, come left to course Two, Seven, Zero. Set the underway watch."

His hands on an aft railing, he looked back on the thick black smoke blotting out the lights of Danang. With a slow headshake, he emptied his lungs through a sigh.

"That was too damn close. Maybe the Lord in His infinite wisdom was trying to tell me something. Like maybe I'm too old for this crap. That I should think about retiring."

"He *does* work in mysterious ways, sir," I said.

"That He does, Lar. That He does." Turning to Barry, "You got the next watch, Lieutenant?"

"Yes, sir, I do."

"As soon as you settle in, lay out a course for Cua Viet. Despite the attack, we've still got a load of anxious Marines waiting to go home. And I wouldn't want to disappoint them. If they're still there."

"Aye, aye, sir," said Barry. "Um, I hate to be the bearer of more bad tidings, but when we pulled off the beach, we weakened our aft cables. The torque from the bow doors shredded several strands of wire. I don't think they'll take the additional strain."

"Can they be bolted back together with a pair of clamps?"

"My men are welding them in place as we speak. But there's no telling how long they'll last."

"A jury-rig on top of a jury-rig?" Skip scratched his stubble and looked to the heavens for the second time that night. "Well, I guess we should count our blessings. At least we're better off than poor *Luzerne*."

"What if one of those cables snaps again?" asked Barry.

"We'll have to jury-rig something else. When you get off watch, drop by my cabin. I have to draft a message to headquarters listing our damage, and I need specifics. If and when we make it to Okinawa,

I want those bow door hinges fixed properly. I think Yokosuka is the nearest facility capable of the job. I know it's a long way, but we'll already be halfway there. If it takes a sit-down strike on my part to get headquarters' attention, then so be it. I've had it up to here with those damn doors."

―――――――――

Still discombobulated by the sneak attack on Danang, that night everybody stayed up for midrats. Nobody could even think about sleep. After four rubbers of bridge, our longest session to date, Skip and I stood on the catwalk, trying to savor a cool night breeze as we watched the glow that was now Danang dip slowly below the horizon. Lieutenant Davidson had already sent off his message to headquarters demanding in no uncertain terms that things be set right with the bow doors. He didn't use the word *mutiny*, but I'm sure the threat was implied. Skip may have been a simple farmer's son from Missouri, but he had a way of getting his point across.

"I see they're still going at it in Danang," he said from under his binoculars. "And probably will be all night."

I took a gander for myself through the ship's forward scope.

"Lucky for us Tet only comes around once a year, Captain."

"Thank heaven for small favors," he said.

"Not to bad mouth our superiors, sir . . . but you'd think headquarters would have their shit together by now. Bunch of birdbrained dickwads. No fucking way we should have been anywhere near that beach this close to Tet."

Seven months on board and already I was talking like an old salt. After what I'd seen so far in Nam, I thought I'd earned the right. From a wet-behind-the-ears rookie to grizzled veteran in two hundred days, time flies when you're having fun. Or being shot at. On the positive side, however, another few months and I'd be a short timer.

The captain took time lighting his next Camel.

"By the way," he said. "Not to change the subject, but before the shit hit the fan, a message came in over the wire." After digging into his pocket, he tossed me a pair of single silver bars. "Here. It's official. You're now a lieutenant junior grade."

"I made JG?" I said, surprised. "Hot damn!"

"Congratulations. You deserve it."

"What, no ceremony?" I said.

Skip grinned. Popped one eyebrow.

"On this ship? Get serious. Consider yourself lucky the wardroom sprung for your bars. Here, let me do the honors."

I'd never given much thought about promotions, but it felt damned good when he pinned that silver bar on my collar. Call it a validation of sorts, perhaps a coming of age, but at that fleeting instant, I knew I belonged in those tattered khakis, that I was no longer a bumbling ensign. I'd earned my spurs. I'd still make mistakes, of course, but now I could make them with confidence. It was a feeling I'll never forget. I would achieve other ranks during my time in the Navy, but this one was special. One that choked up even a cynical bastard like me.

After the *ceremony*, Skip leaned over the rail to toss his cigarette butt into the sea. After watching it spark out, he assumed his normal position in his bridge chair, one leg propped up on a railing. His thoughts light years away, he pulled on his neck. Finally.

"I wonder if all this is really worth it," he said. "Or if in a hundred years from now, on some mystical tote sheet in the sky, this won't be worth a hill of beans."

"Who knows?" I said. "It might. One thing for sure, in a hundred years, none of us will be around to worry about it. Some say everything is interconnected in the world, that things happen for a reason. According to the existentialists, a butterfly's death in Brazil could affect a taxicab driver in Sheboygan."

Skip looked out to sea. Thinned his lips.

"Never studied much philosophy. Sheboygan, you say?"

"Sheboygan," I said. "It's in Wisconsin, I think."

"Remind me to never go there."

After two minutes of comfortable silence, he extracted a folded piece of paper from his shirt pocket.

"Speaking of ridiculous things, I've been working on a ship's motto."

"Don't we already have one?" I asked. "It's engraved on the ship's plaque. *Possumas Quae*, something."

"I never cared for that one. Too stodgy. I'm thinking we need something more modern. Something with a kick to it."

Skip unfolded the paper. Spread it across the chart table. He'd made a rough sketch of a medieval shield overlaying a pair of crossed anchors. A constellation of some sort hung in the background. I'm no astronomer, but it looked like Pisces to me. Then again, it could have been Taurus, the bull.

"The artwork needs a little tweaking," he said, "but I like what I came up with for the inscription. Like all good mottoes, it's in Latin."

Taking a closer look, I saw the words *Armageddon Sic* stretched across the top of the shield. The phrase *O' dis Navi* was scrawled across the bottom.

"I picked Armegeddon because it hints of power," he said. "A final conflict between good and evil, that kind of thing."

"Sounds impressive," I said. "My Latin's a bit rusty. What's it mean?"

"Read it aloud," he said, a slow grin emerging. "*Real* slow."

"*Armegeddon Sic O' dis Navi*," I said once. Then said it again, even slower.

The second time around, it slapped me in the face, like all puns do. I broke out laughing.

"*I'm getting sick of this Navy*?" I said.

"Bingo!" said Skip.

"You've got the makings of a first-class comic, sir." I pulled at an ear. "However, I'm not sure headquarters would be amused."

"Screw 'em if they can't take a joke. No matter, it's probably over their heads anyway. Just between you and me, most things are."

Sleepless in my bunk that night, I contemplated the captain's new motto. He was right. It was a lot better than our old one. He didn't have a snowball's chance in hell of pushing it through, but it proved both his heart and, most assuredly, his mind were in the right place.

"*Armegeddon Sic O' dis Navi*?" I chuckled just before I fell asleep. "Wish I'd thought of that."

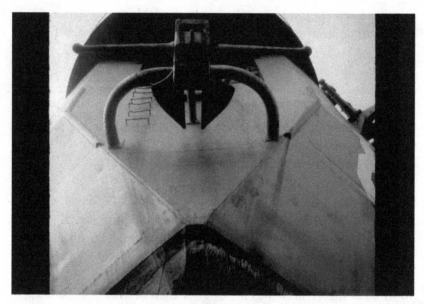

Our cantankerous stern anchor that almost got us killed.

SIXTEEN
Cua Viet and the Long Green Laundry Line!

Our second night out of Danang, Skip and I were once again kicking some serious butt at the bridge table. Hank and Barry didn't know what hit them. Three hands in, we'd already made a six spades bid. The seven no trump that followed was like throwing a no-hitter in the World Series.

"What's Cua Viet like, Hank?" I asked, casually throwing out the jack of hearts.

"Cua Viet?" said Hank. "It's a nothing pimple of an outpost five miles south of the demilitarized zone."

"I hear the enemy has a couple of big guns up there. Will we be within their range?"

"They won't need big guns," said Hank. "We'll be so close Charlie could spit on us."

He pondered his hand for a few seconds, then placed down a slow queen of hearts, which Skip promptly jumped on.

"Damn!" said Hank. "I *knew* he was going to do that."

"If you knew," I said, "then why'd you play it? Tell me more about Cua Viet."

"A pain in the ass landing, it's tucked away in this narrow inlet. After two back-to-back hairpin turns, we slow to a crawl, then have to reverse engines and sashay onto the beach. Sitting ducks all the way."

Skip led out the nine of diamonds. Barry climbed on it with a ten that I, in turn, clobbered with a jack. Chalk another one up for the good guys.

"Not to worry," Skip said. "Charlie will shoot off a few rounds for show and make a lot of noise, but the last thing they want is to come anywhere near us. Dollars to donuts, over half the stuff we're carrying ends up in their camp within a week."

I was shocked.

"Are you serious?"

"Damn straight I am. North of Danang, we're the VC's biggest and most dependable supplier. Most of their underground tunnels are shored up with prime Washington state Douglas pine. All that lumber sitting down on our tank deck. The same lumber we busted our humps to load two days ago. Most of it is destined to disappear down one of their hidey-holes."

Confused, I almost led out the wrong card.

"That's discouraging," I said.

Hank covered my queen with a king. And the captain promptly chopped its head off with his ace.

"Tell me about it," he said. "It's a funny war over here, that's for sure."

———

The following morning, a fast rising sun made quick work of the morning mist. Soon Cua Viet was dead ahead in our binoculars.

"It *does* look a bit like a pimple," I said. "Not a tree for miles."

"Garden spot of Vietnam," said Barry. "You can thank Agent Orange for that. To keep local *unfriendlies* from sneaking up on us, we've dropped so much of the stuff on it, nothing will grow there for the next fifty years."

"And yet they're *still* able to rob us blind?"

"If anything, Charlie's resourceful," said Barry. "He'll swipe your back fillings if he thinks they're gold-filled."

I lowered my binoculars. Turned to the captain.

"I hate to ask a stupid question, sir, but if we know Charlie's going to steal our cargo, why are we hauling it up here in the first place?"

"We? You mean the *Hampshire County*?"

"No, *us* in general. America." I made a sweeping gesture toward the beach. "Look at this place. Cua Viet is a dump. Unless there's some strategic value to this *nothing little pimple* I'm not aware of, why is it important to anyone? As Hank so eloquently pointed out, it's a miserable little bay, difficult to navigate, and completely useless as a commercial port. On top of that, as far as I can tell, there's not another settlement for miles."

Skip took a long swig from his coffee cup. Thought for a few seconds.

"You want the official party line? Supposedly, Cua Viet was established to monitor traffic on the Ho Chi Minh trail."

"You believe that?" I asked.

"Not for a second. Maybe it's there to establish what the higher-ups call a *presence*. We seem to be doing a lot of that lately."

Returning to my binoculars, I decided not to press the point. While scanning the far mountain ridge, I spied a gigantic flag waving in the breeze. The flag of the enemy, it had to be at least fifty feet long.

"Holy crap! Look at the size of that thing!"

Skip drained the last of his cup.

"Impressive, isn't it? Charlie raises that damn flag every time we pull into Cua Viet."

"To establish his *presence* while he shoots at us?" I said. "And since you brought it up, what the hell is *presence* anyway? I thought that's what you put under Christmas trees."

"Touché," said Skip. "Now that you mention it, this little dance we're doing does seem a bit idiotic."

"I'm no politician," I said, "but in the long run, wouldn't we be ahead of the game if we packed up our Quonset huts, along with all our lumber, and went south for the duration? Maybe a lot of enemy tunnels would never get built."

"Can't argue with your logic, Lar."

Three short blasts from the ship's horn cut our debate short. We had lined up with the ramp and were preparing to beach. Right on cue, the North Vietnamese opened fire. I counted several puffs of smoke from the distant ridge, just to the left of Flag Hercules.

Thankfully, Skip was right. They missed us by a mile, their shells landing harmlessly two hundred yards down the beach. Either Charlie wasn't trying to hit us, or his gunners had gone blind.

After our fastest off-load to date (no sense in pressing one's luck), we pulled off the beach with only one minor mishap. The newly promoted supply officer didn't watch where he was stepping and accidentally slipped on one of our bow ramp's many mossy patches. Sliding on my back like an overturned turtle into the water may not have been the most embarrassing thing I've ever done, but it's way ahead of whatever is in second place. At least the crew got a big laugh out of it.

Satisfied that we weren't going to overstay our welcome, the minute we headed out to sea, Charlie stopped firing. He probably had more important things to think about. Namely, how he was going to *appropriate* the tons of lumber we'd just deposited on the beach. I was sure their equivalent of SK3 Mantle was already fast at work, conjuring up a special heist.

Charlie was looking forward to building his new tunnels, and we had our Marines onboard, safe and sound—a win-win situation for everyone. Best of all, other than a few unfortunate soldier crabs two hundred yards down the beach, no one got hurt.

Maybe all wars should be fought that way. *You shoot here, and I won't go there?* Makes perfect sense to me.

———————

The fifty Marines we'd picked up at Cua Viet were ecstatic to be onboard a live, large, and most importantly, *safe* Navy ship. After twelve months of sweating their balls off in the steamy jungle with everybody and his uncle shooting at them, they were going home. Well, at least back to Okinawa. Not having showered in over a month, they stunk to high heaven, but we welcomed them with open arms, like banded brothers.

You'd think they would have been glad to see us. But they treated us like second-class citizens. Battle hardened veterans, they referred to us as *pansy-assed squids, bell-bottomed pussies, camel-toed deck apes,* and worse. What they called us behind our backs was unprintable. After what they'd been through, I suppose they'd earned the right to look down on us as *rear-echelon pukes.*

Several sported *ear trophies* on strings around their necks. I must admit, compared to those Marines, we *did* have it soft. We'd worked our butts off in-country many days around the clock, but the only thing we'd shed so far in 'Nam was sweat. They'd shed blood. Lots of it.

As officers, we told our men to *cool* it, to give them wide berth. Let them vent. Aggravating hardened killing machines was never a smart move. For the most part, the crew swallowed its pride and bit their collective tongues. Except for Chief Holms. He wasn't about to take guff from anyone. And especially not a bunch of loudmouth leathernecks.

"I can see by that glint in your eye, Chief," I said, "You're planning something special for our newfound passengers."

"Nothing that won't happen naturally," he said, pure evil in his tone. "Of course, I might help it along a wee bit."

"What nastiness have you got up your sleeve this time?" I asked.

"Not up my sleeve," he said, pointing out to sea. "Out there. When we clear the break wall, those devil dogs will be barking a different tune."

"Anything I can do to speed up the process?" I asked.

"You could have your cooks add something greasy to their dinner menu. The smellier, the better."

"How about fish and chips? Maybe with some grilled liver and onions on the side."

"That should do the trick," Chief Holms said. "You're a good man, Lieutenant."

"Glad to be of service. Anything to help the cause."

Just then, our skipper walked up, a pinched look on his face. Steam coming from his ears.

"Damn fool Marine captain! I told him I didn't want those friggin' ears on my ship, and the fuzz-faced SOB sloughed me off. Said it wasn't my call. That his men had "earned those ears." I should have read him the riot act, but didn't want to do it in front of his men. The last thing we need is a ship full of pissed off grunts."

Chief Holms snapped to attention. Saluted, then grinned.

"Say no more, sir," he said. "I'll take care of it. Come sunset, those ears will be history."

"I don't want any rough stuff," the skipper said.

"There won't be any. Mother Nature will do the dirty deed for us. In fact, I think she's warming up to the task right now."

When the Fat Lady plowed into the first heavy swell, we started to pitch and roll. With a vengeance.

"Good thinking, Chief," Skip said. Turning toward the bridge, "Officer of the watch! Come left to Two, Nine, Zero!"

"Are you sure, Captain?" asked Barry. "That'll run us parallel to the swells. We'll bob up and down like a cork."

"That's the chief's whole point, Lieutenant."

"Aye, aye, sir," said Barry. "Two, Nine, Zero it is."

Angling left increased our rolling to seasick levels. Spreading his sea legs, the chief shot a thumb toward the gaggle of Marines laughing and telling squid jokes by the forward hatch.

"Won't be long now," he said.

"The long green laundry line?" Skip asked.

"You got it," said the chief.

Sure enough, two minutes later, the first Marine stopped laughing. A green pallor came to his face. He grabbed his stomach, lurched to his right. With a twisting motion, he draped himself over the railing to wretch up lunch. Two of his buddies followed his lead. Soon, six more joined the laundry line. All calling out for somebody named "*Ralph*."

No more laughing, no more jokes. Before sunset that night, nine-tenths of those hard-ass Marines would be flat on their backs in their bunks, moaning and groaning. The tenth would still be draped over the side of the ship, ralphing up what was left of breakfast. Satisfied with himself, the chief turned to me with a smile.

"Got any of those canned sardines left in your storeroom, Lieutenant? The big ones drenched in oil?"

"I think I can rustle up a can or two, Chief. Got something special in mind?"

"Just a little extra treat for our green shirted friends. The *coups de gras*, so to speak."

I was told the chief and his open can of smelly sardines made a tour of the Marines quarters later that night. The mess left in his wake was awesome. Battle-hardened leathernecks should watch what they say. It's always wise to add a pinch of sugar now and then to your words. As every last one of those Marines learned that day, sometimes you might have to eat them. Or in their case, puke them up. If you're a guest on the worst-riding ship in the Navy, you should never, ever, upset the hand on the tiller. What goes around, comes around.

I had other plans for Captain Jarhead. A special glass of milk, laced with expired cream, was waiting for him at dinner. Have to give the man credit, though. As sick as he was, he drank it all down. The slab of undercooked liver on his plate, however, did him in. That, and the double dose of grilled onions it was swimming in.

"Excuse me, Captain," he said. "I'd better see to my men."

Urp!

After he left, Skip turned to me.

"The liver was a nice touch, Lar. My compliments to the chef."

A knock at the door and Chief Holms ducked his head into the wardroom.

"Sorry to disturb your dinner, Captain. But that little matter I promised to take care of? Consider it done."

"And the *trophies*?"

"Soon as I bit into that first sardine, our guests threw every last one of those ears overboard. Seems they no longer had the stomach to keep them."

"Glad to hear it," the captain said. "Keep up the good work."

"Just doing my job, sir." And with a tip of his cap, Chief Holms was gone.

Turning back to us, Skip raised his glass.

"Gentlemen, a toast! Here's to the brave Marines who protect us all!"

"Here! Here!" we shouted.

"And to the sailors who put them in their place," he laughed. "Now maybe we can get on with the business of running a tight ship. Pass the mashed potatoes, Lar. For some strange reason, my appetite has returned."

Mashed potatoes? I thought.

After a slight hesitation, I passed them along. The memory of my wayward cook still lingered.

For the rest of the voyage, we didn't hear a single disparaging word from anyone dressed in camouflaged greens. It seemed as if the Marines had found a new appreciation for the men who go out to sea in ships.

Cua Viet, near DMZ—where Charlie's aim was bad.

After we dropped off our subdued, and no longer mouthy, Marines at Okinawa, several pounds and four dozen ears lighter, we headed for Yokosuka's first-rate shipyard. If anyone could repair our cantankerous bow doors, it would be the Japanese. Hard to believe, twenty-five years earlier, we'd dropped the Bomb on them. Not once, but twice. Now, here they were, possibly helping us to fight a different kind of war.

As we approached Yokosuka's majestic cliffs, I wondered what the souls of all those sailors still trapped in the bowels of the Arizona must have been thinking. Or those of the thousands of civilians vaporized at Hiroshima and Nagasaki. If any of the ironies of history held true, perhaps in another thirty years, I'd be watching a Vietnamese TV and eating nuoc mam from a can. Well, maybe not nuoc mam. I still haven't warmed up to sushi.

Whereas Guam fixed us up in a month, sort of, Yokosuka

promised to complete the job in five days. A week at most. That included removing the bow doors and gears, realigning everything, and overhauling our hydraulics. For good measure, they promised to tweak our cantankerous vaps, wash the windows, and kick the tires.

A crew of shipyard workers in immaculate uniforms was standing by when we tied up to the pier. As soon as the gangway dropped, they swarmed aboard like a sea of carpenter ants. Brandishing an impressive array of immaculate tools, they were off and running the second their highly polished work boots hit the deck. Before we could blink, they had the first door detached and ready to be lifted off by crane.

"Makes you wonder how they lost World War II," said Chief Holms.

Munching on his cheesy eggs at breakfast the following day, Skip was super impressed.

"I never saw such hard-charging ship workers in my life. You'd think they were running a race."

"Any special orders for the day, Skipper?" asked Barry, reaching for seconds. A four-egg-a-day man, Barry had a thing for omelets stuffed with double cheese and spicy pepperoni. Complete with bacon and hash fries on the side. How that man's arteries survived our deployment is beyond me.

"Just enjoy your free time," Skip said. "I've ordered maximum liberty for everyone. That goes for officers, too. Relax, see the sights. Tokyo's just up the pike, and I understand the World's Fair is in full swing at Osaka."

Popgun and I exchanged glances.

"Sounds good to me," he said.

One of the reasons anyone joins the Navy is to see the world, so right after breakfast, I booked the two of us on the Bullet Express, the two hundred miles per hour rocket train running from Tokyo to Osaka.

Vietnam had been a cultural shock for all of us on the ship, but nowhere near what was waiting for Barry and me on mainland Japan. At least in 'Nam you could read most of the signs. In Yokosuka, we were greeted by a series of undecipherable squiggles and scratches. And wonder of wonders, *snow*!

After the steamy confines of 'Nam, where the temperatures

seldom dipped below ninety, the nippy weather was a pleasant surprise. For all of about twenty minutes. After that, it was just too damn cold. To keep me from freezing my skinny butt off, my first purchase consisted of a pair of ill-fitting corduroy pants, some fur-lined gloves, and an overly snug winter jacket. At well over six feet tall and now in the land of mostly little people, my choices were limited to a dust covered shelf in the back of the only store in town that catered to *gaijin*. Where the coats were at least two sizes too small, and the pants three inches too short.

"You look like two hundred pounds of string beans stuffed into a hundred-pound sack," said Barry. "Nice ankles, Lar. Good thing highwater pants are making a comeback."

"Says the guy who buys his clothes in the kids' department at Sears," I said.

Not much of a comeback, but it was all I could come up with. A quick wit, I have not.

While Barry and I waited to board the subway train to Tokyo, two things leaped out at us. First, there must have been a million people waiting on the platform, all of them at least three inches shorter than Barry. And lots shorter than me. Second, there was no way all of us were going to fit into any subway car, no matter how long it was.

But this was Japan, not New York City. When that spotless, graffiti-free subway car pulled in on time, the crowd moved forward in an orderly fashion. And to my utter amazement, over half of us were able to squeeze onboard.

"Looks like the rest will have to wait for the next train," said Barry.

"I don't think so," I said. Then pointed at the dozen uniformed officials in white gloves lined up on the platform.

With wide padded planks the size of ironing boards, they nudged the remaining crowd into the cars, respectfully mashing everyone together tighter than a pack of cheap cigarettes. In America, people would have screamed and cursed. Fist fights would have broken out. For the Japanese, however, it was business as usual. Just another morning commute ritual.

When the dust settled, I found a tiny woman pressed face first into my belly button. I could feel every curve, every nuance of her body. And she could feel mine. The only thing we didn't do was actually have sex.

"I can't breathe," I said to Barry.

"That's nothing," said Barry. "My feet aren't touching the floor."

He smiled down at the girl crushed into him. At least thirty years younger than the one crushed into me, she was also much prettier.

"I think I'm in love," he said.

"Don't dwell on it," I said. "You'll give yourself a hard-on."

"Sorry. That train left the station ten seconds ago."

"At least don't let her know."

"Too late for that. What's more, I think she likes it."

"Dream on, pervert. She probably thinks you're just another ugly American with a pencil in his pocket."

"Spoil sport," said Barry.

———

Americans have it easy. Historically, we've always been a sprawling country. Land of the big sky, endless plains, majestic purple mountains, etc. We have plenty of room to spread out, take a deep breath, stretch our legs. When city dwellers get tired of the urban rat race, they can jump in their gas guzzlers, hit the freeways, and get away from it all. Not so in Japan. With land at a premium, especially in their metropolitan areas, the Japanese are forced to live in close proximity. *Very close* proximity.

Every human being has an acceptable bubble of life, a comfort zone other human beings shouldn't violate. For Americans, that bubble is approximately two feet. As Norman Mailer once said, "get any closer and you'd better be ready to fuck or fight." Japan's comfort zone is more like an inch and a half. And on their subways, it's considerably less than that.

After Barry calmed down, we enjoyed the trip, despite the cramped quarters. Thank goodness our subway ride only lasted twenty minutes. A minute longer and I would have been obligated to propose marriage to my *woman*. At one time, I actually caught Barry's *girlfriend* smiling. Two hops, three skips, and a half dozen jumps later, we were safely onboard the Bullet Express, Japan's superfast cross-island train. Thankfully, in our own reserved, albeit undersized, seats. Out our window, I watched the scenery careen by in a blur of fuzzy shapes and blended colors.

The human eye has trouble focusing on anything whizzing by at over two hundred miles an hour. Telephone poles look like a picket fence. Whole city blocks melt into indiscriminate gray smudges. People? I knew they were out there, but I couldn't pick them out. Ten minutes out of the station, I felt lightheaded.

"I think I'm going to throw up," I said.

"Look farther away," said Barry. "Focus on something in the distance."

And thankfully, I didn't embarrass myself.

Osaka, the site of that year's World's Fair, is located one hundred and eighty miles due west of Tokyo. As the crow flies. We arrived on time, a little over fifty minutes after leaving the station. You do the math. That train was the fastest conveyance without wings I'd ever been on. Also, the smoothest. For most of the trip, however, one thought kept rattling around in my paranoid brain. *What if this thing jumps the track?* My vivid imagination came up with the mother of all train wrecks, one stretching for miles. Always observant, Barry noticed my worried look.

"Relax," he said. "You worry too much. Enjoy the ride." Then opened his second Sapporo beer.

"Easy for you to say. You're the one getting a buzz on."

"Being drunk has its advantages," he said. "I know you don't drink, but now might be a good time to start."

"If this train goes any faster, I might take your advice."

"First one's on me," said Barry.

"Thanks, but I'll pass. The last thing this outing needs is another alcoholic."

"Your loss, my friend. Beer!" he said, raising his bottle in a toast. "It's the only way to fly. Or ride on a bullet train, for that matter."

Our first order of business in Osaka was to check into our hotel. We'd decided to shun the many tourist traps and go natural. To sleep where the natives slept. Anyone can stay at a Holiday Inn, but what fun is that? It's like going to Paris and ordering a cheeseburger. We expected the accommodations to be on the small side, so we reserved two rooms. That way, we both could get a good night's sleep. When Barry has a few beers, he snores like a runaway blender.

Small doesn't come close to describing our rooms. Since I'm far from small, I was in for a long night. More like an elongated cubicle, my room measured exactly five-and a-half-feet long by four-feet wide. And five-feet ten-inches tall. I know because I measured it. That meant I could neither stand up straight nor lie down stretched out. I'd have to sleep in the fetal position. Considering my so-called mattress was a half inch thick pad of woven rice reeds, and my only pillow a fragrant but very hard block of knotty pine, tossing and turning was a distinct possibility.

"Can you believe this?" said Barry. "I have bigger closets back home."

"At least you can stand up. I can't even turn around."

"You're the one who insisted on going native, *Stretch*. Maybe now you'll stop razzing me about how short I am."

"Not much we can do about it now," I said. "When in Rome—" *THAT expression again.*

"I'm starved," said Barry. "A restaurant down the street serves Kobe beef. You up for it?"

"Lead the way," I said. "Maybe a good steak will take our minds off these cubby hole rooms."

My steak was fabulous! Beyond anything my unsophisticated taste buds had ever experienced. Once you've wrapped your lips around a medium rare Kobe filet mignon, I guarantee you won't be satisfied with anything less. I'm not much of a meat eater, and never order veal, but when it comes to Kobe beef, I'm two hundred pounds of salivating putty.

After the finest meal of our lives, we retired to our cubicles early. With only one day to see the World's Fair, we wanted to get an early start the next morning. Lots to see, even more to do.

I must have kicked out during the night, a bad habit of mine whenever I find myself in a strange bed, and especially a strange rice pad. When I woke, I noticed my right leg had disappeared up to the knee into the next cubicle, punching a hole in the rice paper wall in the process. After gingerly extracting my size eleven foot, I bent to peer through the hole, fingers crossed that I hadn't kicked someone in the face. In the far corner of the next room, a tiny elderly couple huddled under a quilt, their eyes wide as teacups. From the looks of terror on their faces, they must have thought I was Godzilla incarnate.

Flustered and red-faced, I backed up, bowed low three times, and said the only two Japanese words I knew.

"*Moshi, moshi!*"

Actually, it's only one word, but I said it twice. Later, when I looked it up in my pocket *Berlitz,* I discovered it was a phrase the Japanese used to greet each other on the telephone. Saying "Hello, hello!" and bowing profusely may not have been an appropriate apology, but once again, it was all I could think of.

After checking out, and leaving a colossal tip to cover the damages, we were packed into another subway to the World's Fair.

———

Shockingly modern and immaculate, the one thing I remember about the fair was how organized everything was, including the fairgoers. Fairs in America are a mish-mosh of sights and sounds. A wonderful explosion of smells and colors. Even Disneyland, the pantheon of efficiency when it comes to theme parks, goes to great pains to make things look natural. The lines are often long, but the people aren't treated like cattle. Contrasts are everywhere, and for the most part, everyone's happy. In Japan, those contrasts are not so evident.

Everyone non-American at the fair belonged to a group of some sort. There were no singles, no bunches of two, three, or four. All wearing the same-colored ball caps, and in most cases, the same T-shirts, these groups of forty or more marched in lock step behind a leader waving a same-colored flag with one hand while brandishing a powerful bullhorn in the other.

Hup! Two! Three! Four!

They looked like drill teams on maneuvers, scurrying from one exhibit to another in single file, probably chatting about what fun the fair was. As if I could understand a single word.

When Barry and I strolled over to our first line, we found ourselves behind at least thirty yellow ball caps. With Barry comfortably in front of me, I settled in to wait my turn. Before I could take a single breath, someone slammed into my backside. When I turned and looked down, I saw a little man wearing a green ball cap, obviously from a different army, tucked into the curve of my buttocks. He was followed in domino fashion by the rest of his green clan.

My bubble of life burst immediately, along with my patience. On the subway, I had no choice but to accept the close quarters. It had been a matter of survival, of getting on the train. Out in the open, however, no one was scrunching us together with an ironing board. It wasn't as if I was asking for all my two feet of living space. A mere three inches would have been fine. In addition, this was a *man* pressed to my butt, not a woman like there had been on the subway. Big difference. Back in recruit training, where nuts to butts was the order of the day, I had to put up with such nonsense. But not here.

To get the guy's attention, I cleared my throat. Although, to him, it probably sounded like a growl. Combined with my steel-eyed stare, the effect was immediate. Godzilla strikes again! And Mr. Green Ball Cap backed off a full foot. My half bubble of life restored, I muttered a thank you, then returned to my place in line. Which I thoroughly enjoyed for the rest of my wait.

I have the utmost respect for the Japanese. Organized to a fault, efficient, respectful, and unbelievably clean, their culture has much to be admired. They are also enthusiastic, curious, and friendly. So friendly that I signed over fifty autographs at the fair. Little kids kept coming up to me with pen and paper, asking me if I was John Wayne. I hope it was my height and not the hitch in my get-along. Not wanting to disappoint them, I scrawled *John Wayne* on everything. Even added a *There you go, Pilgrim!* now and then. John Wayne they wanted, John Wayne they got. I figured his signature was worth a lot more to them than mine.

The rest of the fair was a whirlwind of futuristic gadgets and gizmos, something else at which the Japanese excel. But after a few hours, it was too much. It was like being rushed through an all-you-can-eat buffet with only a demitasse cup in your hand. The phrase *information overload* comes to mind.

We got back to Tokyo at three in the morning, bleary-eyed, our brains swimming with a kaleidoscope of the sights and sounds we'd seen, or been rushed by, that day at the fair. On the subway ride to Yokosuka, Barry fell in love all over again. I was stuck with, make that to, a chatty grandmother who wanted to try out her English. Understanding maybe a tenth of what she was trying to say, hopefully I nodded at the appropriate times.

Glad to be back aboard the spacious confines of the Fat Lady, we headed for the wardroom pantry. After a quick peanut butter and jelly sandwich and two glasses of milk, I staggered off to my stateroom, dead on my feet. My full-size bunk and adequately padded pillow never felt so good.

Cherry blossom time in Yokosuka, Japan.

Ltig Lindsey (aka John Wayne) at the Osaka World's Fair.

EIGHTEEN
Beware Little Guys in Black Pajamas!

We made three more double-time extracts from Cua Viet under *heavy* fire again, but never took a single hit; then we received orders back to Danang. Along the way, we hauled supplies to outposts up and down the coast, from Hue in the north to Cam Ranh Bay in the south. From tarps to toilet seats, bed pans to bullets . . . you name it, we moved it. Boxes of all shapes and sizes disappeared into the Fat Lady's gaping maw to be regurgitated the next day onto whatever beach our headquarters had ordered us to. Phu Loc, Qui Non, Quang Ngai, Tam Ky, all were singsong sounding places we couldn't tell apart.

Despite the nightmare of Tet still being fresh in our minds, we were relieved to be off ferry duty. We'd had it up to here with cleaning up after seasick Marines. We were three thousand yards offshore, a hundred miles from Danang, cruising at a steady, if unremarkable, nine knots. If we didn't run afoul of a headwind, we were scheduled to make its bombed out LST beach early next morning. We were hoping they'd patched it up by now. Mortar craters can complicate landings.

At 2200 hours, our bridge game had just broken up, with Skip and I once again victorious. A calm sea and cloudless night enabled a twinkle of land lights to penetrate the thickening evening mist. A welcome breeze tickled our port quarter. Barry and I had assumed our usual position in the forward gun tub to shoot said breeze and ruminate on life in general. More specifically, what lay in store for us in Danang.

"I hear the higherups went bonkers after the Tet fiasco," said Barry. "Some pissed off three-star promised heads would roll."

"Not surprising," I said. "On the positive side, Captain said the Seabees rebuilt the blown fuel tanks in less than a week. Thank God New Year's over."

A not so devout Catholic, Barry crossed himself.

"Amen to that! My eyebrows still haven't grown back."

"You're lucky you're a blond," I said. "It's hardly noticeable. Speaking of explosions, Hank told me we received a secret message early this morning. The wardroom has been ordered to attend a special demonstration of some kind when we arrive."

Barry lit a cigar. Took time to blow out a perfect smoke ring. Watched the breeze hijack it away.

"Makes sense. After that Chinese fire drill, every full bird in Danang went batshit paranoid. The entire city puckered up tighter than a drum. Security tripled the very next day. Even ships anchored in the harbor have to attend this demonstration."

"Oh, great! Being stuck in a smoke-filled room for an hour, listening to some long-winded instructor tell me how to duck? Just what I don't need."

"Try *three* hours," said Barry. "And from what Hank tells me, this particular demonstration is going to be held outdoors on the Freedom Hill compound. Rumor has it some sapper expert will strut his stuff."

"Even worse," I said. "The mosquitos will eat us alive. I'm a supply puke, not a line officer. Do I *really* have to go?"

"The message said it's mandatory for all officers, including lowly pork chops. No exceptions. Consider yourself invited."

"Damn!"

Barry blew out a final smoke ring.

"Look on the bright side, my friend. You might learn something."

"My mother didn't raise heroes. I'm smart enough to beat feet when the shooting starts. And I've already mastered the art of ducking. Lord knows I've had enough practice."

"Then why do you still have that scar on your forehead? Keep bumping into your office beam and it'll never heal."

"Some of us were born clumsy."

As it turned out, I actually *did* learn something at the demonstration. I learned we all should be scared shitless of sappers.

———

At least two hundred Army, Navy, Marine, and Air Force officers gathered atop Freedom Hill for the demonstration. Included in that gaggle were two dozen full birds, four three-star generals, two admirals, and one LST pork chop. In front of us sloped a gentle embankment. Two hundred yards long, two hundred yards wide, and bathed in floodlights, the entire eight acres lit up brighter than a Friday night Texas high school football game.

Bushwhacked free of all vegetation and draped with at least ten rows of concertina wire, it presented a formidable obstacle for the Viet Cong. To me, it looked impenetrable. On either side of the slope were two fields of cropped, ankle-length grass bristling with claymore mines. Guards armed with M-16s and grenade launchers had been stationed at ten-yard intervals, stretched out in a row fifty feet below us. A last line of defense, each had a pair of night vision goggles dangling from his neck, just in case the flood lights went out. A hundred feet behind us was an elongated pill box, about the size a double-wide mobile home.

As we milled about waiting for the fun to begin, a festive air settled over the crowd. We were reassured by the impressive security measures arrayed before us—confident in the safety of our position. Most of us were expecting a flag-waving good show. Except for all the camouflage present, it felt a lot like drive-in movie. All I needed was a bucket of popcorn and a king-sized Diet Coke. Maybe some Milk Duds.

"Gentlemen, may I have your attention!" said a Marine general, obviously in charge of the whole shebang.

After a few murmurs, the crowd quieted.

"First of all," he said. "I'd like to welcome you all to this demonstration. I'm sure you'll find it enlightening."

Barry leaned in to whisper.

"I'm hungry. Did anyone think to bring snacks?"

Barry was always hungry.

After clearing his throat, the general made a sweeping motion toward the slope with his right hand.

"As you can see, we've gone to great pains making this hill secure. Mines, concertina wire, lights, armed guards, special landscaping, and we've even buried motion detectors to prevent an unseen enemy from getting in."

A buzz of approval snaked through the crowd.

"In short," he continued, "you would be safe in assuming that we are impregnable."

My exact thoughts. Although I think the word that popped into my head was *impenetrable*.

"Tonight, we're going to test that theory," he said. "I'd like you to meet Kit Carson, one of our special scouts."

"Kit Carson?" whispered Barry. "What is this? The wild, Wild West?"

"His given name is Dung Lai," said the general, "and he's a charter member of our Chieu Hoi program. It's a top-secret organization, part of a repatriation effort to lure disgruntled Viet Cong to join up with us. Their assistance has been invaluable in finding out how the enemy lives and thinks."

From the shadows emerged a waif of a man dressed in black pajamas, his complexion lighter than most Vietnamese. Not quite five feet tall and no more than eighty pounds soaking wet, a robust sneeze would have blown him away. His pallid skin and sunken eyes gave him the mien of a hungry mole. I'd seen healthier looking cadavers.

My first thought, *If this is what the enemy looks like, we should have won this war years ago.*

The general must have read my mind.

"Don't let his slight appearance fool you. Kit is one tough cookie. He has over twenty successful raids to his credit and there are hundreds more like him lurking out there in the jungle, ready to slit your throats. I, for one, am glad he's on our side now."

"Yeah," whispered Barry. "But for how long?"

"Good point," I whispered back. "I wonder how much we're paying him."

"Probably more than they pay us," said Barry.

When I took a closer look at the man in black pajamas, a chill trickled up my spine. Kit may have been thin and undersized, but he radiated a wiry strength. A lightning quick strength that could devastate without fanfare or disclosure. Like a razor blade floating on the wind. Kit had the look of a killer, especially in the eyes. I had the feeling that, in his element, this little man was more than a match for the best we had to offer. And that might have included the Green Berets.

The general nodded toward the impregnable slope.

"The object of this evening's exercise is to see just how good Kit really is. And to find out if our defensive measures are up to snuff."

For the next minute, he talked with a translator, who then conveyed his words, probably orders, to Kit, who merely nodded twice. The general then handed a satchel to Kit, who, after strapping it to his back, set off at a trot toward the bottom of the slope, somersaulting over the rows of concertina wire like a circus acrobat. Our searchlights followed him all the way until he dodged into the distant underbrush like a swivel-hipped halfback. Impressed murmurs wafted from the crowd.

"Wow," I whispered to Barry. "That guy could play for the Browns."

"Nah," said Barry. "He's way too small. NFL linebackers would eat him alive."

"Not so sure," said I. "They'd have to catch him first."

The general raised his arms. Called for quiet.

"I gave Kit orders to come back up this hill in view of everyone. For his own safety, I told him to avoid the mine fields on either side of the slope. His objective is to place the empty satchel I gave him on the desk in that pill box behind us. Then bring me a souvenir from its desk. All without being detected. The guards have been instructed to blow a whistle when they sight him. If any of you spot him first, you're welcome to sing out. He has only thirty minutes to pull his insertion off."

"Twenty bucks says he doesn't get within fifty yards of us," said Barry.

"You're on," said I.

———————

Thirty minutes and three false whistle alerts later, we were still standing there, our eyes glued to the slope in front of us. Nothing had moved. Not even a lizard.

"I think Kit's gone back to the other side," whispered Barry. "Laid a con job on us to get our defensive layout."

"Could be," I said. "It's probably been done before. And the crowd's getting restless."

That's when I noticed the short dude in the swimmingly large Army uniform standing next to the general. At first glance, I thought he was an aide.

"Holy crap!" I said, loud enough for everyone to hear. "It's him!"

On cue, the aide handed an object to the general. It appeared to be an official Marine Corps paperweight. A paperweight that a few minutes ago had been sitting on the desk in the pill box. When the ill-fitting uniform hit the ground, there stood Kit in his black pajamas. He bowed once, then said something to the translator.

"Easy come, easy go," whispered Barry, reaching for his wallet.

Still dazed, I stuffed my winnings into a pocket. The twenty made up for that herd of deuce and a halves that jumped ship on me a few months back.

A shocked silence settled over the crowd. Full birds and two stars alike gaped. Even the general looked dumbfounded. Finally, he turned to the translator.

"Um, what did Kit say to you?" he asked.

The translator took a few seconds to clear his throat.

"He said 'mission accomplished,' sir. He also said 'Boom! You're all dead.'"

The general sucked in a lungful of humid night air. Maybe two lungs full. Crossed his arms. Then turned to face Kit.

"How long have you been standing next to me?"

Through the translator, "About five minutes."

The crowd let out a collective gasp. A few came close to wetting themselves. Myself included. The general coughed twice. Almost choked on his own tongue.

"Holy shit! You mean you came through—" Waving a hand at the heavily fortified slope, "all *that* in just twenty-five minutes?"

Kit politely shook his head.

"Not there." Nodding toward the minefield to the right. "*There!*"

The general went ballistic. Threw down his clipboard. Grabbed the translator by his shirt. "Goddamn it! I specifically told you he was *not* to go into the mine fields! He could have gotten killed! Got some of *us* killed! The sonofabitch disobeyed my fucking orders! Tell him he's in a world of shit. Go ahead! Tell him!"

While listening to the translation, a slow grin inched onto Kit. He bowed once to the translator, then turned to the general with a look of disdain. To the amazement of everyone on that hill, he began to speak in halted English.

"Sorry I offend you, General. But your orders made no sense. You tell me show your people how we do it. Then say, 'Go here, but not there.' Viet Cong don't work that way. Safest route not always best route. I'm surprised you Americans have not learned that by now."

Several pins dropped in the crowd.

"You think we dumb enough to come through all that wire?" continued Kit. "Under all those lights, with soldiers watching? You have expression back in States. *Not on your tintype.* You wanted real test. You got real test."

The man in the black pajamas was right. Dead right. And the general knew it. He pulled at his chin. Looked down the slope, then over to the mine field. Took another deep breath in through his nose. Probably the deepest of his career.

"Well, shit on a stick! Maybe we *do* have a lot to learn. All right, Kit, show me how you made it through all those claymores without getting blown to bits."

From a safe distance, Kit pointed out the route he'd taken, inching along on his shoulder blades, the satchel pouch strapped to his belly, feeling ahead for obstructions with his fingers. Camouflaged with leaves and twigs the way he'd been, and with everyone's eyes glued to the hill, he'd managed to avoid detection. Bottom line, if he'd been working the other side of the street, all officers within a fifty-yard radius of where the general had been standing would have been turned into ground sirloin.

Every American on the hill that night ingested a double dose of reality. And as hard as it was to swallow, a triple helping of humility. Despite our best efforts to secure that slope, despite the wire, the mines, the guards, the whistles, the floodlights, and the extra four hundred eyes of an overconfident audience, Kit Carson still got through. With minutes to spare.

A full week would pass before I could sleep soundly again. And only after we put back out to sea.

NINETEEN
Tedium, then Hong Kong!

The next six months sailed by in a blur—March, April, and May pretty much the spitting image of June, July, and August. Weatherwise, workwise, and quality-of-life wise, it was more of the same old, same old. By mid-June, the crew began to forget what day it was.

On duty seven days a week, twenty-four hours a day, the weekends came and went. First without fanfare, then without notice. Dulled by the repetitious, backbreaking work, we stopped counting the number of beach landings. An onload here, an off-load there; *monotony* soon became the word of the day.

Thousands of tons of gear passed through the Fat Lady's cranky bow doors. For all I know, it could have been into the millions. After eyeballing a gazillion cartons, crates, and pallets of indiscriminate shapes, sizes, and smells, we no longer cared. Days turned into weeks. Weeks into months. We learned to accept the tedium, taking reassurance that despite the heat, humidity, and doldrums, and our aching backs, we were doing an important job. And doing it well.

For our latest assignment, we'd been outfitted with a dozen ten-by-twenty-foot refrigerated Conex boxes on our main deck, each attached to a portable generator. In addition to the normal jam of military rolling stock on our tank deck, this time we carried perishable foodstuffs. From frozen hamburger patties and fish filets to chicken breasts and veal cutlets. Along with the required poundage of liver. From bananas, apples, and oranges to string beans, carrots, and black-eyed peas. And, of course, onions.

With all that produce on board, we felt like a mobile grocery store. I even thought about offering coupons.

"*Attention, friendly shoppers! Today's special is frozen rump roast. You'll find it in Conex box number two, right next to the fresh eggs. Get it while you can!*"

At least it kept me busy.

Everything was susceptible to the heat, so time was of the essence during an off-load. All my men, including me, worked shoulder to shoulder hauling frozen meat out of the boxes. In a week, we'd moved enough food to feed two armies. Ours and, sorry to say, probably the enemy's. I can honestly say I got more gratification hoisting cases of flank steaks than I did trying to balance the ship's books, something I never did that well. Tote that barge, lift that bale; working with my hands, sweating with my men, was much more satisfying than totaling up a string of columns. At the end of the day, I'd actually accomplished something. And it did wonders for my scrawny biceps.

Once again, however, we found ourselves steaming up and down the rivers to remote locations, in some cases to old LSTs converted to floating work barges. That meant more sandbags along the sides, flak jackets as the uniform of the day, and more incoming fire. And unfortunately, more outgoing fire from our still incredibly loud 40-millimeter guns. As a stopgap measure, I was reassigned to the forward battery as fire director. Goodbye cool, dark, quiet decoding room. Hello, hot, sweaty, earsplitting gun tub. *Arrivederci*, naps. Welcome back, headaches.

We had just retracted from a beach (I forget which), this time off-loading five thousand pounds of beef, three thousand pounds of chicken, two hundred bushels of beans, and enough potatoes to feed the Irish underground for a month. Hank and I were on the bridge behind a double row of sandbags piled as high as our Adam's apples. He had the con and I was there to catch a breath of fresh air. It was 1000 hours, already a hundred and twenty degrees down in my office.

"Starboard ahead one third! Port back one third!" Hank shouted into the voice tube. "Rudder hard to starboard!"

And the Fat Lady started to turn on a dime. Well, more like a silver dollar. Nothing that big turns on a dime. Over his many months onboard, Hank had become an expert ship handler, almost as good as our skipper. He had worked his way up to sea detail OOD, a position of esteem for any officer of the line. If you wanted to command a ship of your own someday, it was a required checkoff on your fitness report.

"Haul in the stern anchor! All stop! Rudder amidships!"

After witnessing the procedure many times, I recognized the sequence.

"All ahead one third!"

And out into the murky Mekong we surged, churning up a cloud of dark silt behind us. Well, maybe not *surged* exactly. More like *ambled.* As we were turning downstream, Barry came hustling up the port ladder, a crumpled piece of paper in his right hand.

"Great news, guys! We're headed back to Guam!"

"Big deal," I scoffed. "It's only Guam."

Barry waved the message under my nose.

"But *this* says we're also authorized a one week's layover in Hong Kong along the way. Bless their little black hearts, headquarters has granted us some real R & R!"

"*Yessss!*" said Hank, pumping his fist. "What's it been? Over a year now?"

"When's all this supposed to happen?" I asked.

"After our next run," said Barry. "If all goes well, tomorrow we'll be on our way. Hong Kong, here we come!"

Word about our trip to Hong Kong spread like wildfire, and within nanoseconds, it was all over the ship. The crew stepped livelier, worked harder, smiled more. People were actually civil to each other. Hong Kong! Pearl of the East! It's amazing how two little words can shatter the bonds of tedium and bring new life to overworked men. A whole week of R & R in the most exotic city in the Orient? Good food, good women, fabulous sights, and the best and cheapest tailors in the world? Don't throw me in the briar patch!

Hot damn!

In addition, Hong Kong was the only place on the planet where you could get a ship the size of the Fat Lady painted out in just one day. For the reasonable price of a few hundred pounds of expended brass shells and the ship's garbage, Queen Mary, then the reigning matriarch of Hong Kong Bay, would turn her army of female *coolies* loose to repaint the ship any color we wanted. In our case, a plebian shade of battleship gray. All we had to do was provide the paint and prepare the surface. Not a bad deal for our overworked deck department.

The Fat Lady set a speed record on our final in-country off-load. We threw so much food at the Marine contingent at Dong Tam; they didn't know what hit them. *Want an extra case or two of prime steaks? Go ahead, take three or four. Five, if you've got the room.*

So, what if the books didn't balance? We were going to Hong Kong! To hell with paperwork!

After a year as the resident pork chop, I'd learned how to *doctor* my ledgers. *Cooking the books*, it's called in some circles. To hasten our departure, in no time flat, we emptied every Conex box, every nook and cranny on the ship. When we finally pulled off that beach, we were Mother Hubbard empty.

Down the river at full speed, up the coast at flank, after an official sign off from Danang, we were on our way. Hong Kong tailors could fabricate anything from merely looking at pictures, so glossy magazines were a hot commodity on the mess decks. Old *Playboys* were pawed over, not for the naked women this time, but for the fashion adds.

Conversations ran from, "Think this double-breasted suit would look good on me?" to "I'm going to have these shoes custom-made but without the buckle." It was refreshing to contemplate some new and "spiffy duds." Skip's very words.

Blessed by calm seas and fair skies, except for an impulsive action on my part (one I regret to this day), the trip to Hong Kong was uneventful.

I was on my weekly inspection tour of the crew's living quarters, as usual being as lenient as I could. When your men live in spaces hotter than Hades, you throw away the white glove. If you closed one eye and squinted with the other, the supply compartment looked halfway clean. Sort of.

Passing through, I noticed CS3 Durton—formerly piss-in-the-mashed-potatoes CS2 Durton—sound asleep in a top rack. Lying on his back with his mouth open, he was snoring louder than a runaway buzz saw. Since he'd stood the dog watch, he was authorized to be there. In an attempt to make the dirtball hall of fame, he'd resorted to his slovenly ways. One more muck up and I'd bust his ass down to seaman. Two, and it would be bootsville from the Navy, with a bad conduct discharge stapled to his chest.

Durton must have been enjoying the mother of all wet dreams because his sheet stood up like a circus tent. It may have been two of the three most disgusting sights I'd seen in my life. Fighting off a gag reflex, I had to turn away.

I had a removable clamp attached to the clipboard I was carrying. Wide and powerful, with jagged serrations that looked like shark's teeth, it inspired me.

Don't do it, Lar, said my practical half. *Nothing good will come of it. You're an officer. For God's sake, act like one!*

Yeah, said my sadistic half. *But chances like this come along once in a blue moon. Go ahead, do it. The dirtbag deserves it. The coast is clear. Who's to know?*

The deed done, I was out the hatch and halfway down the next passageway before Durton tumbled from his bunk. Being jarred from a sound sleep to find yourself being attacked by a rabid sheet attached to your privates would confuse anyone. He just stood there, mouth ajar, trying to figure out how a sheet could have teeth. And why it wouldn't let go of his erection.

Hidden behind a life-jacket locker, it was all I could do to keep from cracking up. When Durton began to hop around, trying to pull that sheet off, the clamp only bit deeper, and his whooping was heard all the way topside.

Time to make my escape, I headed for the nearest ladder. Up, up, and away, I was gone without a trace, leaving behind nothing but a cackle and a question.

Heh, heh, heh! Who knows what evil lurks in the hearts and minds of men? The shadow knows!

———

Pulling into Hong Kong takes your breath away. One of the most beautiful natural harbors in the world, the city is a feast for the eyes. With majestic Mount Victoria looking down from the main island on one side and the bustling hills of Kowloon on the other, Hong Kong left the entire crew speechless. Distracted by the sights, and unfamiliar with the harbor's layout, we missed our anchorage and had to back down, a common occurrence for ships on their first visit.

Waiting for us was Queen Mary and her flotilla of three barges. Two were to cart away our garbage during the week; the third was filled with female worker bees. Well over seventy years old, Mary scrambled up our Jacob's ladder faster than a monkey climbs a mango tree. We even piped her aboard, a courtesy reserved for high-ranking officers and royalty. In Hong Kong, Mary *was* royalty. Nothing moved in and out of the harbor without her approval.

The skipper bowed once to her, and she bowed in return. He raised one finger; she raised seven. He raised two; she raised five. He raised three; she stayed at five. Negotiations over, the deal was struck at four hundred pounds of brass. All without uttering a single word. Queen Mary spoke perfect English, but seldom did. Since she held all the cards, English only complicated things.

Turning to her number one girl, she snapped her fingers. Immediately, fifty women in straw funnel hats and white sneakers scurried up the ladder to line up in two neat rows. Neater and cleaner, I might add, than the ship's crew had ever stood during an inspection. Mary pointed two fingers aft, one finger forward. And three groups of women rushed forward. Strapped to the back of each was a bundle of towels. After dividing up the paint we had supplied, her army turned to. We had also laid out a variety of brushes, rollers, pads, and pans, but they ignored them.

Instead, they wrapped their hands with towels up to the elbows, securing them with thick rubber bands. In unison, they dipped their forearms into the paint and took their respective positions, all eyes turned toward their queen.

Mary glanced down at her watch. Looked up at the sun. Then

gave a quick nod. And in less time than it takes to butter your toast, the four women to my right had painted, or rather, dabbed, their way past two portholes and were bearing down on a third. Without spilling a drop of paint. Barry's chin dropped a full three inches.

"Wow! They're ten times faster than my men. At that rate, they'll be done by nightfall."

"Maybe it's the towels," I said.

Up strolled Chief Holms, coffee cup in one hand, a half-smoked Camel in the other.

"Better stand back, gentlemen. Get too close and they'll paint right over you."

"This give you any ideas, Chief?" asked Barry.

"I'm one step ahead of you, sir. To hell with paint brushes. From here on, it's towels for our paint crew."

I saw Mary heading for the ladder.

"She's leaving already, Chief?"

"Her work here is done. Mary won't return until it's time to settle up." Nodding toward the British battle cruiser at anchor farther up the bay, "Besides, she's got her eye on bigger fish. We're small potatoes."

Skip hustled over to escort Mary across the quarterdeck. As she was being piped over the side, he snapped off a salute.

A knowing smile, Chief Holms emptied his coffee cup overboard.

"The captain knows what's what. Ain't too often you see him salute a civilian. And a foreign one to boot."

———

Leaving the ship in Mary's crew's capable hands, Barry and I hustled off to change into our civies. Places to go, things to do, tailors to see. And we only had a week.

First thing on our dance card that morning was ordering a new set of threads. So, bright and early, Barry and I trotted our ill clad butts down to the Fleet Landing tailor shops to get measured. When in Rome, you visit the Coliseum. Or whatever ruins you can fit into your busy schedule. In Hong Kong, you buy all the clothes and shoes you can fit into your locker.

I made fun of Barry for ordering ten suits. But I ordered six myself, including a pale-green Nehru jacket that would be out of style before I got back to the States. After our fittings, we were free to do the town up royal. And that, we did.

At the end of the sixth day, Hank, Barry, and I found ourselves sitting high atop Victoria, looking down on Hong Kong's idyllic bay. Hank and Barry nursing their British Royal Ales, me cradling my usual Diet Pepsi. The view was spectacular, the weather munificent, and thanks to three pints of potent dark brew, my shipmates were feeling no pain. Despite a moderate buzz, Barry was the first to spot the Fat Lady, way, way down in the middle of the harbor. From where we were sitting, our ship looked like a bathtub toy.

"Are you sure that's her?' I asked.

Barry pulled out the folding pair of binoculars he always carried on our sightseeing trips.

"Yep. That's the *Hampshire*, all right. No mistaking her bashed in snout and that squat profile."

Hank raised his beer bottle.

"To the ugliest ship in the whole damn Navy. Ours, or anyone else's navy, for that matter."

"To the *Hampshire!*" we said, clinking bottles. Or in my case, a can.

"May she never sink," said Barry. "At least not with us on board."

Following a round of ribald jokes about the Fat Lady's matronly figure, a reflective silence settled over us. After a year of being tossed around like rag dolls on her pitching decks, we'd earned the right to bad-mouth our ship. We hated that floating piece of crap. But we also loved her. And in many ways, revered her. Heaven help a non-shipmate who denigrated her. Noticing something, I leaned forward.

"Wait a minute," I said. "Are my eyes playing tricks on me or did the starboard bow door just swing open?"

Barry refocused his binoculars.

"Yep. It broke loose all right." Handing me his binoculars, he said, "Take a look for yourself."

"Talk about a gap-toothed smile," I said. "Whoops! There goes the other one."

Hank ordered another ale.

"We should be grateful it happened now, while we're at anchor. And not in the middle of the friggin' ocean."

"This means a stop at Subic Bay for another patch job," said Barry.

"The skipper will be pissed but won't chance the long haul to Guam. The crew's gonna love it, though."

I was confused.

"I'm not following you."

"Subic is every sailor's wet dream come true. Cheapest booze and women in WESTPAC. If you can't get laid there, you're officially dead. Five bucks will get you a piece of ass and a six pack of San Miguel. With a dollar back in change."

"San Miguel?"

"Nastiest beer in the world. Tastes like three-week-old panther piss in a jar. Smells even worse. You don't drink the stuff; you just lease it for a few hours. Goes through you like yesterday's paycheck. Makes you pee green for a week. But beer's beer, I guess. Unfortunately, the women aren't much better."

"Ugly?"

Barry shuddered. Made a face.

"Real clock stoppers. Most have to sneak up on a glass of water. Half of them play goalie for dart teams."

Hank laughed so hard, ale snorted out of his nose.

"Of course," continued Barry, "after three San Miguels, it doesn't matter how ugly a girl is. Drink four and—" He broke out a popular song of the day, "*. . . everyone is beautiful.*"

Hank leaned in to put a hand on his shoulder. Cleared his throat. Then joined him at the chorus.

"*When you can't be with the one you love, love the one you're with.*"

Even though I hadn't had a drop to drink, I broke down and sang along.

After a few seconds, our buffoonery drew stares from nearby tourists. Loud, drunk, and obnoxious does not make a favorable impression, especially when we were so obviously American. We finally calmed down and our attention returned to the magnificent view.

"Well," said Barry. "Shall we head back to the old girl? I'm sure the crew could use some help with those bow doors."

Hank shook his head so vigorously he spilled his drink.

"Hell, no! In our condition, we'd only botch it up. Besides, we've only got one day of liberty left. And I'll be damned if I'm gonna waste mine on those stupid doors."

We stayed out until the wee hours of the morning, closing as many bars as Hank and Barry could find. By that time, they were three sheets to the wind and fading fast. They staggered back on board around four in the morning, each holding on to one of my still sober arms. I was exhausted and a little miffed. Being the designated driver all the time can be a pain in the ass. However, I was better off than those two. I didn't have to stand duty the next day feeling like the bottom of a bird cage.

Leaving Hong Kong's harbor, I took a page from Chief Holm's book of payback etiquette. Far out to sea, I showed up on Hank and Barry's bridge watch with a liver and onion sandwich in one hand, an open can of sardines in the other.

"How's it going, boys?" I said with a shit-eating grin. "Still under the weather, are we?"

Hong Kong harbor—The *Hampshire* is down there somewhere.

TWENTY
Up Shit Creek!

During the Vietnam War, the Navy used a large repair facility in Subic Bay, one twice the size of Guam's. Unfortunately, Subic's reputation had little to do with how well she fixed ships or resupplied the fleet. Her better-known claim to fame came from the hodgepodge of seedy night clubs camped out on her doorstep. Larger than a town but smaller than a city, Olongopo was the hodgepodge's name, and prostitution was its very profitable game.

Lurking across the Olongopo River (a.k.a. *Shit Creek*) were twenty to thirty (depending on the number of fires that month) disreputable honky-tonks. On any given night, at least two hookers were available for every sailor in port, able-bodied or not. Drawing eager women from all over the Philippines, most not so young, Olongopo could supply the needs of the fleet at a moment's notice. Whenever an aircraft carrier pulled into Subic Bay unannounced, an additional thousand ladies of the night miraculously materialized on *The Strip*, the settlement's one and only paved thoroughfare.

The Strip was filthy, disgusting, morally bankrupt, religiously reprehensible, malodorous beyond belief, disease-ridden, hot, sweaty, and bust-your-eardrums loud. And most importantly, dirt cheap. Drink the water there or forget to wear a condom and you'd come down with a list of diseases as long as your arm. Many of which had no name, much less a cure. Despite all this, sailors loved the place.

As we were pulling up to the dock, I noticed a lanky hospital corpsman chief leaning against a bollard, an oversized briefcase in his right hand. Lean and wiry, with the body of a swimmer and the eyes of a commando, he looked like he'd munched on a bowl of nails for breakfast. Next to him was a pudgy third class, carrying a portable slide screen.

"There's Chief Shortarm and his flunkie," said Barry. "Right on time. His name is Sorenson and he's one tough son of a bitch. Looks like he's ready to lay his famous slideshow on us."

"Slideshow?" I asked.

"Standing orders. In Subic, the crew has to listen to the chief's VD lecture before we turn them loose. Gross beyond belief, his slides will pucker your scrotum. But given how horny our men are, I think it's a total waste of time. His, and ours."

"The men don't listen?"

"With all that blood rushing to their dicks, they can't hear a word he's saying," said Barry. "After months at sea, they've only got one thing on their minds. And I'm ashamed to say I'm just as bad. You'd think I'd wise up by now, but you know me when I get up a full head of steam."

"Tell me about it. I've seen you in action."

"Seems to me I remember a certain pork chop who wasn't exactly a wallflower in Bangkok."

"All right, all right. So I slipped a little."

"Slipped?" said Barry, "More like plunged. Headfirst, I might add."

The pot calling the kettle black, he had me dead to rights.

———————

Except for a skeleton watch, the entire crew had assembled down on the tank deck, most sitting cross-legged in front of a battered screen. I have to give Chief Sorenson credit. Starting his talk off with a bang, he slapped a slide of a syphilis-ridden penis into the projector. A close- up shot, it indeed shriveled every scrotum present. When those giant canker sores hit the screen, ninety sailors gasped in unison.

"See this broke dick?" he said, slamming his pointer to the screen. "This is what happens when you think with your willie and not your head!"

Silence reigned on the tank deck. Most of the crew winced. Several covered their privates.

"This place has the highest VD rate in the world," said the chief. "Go bare back in Olongopo, and I guarantee your gigglestick's gonna drop off before sunrise. Rubbers, gentlemen! It's the only way to go. Any shit-for-brains who doesn't wear one deserves to be castrated on the spot. And if I were you, I'd slap on two. Just in case."

That guy again.

Chief Sorenson plopped another slide on the screen, more nauseating than the first; my stomach lurched to the right.

"Think that last slide was disgusting?" he said. "How about this beauty!"

Another ravage job, slide number three was even more graphic.

"And then there's *this* gem!"

Number four boggled my mind.

"And this!" Number five was the ultimate; so sickening, I had to look away. A radioman in the back row twisted to the side and ralphed up breakfast.

Pacing in front of the screen, like a predator sizing up his prey, the chief gave his queasy audience a few seconds to digest the genital carnage. Then leveled an accusing finger at us all.

"And if any of you dumbasses gets tanked up and falls into that godawful excuse for a river, the shore patrol will shoot you on the spot and let your body sink. No sense in bringing your sorry ass back to my clinic because we can't save you. Ain't no antibiotic powerful enough to counteract what's spawning in Shit Creek. Personally, I'd rather go skinny-dipping in an outhouse."

Thicker silence from the tank deck. Someone coughed. Somebody else dropped his lighter. With a nod, the chief turned and pointed at slide number six.

"And if you think I'm shitting you, take a look at this poor, dumb bastard. He has a wife and two kids. Can you imagine what the missus said to him his first night home? The man used to work for me, so I can tell you firsthand his welcome was far from pleasant. Any questions?"

My man Markovich cleared his throat. Raised his hand. Thought better of it, and quickly lowered it.

The chief turned off the projector and the screen went dark. I, for one, breathed a sigh of relief.

"One last thing," said Chief Sorenson. "I can see from the looks on your faces most of this went in one ear and out the other. *Never happen to me*, you're probably thinking. Well, don't kid yourselves. It can, and it *will* happen if you aren't careful. You were given a brain when you popped out of your momma's womb. For God's sake, use it!"

He took off his hat. Ran a hand through his thinning hair. Then lit up a cigarette.

"Last chance. Are you sure there are no questions?"

Tomb-caliber silence on the tank deck. The chief nodded to his assistant who then began to take down the screen.

"Okay. I'm outta here. Good luck to you. Something tells me you're going to need all you can get."

The wardroom drew straws for shore patrol duty our first night in Subic and I came up with the short stick. My only saving grace was that Chief Holms was tapped as my duty petty officer. After Chief Sorenson's vivid VD lecture, I had serious doubts about the watch, my duties, and whether I was up to the challenge of Olongopo's sin city. To reassure myself, I corralled the chief on the mess deck.

"Is it as bad as they say it is, Chief?"

Holms rolled his eyes. Pulled out a pack of Camels from a shirt pocket. Straddled a chair to light up.

"It's worse," he said, blowing a smoke ring. "Sorenson never brought up the banana knives."

Just what I wanted to hear. A sentence with the word *knives* in it.

"Banana knives?" I asked.

"Nasty little suckers with curved blades about four inches long. Hooked at one end and sharp as a razor, they can slice through flesh like a hot knife through butter."

Sharp, slice, and *flesh.* Three more unwelcome words.

"Pimps on the street are experts with them," added the Chief Holms. "Cut your ear clean off and you wouldn't feel a thing. Throw a silk scarf into the mix and you've got some serious problems."

"Silk scarf? This isn't another of your tall tales, is it, Chief?"

"It's a no shitter." Holms put a hand over his heart. "On my mother's grave."

"Okay, lay it on me."

He filled his cup to the brim. Pulled out another cigarette and laid it on the table. Leaned back and tugged on his neck. Something told me this was going to be a long one, at least two cigarette's worth, so I made myself comfortable.

"Back in the summer of '64," he said. "I was on the *Bernstein* at the time, a destroyer out of San Diego. I'd just made chief. The *Bernie* wasn't a bad ship as destroyers go, but that's another story. We'd tied up to this very same pier here in Subic, and I was pulling my first watch wearing khaki. It was a Friday, I think."

He took another swig of coffee. Squinted up at the overhead for a second or two.

"Or maybe it was a Saturday. No matter. Anyhow, I was down in chiefs' quarters watching a skin flick when the messenger of the watch hustled up, out of breath, his eyes big as saucers. I knew it wasn't good news.

"'We got trouble on the quarterdeck,' he says. 'Smitty was knifed. Some pimp cut his throat.'"

The chief tugged at his right ear. Thinking back on the incident, he nodded slowly. Then continued his story.

"'Is he dead?' I asked the messenger."

"'No. Not yet anyway,' said he. 'The handkerchief's still in place.'"

"'Handkerchief?' I asked. 'What the hell are you talking about?'"

"'You'll have to see for yourself, Chief,' he said. 'Words won't do it justice.'"

Chief Holms took one more swig of coffee. Swished it around in his mouth for a few seconds. Then swallowed it real slow.

"When I got to the quarterdeck, there was Smitty sitting in a chair, his chin tucked down on his chest. Other than a thin trail of blood down his shirt front, he didn't look that bad. For a man who just had his throat cut. Smitty was a second-class quartermaster, pretty smart guy, but he couldn't handle the booze. But he was now stone-cold sober. And in deep kimchi.

"When I bent down to take a closer look, I noticed something sticking out of his neck. It was a thin silk handkerchief. When I reached out to touch it, he batted my hand away. In a raspy voice, he told me in no uncertain terms to 'back off.' Good thing, too. Had I pulled it out, he would have expired on the spot."

"What did you do?" I asked.

"Wrapped his neck in gauze and waited for the ambulance."

"How did he—?"

"Get his throat cut?" said the chief. "Good question."

Another sip of coffee, another drag on his cigarette, and he launched into his explanation.

"Seems as if Smitty had a few too many beers that night, something he did quite often. Only this time, he pushed one of the girls. 'By accident,' he said. Her pimp across the way took offense and waved his banana knife in front of Smitty's nose. Told him he'd cut him bad if he didn't settle down. Well, Smitty wasn't thinking too straight, so he told him what he could do with his damn knife. Something about sticking it where the sun don't shine."

"Sounds like a bad idea," I said.

"You got that right. Anyhow, it would have ended there if Smitty hadn't pushed the girl again. A little nudge to make his point."

"I can see where this is heading," I said.

"Unfortunately, Smitty didn't," said Chief Holms. "Push came to shove again, and before Smitty could draw back to coldcock the pimp, the guy slapped a silk handkerchief on his blade and slit Smitty's throat. So fast and slick, Smitty didn't feel a thing."

"Throat? As in jugular?"

"Clean through."

"With his throat cut like that, shouldn't Smitty have bled out in the bar?"

"You would have thought so," Chief said.

"What was the silk for?" I asked.

"That's the kicker. The pimp didn't want to *kill* Smitty, just scare the bejesus out of him. Sailors are a pimp's bread and butter, their meal ticket. It would be like killing the goose that laid the golden egg. Instead, he sliced him with the knife carefully, leaving the handkerchief in his throat. Silk is a super coagulant. Doctors use it for sutures all the time. It sealed off Smitty's jugular in two seconds flat."

"But, wouldn't it also stop?"

"Nope. The blood continued to flow through the silk on its merry way to his brain. In effect, it acted like a filter."

"And if Smitty had pulled the handkerchief out?"

"He would have been dead before he got to the door. The pimp told him as much on his way out. That's why Smitty batted my hand away. I'd have done the same thing were I in his shoes."

I leaned back, slowly crossed my arms.

"Let me get this straight. You're telling me you just sat there, talking to a man with his throat cut, a piece of silk hanging out of his Adam's apple, and you merely waited for help to arrive?"

"Nothing else I could do. I wasn't about to say or do anything to upset Smitty. He had enough to worry about. A simple sneeze would have done him in. When the corpsmen finally arrived, I helped him into the ambulance. They stuck an IV in his arm and made him as comfortable as possible. I wished him well and shut the door behind him."

"Did Smitty survive?"

"He was back a week later, thirty stitches in his neck, but none the worse for wear. I haven't the foggiest how the doctors removed that silk from his throat."

Chief butted his cigarette. Drained the last of his coffee.

"I can tell you this, however," he continued. "That was the last time ol' Smitty shoved any bar girl. From then on it was 'Yes, ma'am this' and 'Yes, ma'am that.' Moral of the story. They may be hookers, but you'd better treat them with respect. No matter how ugly they are."

I tapped my nose twice. Raised an eyebrow.

"I'd say about twenty percent, Chief. Twenty-five at most."

"Twenty percent?" Chief Holms asked.

"That's how much of that story I believe."

And we both had a good laugh.

After the chief swabbed out his coffee cup, he stood to leave.

"Silk handkerchief aside, I did learn a valuable lesson that night."

"Which was?" I asked.

"Steer clear of the East Inn Club at all costs."

"East Inn?"

"That's where the ruckus with Smitty took place. Worst hellhole this side of the Pacific. It's the last club on the street. You name the sin; it's been done at the East Inn. A thousand times over. I've wavered from the straight and narrow in my younger days and was there once or twice myself."

Chief Holms put a reassuring hand on my shoulder.

"But don't worry, Lieutenant, I'll have your back on shore patrol. You'll do just fine. As an officer, you probably won't have to leave the watch shack. Unless all hell breaks loose, you'll spend most of the evening watching TV. Maybe catch up on your sleep."

———————

Shore patrol duty turned out to be a snap. At least the first three hours of it did. After writing a letter home, I watched two *I Love Lucy* reruns and started a new paperback. I was on page twelve when my walkie-talkie buzzed off the hook.

"Sorry to disturb you, Mr. Lindsey," said Chief Holms. "I'm afraid we got us a situation here in town. One of your men stumbled into a predicament."

I set down my book. Looked over at the clock on the nightstand. Midnight. The witching hour.

"Who is it?" I asked.

"Your favorite stew burner."

"Durton? What's the lowlife done now?"

"He's got himself stuck on the ceiling. Drunk as a skunk, he's been cussing you out something fierce. I tried to talk him down, but he told me to shove it. He wants to palaver with you personally."

"The ceiling? How'd he get up there?"

"Beats me. But he's swinging around on a chandelier."

"Did you try pulling him down?"

"I couldn't reach the son of a bitch. Says he'll only come down after he talks to you."

Durton again! That man was my personal albatross. I sucked a deep breath through my teeth. Tried to think.

"Shoot the bastard," I said. "That'll bring him down."

"Not a bad idea," said the chief. "But I'm pretty sure the Navy would take a dim view of such measures. Probably hang us both out to dry."

"You know what a dirtbag Durton is. Remember the mashed potatoes? We could plead justifiable homicide. On public health issues alone."

The chief belly laughed.

"Probably get acquitted, too," he said. "But are you willing to take that chance?"

"No, I guess not. I'm on my way. What's your twenty?"

"Sorry to say, but I'm down at the East Inn."

"The hellhole?"

"The one and only."

"I'm going to ring Durton's neck."

"I'm afraid you'll have to wait in line, sir."

———

My duty driver pulled up in front of the East Inn and left the engine running. And didn't get out of the jeep. A bad sign.

"Just in case we have to make a quick getaway," he said.

Justin Case? That man one more time.

I adjusted my official looking Shore Patrol arm band, the one signifying I was the officer-in-charge. Big whoop! After a deep breath, I took a few seconds to assess the so-called inn.

A weathered conglomeration of recycled tin and second-hand lumber, it didn't look that dangerous from the outside. A bit on the shabby side, but as Olongopo night clubs go, it was better than some I'd seen on the way down.

A faint reddish-orange string of neon lights flickered above a row of wide-open windows. Even hellholes need ventilation. A rusty, barely legible Pepsi Cola placard on one wall completed the décor. Parked out front was the owner's diarrhea-tan jitney. I'd been told he used it as an escape vehicle in case a fight broke out. Which happened at least four times a week. Chief Holms came hustling over.

"Glad you could make it to the party, Lieutenant. Welcome to Hell."

I fiddled with the .45 strapped to my hip to make sure the safety was on. Obviously procrastinating since the clip was empty. Regulations prohibited carrying live ammunition in town. Good thing. As experienced with handguns as I was, it probably kept me from shooting myself in the foot.

"What can I expect in there, Chief?" I asked.

"Words won't do it justice, sir. You'll have to see for yourself."

I vaguely remembered hearing those exact same words before. In that order. I sucked in ten gallons of air. Blew each one out separately.

"Okay, lead the way."

Chief Holms stopped at the door.

"Just one thing, Mr. Lindsey. Are you a religious man?"

"Not especially. I can't remember the last time I went to church."

"Good," he said. Then opened the door for me. "Cause this ain't no place for a church-goin' fella."

The smell hit me first. A musty, vinegarish mix of stale sex, rotten meat, green beer, yesterday's piss, and forgotten manners. All undercut by the bouquet of an overly ripe chamber pot. The stench was so bad, I had to pinch off my nose.

"Jesus! What a stink! How can they stand it in here, Chief?"

"After a few beers, you get used to it. A San Miguel doesn't smell much better."

Hellhole, cathouse, bordello, den of iniquity. Nothing comes close to describing the debauchery arrayed before me. Blushing three shades of red, I couldn't believe what people were doing out in the open. And I'm far from a prude.

"Holy crap! Is it always like this?"

"You should see it on a Saturday night."

Lord, have mercy! I thought, ashamed to even have thought of His name in a place like that.

On a shallow stage to my right, a completely nude performer (a euphemism if ever there was one) lay flat on her back, stuffing hard-boiled eggs up her private parts. Using muscle control beyond my comprehension, she was expelling the eggs to the audience rapid fire, squirting them out with a loud sucking sound. Whenever a drunken sailor raised his hand, she'd shoot him an egg. Which he promptly salted, then devoured whole. An expert markswoman, she never missed.

My innards did flip-flops. I knew I'd never be able to face a hard-boiled egg again. On the stage to my left, another nude lady (second euphemism) writhed around in ecstasy, real or faked, I couldn't tell which. Spurred on by the crowd, her moans sounded real. Her back arching, she dripped hot wax from a burning candle down her breasts. When she performed a bikini wax on herself, she screamed so loud, I had to cover my ears.

"Now *that's* something you never see in the States," Chief Holms said.

"No kidding."

My eyes were drawn to the table in front of me. Three oblivious sailors, each sporting a shit-eating grin, were leaning back in their chairs, mewling like kittens, their eyelids fluttering.

"What's wrong with those three?" I asked.

"Look under the table," the chief said.

Three East Inn lovelies were plying their trade, their heads bobbing up and down in fluid strokes.

"A little skin flute action," the chief said. "Been down that road a few times myself. The one on the left seems to know what she's doing."

I cocked my head to the right.

"The one in the middle isn't half bad, either."

I continued to scan. Still no Durton.

"Okay, Chief. Where's my soon-to-be seaman cook?"

The chief pointed to the ceiling. Fifteen feet up and thirty feet to my right, the Fat Lady's mashed-potato menace hung by his naked legs, one hand holding on to a wagon wheel chandelier. Suddenly spotting us, he waved an empty beer bottle in our direction.

"Well, well, well," he slurred. Then pulled his manhood out of his tighty-whities. "If it isn't my shitass departmental officer. How the fuck's it hanging, Lieutenant Dickwad?"

Greetings over, he aimed his shriveled pecker in my direction and took a healthy piss. Bug-eyed and blasted, he missed me by a mile and only dribbled on drunken-table sailor number three, who by now was in the final shudders of his blow job and didn't notice.

"Fuck you, Lindsey!" said Durton, now drained of ammunition. "And fuck the whole damn Navy! You can all kiss my hairy ass!"

Chief Holms pulled at an ear. Grinned.

"You might say that boy is a *tad* pissed off. Literally."

I spied what looked like a pile of fresh dog crap beneath the wagon wheel, radiating steam from the floor.

"He do that, too?"

"Yep," the chief said.

"Then I'd say he's more than *pissed.*"

"What are we going to do, Lieutenant? Durton's beyond reasoning with."

"He was beyond reasoning with before he got drunk," I said. "Are you sure we can't just shoot him?"

Chief shook his head.

"Too messy. I suppose we could let him hang there until he passes out. Course, the fall might break his neck."

"Sounds good to me."

"Then again, he might land on someone."

Decisions, decisions. A half empty beer bottle on the table to my right gave me an idea.

"Mind if I borrow this for a second?" I asked its owner.

"Be my guest," he said.

I positioned myself off to one side of the chandelier. Calculated the projected drop zone.

"Hey, Durton!" I yelled. "How about another beer?"

I tossed the bottle in the air. Made sure it was just out of his reach. Letting go of the wagon wheel to catch the bottle, he lost his balance and cartwheeled free, nose diving to the floor like a dying swan. Tucking at the last second into a perfect half gainer, he landed flat on his back.

Letting out a groan, he tried to raise his head,

"I think I broke my fucking neck!"

Before he could say another word, Chief Holms slapped the cuffs on him.

"After the captain gets finished with you, asshole, you'll wish you *had* broken your *fucking neck.*"

Durton tried to focus on who was talking to him, but his eyes wouldn't cooperate. They swam around in their sockets like a pair of drowning gerbils. Turning to me, he mumbled an incoherent curse, belched, farted, then passed out, his head hitting the floor with a satisfying *Thunk!* The chief and I stood there for a few seconds, basking in the moment.

"Nice work, Lieutenant," he said. "The bottle thing was a neat trick. Wish I'd have thought of it."

"That's why they pay me the big bucks."

He nodded at the form at our feet.

"What'll we do with this piece of crap?"

"I vote for dumping him in Shit Creek," I said.

"You're an officer after my own heart, sir. You'll go far in this man's Navy."

After the corpsman threw Durton's limp ass into the ambulance, a call came over the chief's radio. A slow grimace slid onto his face as he listened.

"We'll be right there," he said into the receiver. Then clicked off.

"Now what?" I asked.

"We've got ourselves another altercation. There's been a slobber knocker down at the Queen Bee."

"I thought you said I'd catch up on my sleep tonight, Chief."

He laughed, then shrugged.

"When it rains, it pours."

I had passed the Queen Bee on my way down to the East Inn and paid it no mind. Sitting across the street from El Camino Club, it was a carbon copy of the Ace of Spades on its right, and not much different than the Hot Spot to its left. The only thing distinguishing the Bee from the other forty clubs on the strip was the disheveled crowd out front, only half of them conscious. Chief Holms pointed out three red *chicklets* scattered on the porch.

"Somebody's missing some teeth."

Given away by their high and tight haircuts, I counted six Marines in blood-splattered civies slumped against a wall, most of them moaning. Four looked like they'd been shaved with a brick, and two had broken noses. One was missing half of an ear. Several tousled bar girls, most with deep scratches on their faces, milled about, whimpering in what had to be Tagalog. Three windows of the Queen Bee had been smashed out. Four splintered chairs, along with a flattened table, were strewn across the narrow porch. The open front door hung by a hinge.

"Looks like an earthquake hit the place," I said.

"Must be a full moon out," said the chief. "I wonder what's left inside."

"Not much," said the owner, appearing out of nowhere.

A short, round mass of acne with a pencil-thin moustache and darty eyes, he sported a bad combover. A tattoo of a woman with gargantuan breasts had been inked onto his right forearm. Missing his left sleeve and at least one tooth, clearly he'd been in the middle of the brawl.

"What happened?" I asked.

He nodded toward the door. Snorted.

"Ask the guy inside," he said. "SOB demolished my club."

"One man did all this?"

"I don't know if he started it, but he sure as hell finished it."

Inhaling slowly, I headed for the door.

"Okay. Point him out to me."

The owner backed away. Waved a hammy hand.

"I'm not going back in there. No way in hell. Not with *him* still around."

"You'll have to. How else can I identify him?"

"You can't miss the bastard. Ten feet tall, one green eye in the middle of his forehead, steel teeth, he's the only one left standing."

The chief and I exchanged glances. I shook my head. He took a deeper breath than mine.

"Looks like we got ourselves a monster on the loose," I said.

Pulling on an ear, the chief surveyed the porch aftermath.

"Or an angry SEAL," he said. "I hear there's a detachment in port. Bad news, those SEALs. You don't want to mess with any of them, especially in no damn bar."

A long night had suddenly grown longer. I let out a soft sigh. Looked to the heavens. No rest for the weary, I hitched up my holster. As if an empty pistol would do me any good.

"Should we call for reinforcements, Chief?"

"A tank or two would be nice. Then again, if it really is a SEAL, it would only piss him off. And we definitely don't want to do that."

"Maybe a flame thrower?"

"He'd just use it to light up a cigarette. Then stick it up our asses. I don't know about you, but I'm not looking for a colonoscopy."

"You make him sound like some kind of Superman."

"Ever seen a real SEAL in action?"

"No."

"It ain't pretty. Look around. Imagine if there had been *two* of them in there."

"Then I guess we'll have to talk some common sense into the guy."

The chief stepped aside, bowed politely, and said, "Be my guest. After you, sir."

"Age before beauty," I said, stepping farther aside.

"You're the one with the college vocabulary," said the chief. "And the silver bar on his collar."

He had me there.

The Queen Bee was even worse on the inside. With most of the furniture in pieces, it looked like a kindling convention had blown through town. There may have been one or two salvageable chairs in the entire place, but I couldn't see any. Broken glass was everywhere, dotted here and there with a few more bloody *chicklets*. Fixtures had been ripped out of the walls, mirrors shattered, and the room-length bar looked like it had made love to a trash compactor. Hovering behind its shattered frame was a terrified bartender, his face a porcelain white, eyes wider than dinner plates. Chief Holms pointed to the far corner where a solitary sailor was sitting quietly.

"That must be *him* over there."

Through the smoky haze, I could barely make out a shadowy figure next to a table missing one leg.

"He doesn't look so tough," I said. "Some monster. The guy's no bigger than I am."

"Size isn't everything, sir."

Our culprit was leaning back in his chair, his right hand cradling a beer bottle, his eyes staring straight ahead at nothing.

"Maybe we should rethink our strategy here, Chief."

"I hope you've got something special up your sleeve, Lieutenant. 'Cause I got squat."

"What's the shore patrol manual say?"

"It doesn't cover pissed off SEAL's."

My mind worked overtime to crank out a cockamamie plan. If it worked, I'd be a hero. If not, I'd get my ass kicked.

"You wait here," I said. "I'll try to lay a heavy dose of logic on him. Keep me covered, Chief."

The chief patted his own bulletless 45.

"With what?"

"A prayer might come in handy. If this doesn't pan out, you can say a few words at my funeral. Something about how I went out with my boots on."

"You got it. Good luck, sir."

Not wanting to confront the SEAL head on, I casually meandered in his general direction. Taking great pains not to make eye contact, I took stock of the wreckage around me. Two minutes passed before I was within comfortable speaking distance. All part of my plan.

Close enough to chance a good look, I saw the guy was still staring into space, maybe thinking how he was going to break me in half. Without a scratch on him, except for a few welts on his knuckles, he reminded me of a samurai warrior. Hopefully he wasn't gathering his strength for the next battle. Wearing a short-sleeved T-shirt strained at the biceps, and taut across the chest, his demeanor screamed physical dominance of the species, the calm, blue-eyed look of a trained killer. Which, of course, was exactly what he was.

I saw a blink, a glimmer of hope; at least the guy was human. Maybe behind all that sinew beat a reasonable heart. Fingers crossed, I plopped my hat down on what was left of the table. I righted a now backless chair and sat at a safe enough distance to the door. I looked around for a few seconds, then laced my hands behind my head.

"What's a guy gotta do to get a beer around here?" I yelled at the bartender cowering behind the bar.

The man crossed himself then, giving the SEAL a wide berth, hustled over with a San Miguel bottle in his shaky right hand. He handed the bottle to me, then beat a hasty retreat.

"On the house!" he called out from behind the bar.

I unscrewed the cap and took what I hoped was a manly swig. The stuff actually *did* taste like panther piss. The vile liquid burned all the way down. Come tomorrow morning, I'd be pissing green. I wiped my mouth, tried to look satisfied.

"Good stuff!" I said, lying through my teeth. I glanced over at the far wall where a velvet nude painting hung at a disturbing angle. Then tipped my bottle in the SEAL's direction.

"Nice place they got here," I said. "A bit on the messy side, but homey. I hate to drink alone. Mind if I join you?"

"It's a free country," he said.

I took off my arm band, undid my holster, and placed them both on the table. After forcing another manly gulp of beer, I stared straight ahead, just like him. Silence once again descended in the bar. *So far, so good.* Inhaling slowly through my nose, I said a silent prayer, then launched into phase two of my plan.

"I wonder what they did with all the longhorns," I said.

"What?" said the SEAL.

"Texas longhorns. The herd of cattle that must have stampeded through here tonight."

He took a swig of his beer, cracked a smile. Both good signs.

"It must have been a hell of a fight," I added. "Too bad I missed it."

He nodded once. "Better than most," he said.

"You want to tell me what happened?" I asked.

"Not particularly."

At least I had him talking. Sort of.

"Damn!" I said. "That means I'll have to make something up for my official report. And just between you, me, and this broken chair I'm sitting on, you don't want to depend on my imagination. Might as well tell me the truth. It'll go easier for you if this mess ever makes it to a court martial."

Thank goodness he smiled.

"You've got a point," he said.

Short version: a group of tipsy Marines had swaggered in, recognized the SEAL insignia on his ball cap, and took it upon themselves to test their mettle against the Navy's finest.

"SEALs and Marines don't get along," he said. A gross understatement, if ever there was one.

One thing led to another, and when someone pushed him, he pushed back. "The rest was history." His very words.

I nodded at the two unconscious pimps draped over a table in the far corner. One appeared to be missing a finger. The other had a banana knife sticking out of his right butt cheek.

"How'd the locals get involved?" I asked.

"In the course of the *conversation*, some girls got jostled. Those two over there took offense. The one on the right threatened me with his pig stabber."

The SEAL shrugged. Cracked his knuckles.

"I told him if he didn't get that thing outta my face, I'd stick it up his ass. He didn't. So, I did. When his friend there objected, I bit off his finger."

I took a closer look at the banana knife. It was buried halfway to the hilt, a good three inches. Amazed there wasn't more blood, I shook my head. Let out a slow whistle.

"Man! That *had* to hurt!"

"Probably did," said the SEAL. "But I gave the man fair warning."

I crossed my arms. Searched for my next words.

"You know," I said, "I really have no choice in the matter. As much as it pains me to say this, I have to take you in. For your own protection."

"Does it look like I need protection?" asked the SEAL.

"Okay. Mostly for *my* protection. But think about it. Sir Knife-in-the-Butt over there probably has some cronies wandering the street who won't take kindly to you skewering their friend like that. Who knows when or where they'll attack you? A lot of innocent people could get hurt in the process. You wouldn't want that on your conscience, would you?"

The SEAL thought for a minute. I'd hit a nerve.

"Yeah, I guess you're right. But no cuffs. I can't stand anything around my wrists."

"Fair enough."

After he finished his beer, we left peacefully, much to the relief of the bartender still cowering behind the bar. When the SEAL was sitting safely in the back of our Jeep, Chief Holms pulled me aside, well out of earshot.

"Slick piece of work you pulled off in there, Lieutenant. That's twice in one night. You'd make a fine lawyer."

"Nah," I said. "I prefer an honorable line of work."

And we enjoyed our second laugh of the evening.

Olongopo's Shit River.

The notorious East Inn Club—den of iniquity.

TWENTY-ONE
The Heart Wants What the Heart Wants (and Sometimes Doesn't Need).

Trouble always travels in packs of three. Two days after my shore patrol stint, my third headache arrived in the form of Seaman Jason Arsenocks, a naïve eighteen-year-old from Omaha. Fresh out of boot camp, he'd only been aboard a month when we pulled into Subic Bay.

"Mr. Lindsey, can I talk to you for a second?" he said, standing in the shadows outside my stateroom, hat in hand. "Um, in private?"

Nine times out of ten, when one of my men said, "in private," it meant he'd come down with a venereal disease of some kind. And in Subic, there were a bundle lurking around every bush. I set down the report I was working on. Turned around.

"Come in, Seaman. Have a seat. What's on your mind?"

Arsenocks fiddled with his hat for a second, then sat down on half the chair. Radiating indecision, his eyes dropped.

Definitely the clap, I thought.

After inhaling half the room's air supply, he looked me in the eye.

"I'm in love and I want to get married," he said.

This was something new.

At first, I thought I hadn't heard him correctly.

"Married? You want to get married? *Over here*? Shouldn't you have taken care of something that important when you were back in the States. When you were with your family? And especially your fiancé?"

"But I only met her yesterday."

Yikes.

"Yesterday? Isn't that kind of quick?"

"Well, er . . . she works at Ocean's Eleven, serving drinks," said Arsenocks.

Serving drinks? Oh, oh!

"So . . . she's a hook—"

I discreetly cleared my throat. *Ye who are without sin, cast the first stone.*

"Um . . . a waitress?"

"Her name is Carla," said Arsenocks. "I know it's sudden, but we love each other. I understand I have to go through my division officer to get a marriage certificate. That's why I'm here."

A lot of servicemen married Filipino women, but usually not after a single night's *courtship*. Hoping this was a young man's hormones talking, half of me was tempted to give Arsenocks a birds-and-bees lecture. The other half filibustered my gut to give the lad a swift kick in the slats.

"Far be it for me to rain on your parade, Seaman Arsenocks, but I have to ask an indelicate question. Were you a virgin before you met Carla?"

Embarrassment radiated from his every pore.

"A virgin, sir?"

"To put it bluntly, was Carla your first piece of ass?"

"Well, yes. But that has nothing to do with it."

"*Au contraire*. It has everything to do with it. Far be it for me to stand in the way of true love, but when it comes to something as serious as marriage, you have to be sure you're thinking with your head and not your heart. It's not like you're asking someone to the prom."

Arsenock's jaw tightened.

"All I know is that I love her, sir. That she loves me. And that we're going to get married. With or without your help."

I admired the kid's nerve. It took guts standing up to his boss like that. I leaned back in my chair. Assumed a Solomon-like pose. This would be harder than threatening to cut a baby in half.

"Tell me, Seaman, do you have a girlfriend back home?"

Arsenocks hesitated for a telling second.

"Yes, sir. Yes, I do. That is . . . I did."

"What's her name?"

"Judy. Judy McIlrath. She turned eighteen last month."

"Do you love Judy, too?"

Arsenocks blushed out to his ears.

"I thought I did. That is until I met Carla. But Carla knows how to, well, you know. She knows things. Things that Judy would never do. Never in a million years."

Now we were getting to the crux of the matter.

"Are you sure?" I asked. "Women don't reach their sexual stride until they're well into their twenties. And beyond. Maybe Judy will learn. You could even teach her."

Arsenocks shook his head slowly.

"I don't think so. Judy is a nice girl."

"There's more to marriage than good sex," I said.

"Sex with Carla is beyond good, sir. It's *great*."

I could tell my man was thinking between his legs, not between his ears. And that reasoning with him would be like peeing up a rope. A barely pubescent rope with a hard-on.

"It looks as if your mind is made up," I said. "Give me a day to check out the regulations, and I'll get back to you."

A walking erection masquerading as a sailor, Arsenocks shook my hand, then left, humming the wedding march as he floated down the passageway. An accident looking for a place to happen, the lovesick puppy was in lust up to his eyeballs. But I wasn't about to give up on the kid.

I knew just the person to help me. Recently promoted, SK3

Markovich was the ship's lothario, knew every girl on Olongopo's strip by her first name. Half of them intimately. I found him on the mess decks, finishing up a hamburger.

"I need your expert advice," I said. "It seems Seaman Arsenocks has fallen for an Olongopo lovely. Her name is Carla, and she works at Ocean's Eleven. Ever seen her?"

Markovich choked on his burger. Shuddered, then went lemon faced.

"Seen her? It's hard to miss her. Uglier than a baboon's butt. Her face is so pockmarked, it could soak up a two-day rain. Hell, half the crew's *been* with her."

"Arsenocks wants to marry her."

"Marry her! Why the hell would he do that? She's old enough to be his mother. Grandmother, maybe. She's got three kids. With one on the way, I think. All she wants is a ticket to the States."

"I was afraid of that," I said.

I knew Arsenock's parents were both teachers. I could imagine the looks on their faces when he brought his not-so-lovely new bride home for the first time.

Mom, Dad . . . I'd like you to meet Carla and her three and a half children. We got married overseas. With Lieutenant Lindsey's blessing.

Mom and Dad would put out a contract on me.

"Somebody's got to have a serious talk with him," said Markovich. "Tell him the facts of life."

"I tried, but he wouldn't listen. He's thinking below the beltline."

"Been there myself when I was a rook. 'Course I never thought once about marrying anyone. Couldn't afford it. Leave it to me, sir. I'll handle this."

"You won't do anything illegal, will you?"

"Immoral maybe, but not illegal. Trust me. I know what to do."

And so, I left it in SK3 Markovich's capable hands.

———

The following morning, I met Markovich on his way to quarters. He was sporting one hell of a shiner.

"What happened to your eye?" I asked.

Markovich grinned to reveal a split lip.

"I had a rough night, sir."

"Sorry to hear about that. Um, did you get a chance to check out Arsenock's *problem*?"

"It's all taken care of. I don't think Nock'll be getting married anytime soon."

"Outstanding! If you don't mind my asking, how'd you pull it off?"

"I bird-dogged his girl."

"You, you *slept* with her?"

"Let's just say I took one for the team. But only after six beers. She was uglier than I remembered."

"What did Arsenocks say when you told him?"

"At first, he wouldn't believe me. Then I showed him the pictures."

"You took pictures?"

"No, her girlfriend did. A dozen Polaroids. We had a threesome going. Carla's what you might call an *accommodating* woman."

"Was Arsenocks pissed?" I asked.

Markovich pointed to his eye.

"How'd you think I got this?"

"Thanks, Markovich. I appreciate your sacrifice. As will his parents. I knew I could count on you."

"Anytime, sir."

———

Our hard luck sister ship, the *Luzerne County*, once again dealt us a bum hand. While the Fat Lady was pulling into Guam, two thousand miles away and unbeknownst to us, the *Luze* was running aground again, this time in the Mekong Delta. A sapper charge had blown a four-foot hole in her hull. By the grace of God and her thick skin, no one was hurt, but she was definitely out of commission. That left America one LST short in-country. Goodbye extended rest in Guam; hello quick turnaround back to 'Nam.

After a hectic five-day patch-up job, we were on our way to Vietnam, our fingers crossed we wouldn't sink in the middle of the ocean. This time, our bow door jury-rig involved a makeshift system of pulleys running from the forward bullnose back to the deck crane. Our chances of making it across the South China Sea during monsoon season were fifty-fifty at best.

The crew took the change of orders in stride, chalking it up to either the misfortunes of war, or the *Luzerne* curse. Having had it up to here with boonie stomping, most of us had our game faces on the day we left port. Guam is good. But only Haf Adai.

After a two-week transit, rocking and rolling through the first monsoon of the season, it was a relief to pull into Danang. One thing in our favor: Tet was still four months away. Bad news: it was still coming down in buckets as we on loaded our first detachment of Marines.

"I can't believe it," said Barry. "We're back to busing jarheads."

"Time to break out the sardines," said Chief Holms.

War dulls the senses, forces one to accept the inevitable with a minimum of grousing. After one trip from Cua Viet to Okinawa and back again, it was as if we'd never left. Since this was the third time in-country for most of us, the brain-numbing routine settled in quickly. Like a well-worn saddle sore.

I'd begun to think the war would never end. The distant millennium would come and go, and we'd still be chugging up and down the coast of Vietnam, in and out of her rivers, like Sisyphus toiling away at his boulder. A tote-that-barge, lift-this-bale purgatory without even a pin prick of light at the end of the tunnel. In thirty years, other than a few added layers of rust on the Fat Lady and maybe a million gray hairs on her crew, everything would be the same. A sea of sunsets would come and go, and we'd still be hauling herds of green buffalo trucks, tons of hamburger patties, and a forest of VC-bound lumber through a river of lime Jell-O. Death, taxes, and Vietnam. Same old, same old.

After a side trip up north to repair our overworked door cable, everything changed. For me, at least. Waiting on the sands of the LST beach at Danang was a fuzz-faced officer wrapped in a brand-new set of khakis. Sporting a shiny ensign bar on one collar. On his other collar, an equally shiny *PORK CHOP*. My relief!

I didn't know it at the time (my official orders arrived two days later), but I'd been ordered to aide duty back in the States. Probably as a reward for my stint in Vietnam. Apparently, some high-ranking admiral wanted a young, semi-presentable, hard-charging junior officer with combat experience and a few medals on his chest to stand tall at official functions and carry his bags.

I still had all my hair, and in a dim light, I could pass for young, but I was far from a combat vet. Never one to look a gift horse in the mouth, I accepted the reassignment. Like a starving man accepts manna from heaven. It had taken a month to get my sea legs and another month to recognize *port* from *starboard,* but I was more than ready to leave. Of course, the wardroom was happy for me.

"Lucky bastard!" said Barry.

"Lucky son of a bitch!" said Hank.

"Lucky fucking prick!" said Chief Holms.

You get the picture.

After a relieving whirlwind of a process, where I probably recounted some of the same cans of beans I counted two years ago, I turned the department over to my dazed relief.

"Bless you, my son!" I said. "May the supply gods be with you!" My parting words.

I said my goodbyes to my men first and then to the wardroom. *I'm going home! I'm going home!* was all I could think of.

———————

Not until I was being bonged off the Fat Lady, a tradition in the Navy when an officer walks off the ship for the final time, did a lump come to my throat. About the size of a grapefruit. When I cast off the *Hampshire County's* last line, another tradition, it finally hit me.

It was probably the last time I'd ever see any of my shipmates. Or that rusting old bucket of bolts disguised as a ship. The last time I'd stand on her bridge, or win a bridge game with the Skipper Davidson as my partner. For sure it was the last time I'd ever put liver and onions on a menu. As I watched the Fat Lady make her way ever so slowly past the break wall, I may have shed a tear or two. Happy, sad, excited, alone, and now hopeful, a sea of emotions washed over me.

I felt as if a ton of weight had been lifted from my shoulders. I was as free as a bird, but I also felt guilty. Guilty for leaving my friends behind. To shoulder their remaining burden alone. Such was the enigma called Vietnam.

If life is unfair, could war be anything less?

TWENTY-TWO
Welcome Home!

I spent most of my flight back to the States mulling over the past two years. Eventually, I got around to the sailor who sat next to me on that plane to Vietnam. The young man with a pregnant wife waiting for him. Was he still alive? And if so, how was he doing? Did he make it back home in one piece? Marry Carol? Buy that farm? Raise chickens? Since he was a dental tech, he probably did. But you never know.

Stepping off the plane in San Francisco was a shock, but nowhere near the eye-opener that was waiting for me in the terminal. I'd read about all the anti-war demonstrations taking place on the West Coast, but still wasn't prepared for the *greeting* that awaited me. During my 'Nam debriefing in Saigon, I'd been advised to get out of my uniform as soon as the plane landed, but I was so excited, I forgot. Coming down the ramp, I tried to blend in by walking next to a pair of airline pilots. My dress blue uniform was somewhat similar to theirs, and at first glance, I looked like I'd just flown into town behind the controls of an airbus from Dallas.

The ruse would have succeeded if it hadn't been for my *chest candy*. When the three of us, two bona fide pilots and one wannabe, turned the corner, we walked smack dab into a banner-waving rally of bandana-clad hippies waving peace signs. When the pilots turned left, I knew I was in trouble. *Uncovered* as I was, a miniskirted girl wearing beads and a fringed top laid the hammer down on me.

"Look!" she said, pointing at my few medals. "He's one of *them!*"

I know it's a cliché, like something you'd expect as the cathartic moment of an Oliver Stone film, but she actually spit on me. A hefty loogie that landed right on my newly shined buttons. At first, I was confused, maybe even a tad amused.

Oh, no, you didn't, I thought. *Give me a break. I only want to go home.*

I should have been pissed off, but I wasn't. I didn't have it in my heart at the time.

Then it got ugly. Shouting, pushing, shoving, the whole nine yards. Since I was outnumbered in the debate, I let the protestors do all the talking. The only thing I remember is some pimple-faced skinny kid in a buckskin jacket getting up into my face, sneering as he hurled a spittle-laced diatribe at me.

"*Fascist killer!*"

Another liberal-minded, free-lover followed up with a hackneyed bromide.

"How many babies did you kill yesterday?"

Not sure I wasn't dreaming, my first thought was to fire a quip back. Something like *None, thanks for asking. But with any luck, maybe tomorrow I'll bag a few.* But I decided against it. Flippancy, at that point, wouldn't have won me any style points.

Just when it looked darkest for Johnnie-Come-Marching-Home, the cavalry arrived. I was wearing a uniform, they were wearing uniforms, so it took the police less than a second to decide which side they were on. An unfair choice, perhaps, but a welcome one from my point of view. Outnumbered as I was, I appreciated all the help I could get.

Wielding their night sticks, the cops formed a protective cordon around me to escort me to my gate, where they stationed two of their burliest at the check-in counter to make sure nobody else bothered me.

Although grateful for their presence, in the back of my mind, I wondered if it really had come to this in America. Hardly a hero of any kind, I knew I didn't deserve a parade. I was just a run of the mill GI, one who had served a run-of-the-mill tour in Vietnam. Without killing anyone. Babies, most assuredly, included. That unlucky crow in Danang never made any of the body counts. I served to the best of my abilities and was lucky enough to come back with all my appendages attached. No big deal.

But I also didn't deserve to be spat upon.

As I sat there waiting for my flight to board, I realized there was nothing I could do about it. When my flight number was called, I shook the two officers' hands. They thanked me for my service and wished me Godspeed. The first friendly words I'd heard since setting foot back in the States.

Knotted in doubts, and with an empty pit where my stomach used to be, I boarded my plane to Ohio in gloomy silence. What should have been the happiest day of my life had suddenly turned sour. I was still excited about seeing Mom and Dad again, but now I was worried about them having to fight their way through an angry crowd. Would there be another peace demonstration waiting for me in Cleveland?

I even contemplated changing out of my uniform in one of the airbus' cramped lavatories; at over six feet tall, not the easiest thing to do on a bumpy flight. Hat in hand, I was about to get out of my seat when the elderly woman across the aisle reached out to touch my arm.

"I saw the whole disgusting thing back in the terminal, young man," she said. Her voice sounding like my grandmother. "Don't let those hooligans get to you. We appreciate what you've done for us, and you should be proud of that uniform."

It's amazing how a few well-placed words from a stranger can lift one's spirits. Life is a series of counterbalancing weights. Some heavy and black as lead. Some lighter and purer than liquid gold. I don't know who that woman was, or where she was from, but I owe her a lot.

By the time we landed in Cleveland, I was back on an even keel. When my mother saw me coming down the ramp, she let out a shriek that must have been heard all the way to Pittsburgh.

My dad stood in the background until her gushing subsided. With a single tear dripping down his cheek, he finally stepped forward to shake my hand with both of his. Then he gave me the longest hug of his life.

"Welcome back, son," he said simply.

It was the first and last time I saw my father cry.

EPILOGUE
On the past. . .

I never felt closer to a group of guys in my life than I did to the crew and officers of the *Hampshire County*. She may have been the slowest, ugliest, worst-riding ship ever to fly the American flag, but a part of me will always be with her. Overworked and underfunded, she was a gator through and through. And anyone who struggled to man her rails should be damn proud of her.

Vietnam?

To this day, I'm still confused about that war. Could we have won? Probably. Should we have been there in the first place? Maybe. And I think I'll leave it at that.

It has been over five decades since I watched the Fat Lady steam away that hot day in Danang, and in all that time I've only run across one of my old shipmates. Ten years ago, purely by chance, I met up with Barry Kott. In a bar, of all places. I bought him a beer; he bought me a Diet Pepsi. We swapped a few lies, shared a few laughs. And then, after a surprisingly short period of time, there was nothing left to say. We'd grown into two different people. I guess you can never go back.

Over the years, I've come to realize the only thing that ragtag conglomeration of men on the Fat Lady had in common was a war-torn country, the conflicted times, and a rusted old relic. Take away the ship and we were just fivescore of wayward souls pinballing through a confusing war. As time and places march on, as they inevitably do, the bonds of friendship, so important and life-sustaining only then, tend to fade. As they must.

The Fat Lady is gone now, sold for scrap in 1995. Melted down to make engine blocks, pots and pans, washing machines, razor blades, perhaps even plowshares. Who knows, twenty years ago, I may have even shaved with a piece of her. It doesn't matter. The memories are still with me, in living, and sometimes painful, color. And that should be enough for even the richest of men.

APPENDIX

USS *HAMPSHIRE COUNTY* (LST-819)—aka The Fat Lady

Statistics:

Length: 328 feet

Beam: 50 feet

Draft: 11 feet

Displacement: 1625 tons

Maximum speed: 12 knots (Empty, and with a brisk tail wind.)

Crew: 105 enlisted

10 or 11 officers

Chronology:

12 Sep 1944—Keel laid in Evansville, Indiana

21 Oct 1944—Launched

14 Nov 1944—Commissioned

18 Dec 1944—Departed New Orleans for the Pacific

23 Feb 1945—Arrived Tulagi

2 Apr 1945—Took part in Okinawa invasion

6 Jan 1946—Arrived San Francisco for decommissioning
8 Sep 1950—Recommissioned for Korea
19 Feb 1951—Arrived Pusan for duty
17 Jul 1954—Arrived San Diego for decommissioning
9 Jul 1966—Recommissioned for Vietnam
8 Nov 1966—Arrived Danang
19 Dec 1970—Decommissioned for the final time at Bremerton, WA
17 Apr 1975—Struck from naval reserve, sold to Singapore
22 Dec 1995—Arrived at Aliaga, Greece for scrapping

Awards earned during the Vietnam War:
Combat Action Ribbon
Presidential Unit Citation
Navy Unit Commendations
RVN Gallantry Cross with Palm
RVN Civil Action Medal First Class with Palm
RVN Campaign Medal with 60s Device
Vietnam Service Medal with (10) Battle Stars

The last and only remaining remnant of the *HAMPSHIRE COUNTY* is her ship's bell. Since 1992, it has hung in a position of honor on the quarterdeck of the Marine Corps Support Battalion, Marine Corps Recruiting Depot, Parris Island, South Carolina. As Marines enter and leave the quarterdeck, they turn and salute in the bell's direction. Having ferried so many seasick leathernecks out of Vietnam, from a place far, far away, she salutes them back.

May the "Fat Lady's" hardworking spirit always have *fair winds and a following sea.*

PERSONAL CITATION (?):

LST819: MSW:an

1650

Ser 569

8 November 1969

From: Commanding Officer, USS *HAMPSHIRE COUNTY* (LST-819)
To: Officer in Charge, US Transit Barracks, Cat Lo, Vietnam

Subj: Verification of heroism in case of LTJG Larry A. Lindsey
USNR, 739915; request for

1. Prior to reporting to USS *HAMPSHIRE COUNTY* (LST-819) for duty, LTJG Lindsey was attached to the transient facility at Cat Lo, Vietnam from 8 April to 19 April 1969. During this period the transient facility reportedly underwent an enemy mortar attack in which LTJG Lindsey distinguished himself in the highest traditions of the United States Naval Service.

2. In the face of overwhelming odds LTJG Lindsey bravely and heroically sought immediate shelter seeking time for which to plan a counter-offensive. A nearby latrine proved to be exceptional shelter for LTJG Lindsey. He quickly extracted unnecessary personnel from the crowded refuge making it possible for him to lower his entire six foot four inch frame into the safety of the shelter. LTJG Lindsey courageously kept his head between his legs allowing him to silence the noise and thus enabling him to plan a counter-strategy. Hours passed, and as the all clear signal sounded LTJG Lindsey bravely burst forward from his refuge hysterically shouting out his plan of attack, yet "Charlie" was nowhere to be found.

3. Despite the fact that the attack plan came too late, this command feels that LTJG Lindsey's courage and heroism should not go unnoticed. It is requested that information and verification of this glorious event be forwarded to this command for appropriate action in recommending LTJG Lindsey for the National Defense Medal.

R. P. Davidson

ODES TO AN LST (LANDING SHIP TANK)

(A potpourri of mostly addlepated ramblings inspired by the *Hampshire County*—all taken from the author's poetry (?) collection entitled *"Graffiti, Frail on Cellophane Walls."*)

Thirty Degrees

I awake to a whistle and a roll.
Through my porthole comes the blue of the sky, the green of the sea. . .
The blue of the sky. . .
 The green of the sea. . .
  Blue, green . . .
   Blue, green. . .
   Blue-green.
I live in a thirty degree world.
I eat a thirty degree meal from a thirty degree plate.
I walk a thirty degree path to a thirty degree job.
I am bombarded by thirty degree words coming from thirty degree people.
Then I lower my thirty degree body into a thirty degree bunk and go to sleep.
Degree by thirty degrees.
Thirty degrees to port, thirty degrees to starboard.
My limit of existence, my arc of life is sixty degrees.
This is not my right angle.

The Sea at Night

The sea at night is a frightening sight.
Strong, silent, vast, a fierce animal at restless sleep,
A rhythm of power undulates from her liquid beat.
To gaze alone upon this slumbering creature, uncharted and deep,
Is to feel the fluid surge of a transgressing darkness.
Night visions reflected from white-topped ripples,
A mirror of time is the sea, to and from the beginnings of infinity.
More than fear or fascination, more than a tide-full bondage:
The sea, night and man . . . a catalytic trinity.

What the World Looks Like Through the Starboard Porthole of an Overly-Tired Navy LST Rolling Around Somewhere in the Middle of the Southeast Asian Seas.

Round!

$%^&**#$!!!

Truyieing to tupe a po(iem in the middle of the ocijah, rolling with the seeaas, is knot eZsy.

On Deck

Standing on a rolling deck, head into the wind, with the taste of salt spray on your lips, can be one of the most rewarding experiences of being a sailor. If you wear glasses, it can also be one of the most annoying.

The Place

When I was young I met an old sailor, who with a tear in his eye said to me, "Son, there's only one place for you, and that place is out to sea."
And so I sailed.
If you ever meet an old sailor, beware the moment's lure of a whim.
When his eyes fill and he looks so far, far away, don't listen to him.

Flame for Thought

Seen on the barrel of a tank's flame thrower somewhere above Cua Viet:

CAUTION: Smoking may be hazardous to your (and/or) the health of others.
—*The American Medical Association*

Relative

Happiness, like most things in the vernacular this year, is relative. A box of crushed cookies, long stale from many journeys, would not register a single flicker on any happiness meter back home. That same box, just as crushed, just as full of stale cookies, brings universal joy in Vietnam. How much more relative could anything be?

Green Fields

Green fields, sun-kissed o'er which we have run,
Soft and wet beneath our gliding feet.
Smiles and laughter, vital parts of life's fun,
There should be more green fields to welcome the sun.

Automatic Love

Automatic love
Is made by automatic people,
With nothing on their minds,
But their hands and their glands.

Tomorrow

A long sigh, a soft goodbye, a tear for our year, and with less than yesterday's fear,
There will be . . . tomorrow.

Do You Believe? (*A Dichotomous Moral Rhetoric*)

"Do you believe?"
"Do I believe in what?"
"*What* is inconsequential. It's the *act* of believing that's important."
"But you have to believe in *something*."
"*Something* is picayune. *Believing* is pervasive."
"What in hell do you mean by that?"
"Oh, never mind. Do you *just* believe?"
"No, I don't believe."

"Why don't you?"
"Because."
"Because why?"
"*Just* because."

Little Yum-Yum Box

I am a soldier
I try to stay alive in the mud and I eat out of a little box.
Today my box contains the following:
Spoon in cellophane wrapper.
Four cigarettes: complimentary, not for sale.
Matches designed for damp climates.
        (But won't light when wet or after long exposure to extremely damp air)
Chicklets, two.
Toilet paper, thirteen single ply sheets.
Coffee, instant: 2.5 grams net.
Cream substitute, dry: Four grams net.
Sugar packet, Six grams net.
Salt packet, Four grams net.
Can of white bread, 1.75 ounces net.
Tin of blackberry jam, seedless: 5.5 ounces net.
Can of pork slices with juices: 5.5 ounces net
Three cookies, very small
C-RATS! Vintage 1955: A very good year.
Aren't you glad you're not a soldier?